WHO IS PHAEDRUS?

Who Is Phaedrus?

Keys to Plato's Dyad Masterpiece

Marshell Carl Bradley

☙PICKWICK *Publications* · Eugene, Oregon

WHO IS PHAEDRUS?

Copyright © 2012 Marshell Carl Bradley. All rights reserved. Except for brief quotations in critical publications or reviews, no part of this book may be reproduced in any manner without prior written permission from the publisher. Write: Permissions, Wipf and Stock Publishers, 199 W. 8th Ave., Suite 3, Eugene, OR 97401.

Pickwick Publications
An Imprint of Wipf and Stock Publishers
199 W. 8th Ave., Suite 3
Eugene, OR 97401

www.wipfandstock.com

ISBN 13: 978-1-62032-151-5

Cataloging-in-Publication data:

Bradley, Marshell Carl.

Who is Phaedrus? / Marshell Carl Bradley.

xxiv + 184 p.; 23 cm—Includes bibliographical references and index.

ISBN 13: 978-1-62032-151-5

1. Plato. Phaedrus. 2. Plato. 3. Socrates. 4. Love. I. Title.

B380 B73 2012

Manufactured in the USA.

For
Nicolas, Sophia, Eva, Olivia

the beloved receives all service from the [true] lover as if he were a god ...
—SOCRATES, *PHAEDRUS*

Now I myself, Phaedrus, am a lover of the processes of division and collection as the very means by which we think and speak; and if I think any other is able to see things that can naturally be collected into one and divided into many, him I follow after and "walk in his footsteps as if he were a god."
—SOCRATES, *PHAEDRUS*

Contents

Preface | *xiii*
    α) Abbreviation: Textual
    β) Abbreviation: Contextual
    γ) Abbreviation: Pretextual
    δ) Index of Abbreviations

Acknowledgments | *xix*

Introduction | *xxi*

1. Situating *Phaedrus* | 1
    α) Chronology
    β) Reading Plato
    γ) Reading *Phaedrus*

2. The Line on Dialectic, Part 1 | 15
    α) " . . . as if he were a god."
    β) Dialectic and Rhetoric
    γ) Dialectic and Discernment

3. The Line on Dialectic, Part 2 | 26
    α) *Dianoia* and the Good: *The Republic*
    β) *Dianoia* and the Beautiful: *Phaedrus*

4. Phaedrus's Ultimate Whence: A Mystery Triad | 35
    α) The Orphic Mysteries
    β) The Eleusinian Mysteries
    γ) Socrates Defeats Triptolemus
    δ) Phaedrus and *Schadenverbesserung Eros*

Contents

5. Phaedrus's Middle Whence: Was Phaedrus Bi-Rebellious? | 55
    α) Why Mutilate the Herms?
    β) Why Profane the Mysteries?
    γ) Alkibiades: Apotheosis by Other Means
    δ) Phaedrus the Nihilist and the Heteratai

6. Phaedrus's Immediate Whence: Athens's and Phaedrus's Decline | 76
    α) The Morychus-Epicrates-Lysias Triad
    β) The Morychus-*Epicrates Triad
    γ) The *Epicrates-Lysias Triad
    δ) The Lysias-Phaedrus Dyad

7. Plato's Rehabilitation of Zeus | 87
    α) Socrates and Teisamenos
    β) Zeus's and Socrates's Dual Duties
    γ) The Lisper *contra* Zeus
    δ) Dodona Devotionals

8. Triads and Dyads of Speeches | 103
    α) Lysias's/Phaedrus's Pederasty Speech
    β) Phaedrus's/Socrates's Pederasty Speech
    γ) Socrates's Half-Comical Halting
    δ) Divining Socrates's Palinode

9. Images of the Image of the Soul | 117
    α) Images of the Soul in the Palinode
    β) The Image Superseding the Palinode
    γ) The Stymied Image

10. Phaedrus: Inverse Cicada | 129
    α) Noon
    β) The Cicada Transformation
    γ) The Transformation of Phaedrus
    δ) The Typhonic Violation of Nature

11. Confounding Dialectic | 138
    α) Phaedrus the Artless
    β) Countering Zeno and Lysias
    γ) The Triad of Speakers
    δ) An *Apologia* for Phaedrus

12. Phaedrus's Whither | 162
    α) Another Return to Athens
    β) From Simple to Simple

13. Conclusion: Two Final Triads | 168
    α) Homer, Solon, Lysias
    β) The Ridiculous, the Clever, the Enemy

Bibliography | 173

Index

Preface

α) Textual Abbreviation

THE INTRODUCTION THAT FOLLOWS makes the beginning of the case that Plato's dialogues are more than elongated pufferies of poetry that buffet the philosophical parts that really matter. However, regarding *Phaedrus* in particular, a kind of textual topology might be established. This is hardly a radical notion. A textual topology of Platonic dialogues has become almost obligatory, especially for modern translators.[1] My aim here is not to provide an abbreviation system for all of the *topoi* in *Phaedrus*; and I hardly mean we might treat the dialogue's *topoi* as if we entirely understood each. Socrates's first speech, which I label *P'/S'*, is easy to quantify in the text; but it has been interpreted variously. Indeed, Tomás Calvo offers a self-described "unusual reading" of that speech as compared with what he calls the "usual" reading.[2]

The point is this: while I pay extraordinary attention to dramatic detail, I shall refer to portions of at least the first half of *Phaedrus* with a kind of shorthand relative to those sections with which many readers are likely familiar. Thus the following abbreviations:

$$L'/P' \equiv 230e–234c$$

$$P'/S' \equiv 237b–241d$$

$$HH \equiv 241d–243e$$

$$PL \equiv 243e–257b.$$

L'/P' designates Lysias's speech, the speech in praise of the non-lover. I append the possessive apostrophe to L and P, as Lysias's speech becomes, in a sense, Phaedrus's speech also, as Phaedrus reads Lysias's written text

---

1. Cobb, *Plato's Erotic Dialogues*, 86; Scully, *Plato's Phaedrus*, xvii–xix; et al.
2. Calvo, "Socrates' First Speech in the *Phaedrus* and Plato's Criticism of Rhetoric," 48.

aloud; and Phaedrus, in *Phaedrus*, is, or has become in effect, identified with Lysias.

P'/S' designates Socrates's first speech, the speech against the lover. I append the possessive apostrophe to S and P, as Socrates's first speech, by Socrates's express declaration, is really Phaedrus's speech.[3] *P'/S'* is really just *L'/P'* in different form; a speech Socrates generates for rhetorical-pedagogical purposes but does not endorse.

Aside from *L'/P'* and *P'/S'*, I offer another abbreviation for another *topos* of *Phaedrus* that, I argue, has long been underappreciated: 241d–243e. I refer to that section as Socrates's Half-comical Halting, or *HH*, for short. With a mix of disdain and satire, Socrates half-comically halts *P'/S'*: thus *HH*.

One excellent translator does indeed bother to recognize Socrates's *HH* in *Phaedrus*, yet refers to it simply as "Transition."[4] Yet, this portion of *Phaedrus* is no simple transition. Socrates's *HH* is hardly a merely functional interlude to move the narrative. (And, yes, I do not find any portion of *Phaedrus* merely accidental.) The significance of Socrates's *HH* will become obvious in due course. Yet, at points in this commentary I will refer to Socrates's dyadic halting of *P'/S'* so often I thought it best to provide an abbreviation.

Finally, as regards textual abbreviations, I offer *PL* as an abbreviation for Socrates's famous "Palinode to Love" or "Socrates's Great Speech," as it is often called. According to my hermeneutical principle (posed previously), even the little things in a Platonic dialogue have great meaning. But the *PL*, of course, is especially powerful and crucial. Graeme Nicholson's commentary on *Phaedrus* even reproduces the *PL in toto* within the commentary.[5]

L'/P', *P'/S'*, *HH*, and *PL* are what may be called textual abbreviations. To say nothing of quality, those letters signify quantifiable parts of *Phaedrus* with which many might already be familiar.

β) Contextual Abbreviation

The reader will also see what may be called contextual abbreviation: *CO*.

This abbreviation represents a phenomenon that occurs many times in all of Plato's work, sometimes openly, sometimes between the lines. It

---

3. *Phaedrus*, 242d.
4. Scully, *Plato's Phaedrus*, xviii.
5. Nicholson, *Plato's Phaedrus*, 89–106.

occurs numerous times in *Phaedrus*, given the almost advertised dyadic elements of this dialogue.

In the Introduction, I noted Raven's reference to the *Republic* as Plato's masterpiece; and I noted, and surely Raven would agree, Plato was capable of more than one masterpiece, despite the singularity of the term. That reference to the *Republic per* the discussion of masterpieces was to help the reader anticipate what follows: my contention that *Phaedrus* was composed in much the same mental frame, and time frame, as the *Republic*.[6] This is hardly a startling claim. However, I bring specificity to it. I argue that *Phaedrus* is an intentionally complex thought-experiment tied profoundly to the *Republic*; that the machinations that move *Phaedrus* are derivative of epistemological elements found in the centerpiece masterpiece, the *Republic*.

More particularly, the term *dyad* in the subtitle, *Keys to Plato's Dyad Masterpiece*, would call attention to the triad/dyad dynamics associated with Plato's presentation of διανοια (*dianoia*) in the *Republic*. In the *Republic*, in the section on the Divided Line in particular, Socrates addresses the question as to what prompts thinking. There the question is this: what activates the mind to operate systematically beyond the encounter with the merely sensuous?

In the *Republic*, Socrates suggests that thinking begins when the mind is confronted with a sensuous triad/dyad: in sum, with the recognition of a "compresence of opposites." The dynamics between and among opposites, and the necessity to discern various forms of similarities and dissimilarities, of identity and difference, are as fundamental to *Phaedrus*, in part and on the whole, as they are to all of Plato's works.

Accordingly, given the many instances of dyadic dynamics in *Phaedrus*, glaringly obvious in the dialogue's famous halves, and in the fact that we see only a dyad of interlocutors, any commentator could use the phrase "compresence of opposites" often. In fact, those very terms have been used in other works on Plato. Mary McCabe uses the terms "compresence of opposites" in *Plato's Individuals*, but in a way different from that to be construed in *Who is Phaedrus?*[7] G. E. L. Owen uses the terms "compresence of opposites" much more narrowly than McCabe; that is, relative to the operations of the soul in the three-finger issue *per* the Divided Line in the *Republic*: "the compresence of opposites that the Form was invented

6. Cf. "Situating *Phaedrus*."
7. McCabe, *Plato's Individuals*, 50.

Preface

to avoid."[8] We might surmise that Plato would disagree with Owen's claim that Plato "invented" the Forms, or Essences; but that is not the issue here.

The issue here is that I will use the terms "compresence of opposites" very much as intended by Owen in the previous quotation, relative to the importance of the Divided Line, and yet by extension for reasons that will become clear in the course of the commentary. Here the point is that the phrase "compresence of opposites" will become such a useful phrase, I shall employ a kind of contextual abbreviation for it. Thus:

$CO \equiv$ compresence(s) of opposites

Should the reader be suspicious of the claim that there is so much dyadic action in *Phaedrus* that a contextual abbreviation is almost necessary, consider how the reader, outside the dialogue, to say nothing of Phaedrus within it, is confronted with one compresence of opposites, or *CO*, after another, after another.

The dialogue's very first line offers a verbal *CO*: Socrates's "whence and whither" question. Consider the two figures of *Phaedrus*: a dyad of interlocutors, Phaedrus and Socrates, a human *CO*. Phaedrus and Socrates are both lovers of speeches, yet they are different in that sameness: Socrates loves speeches because speech is the vehicle by which truth is revealed; Phaedrus loves speeches for their entertaining expressions of cleverness, with maybe a little persuasion in the equation. Otherwise, Phaedrus and Socrates are respective opposites in many other ways: handsome-ugly; rich (or once rich)-poor; superficial-wise; democrat-aristocrat.

Phaedrus offers so many triad/dyad distinctions of so many kinds, with so many *CO* of various kinds, *Phaedrus* often comes across as tension-filled as any portion of Hegel's *Science of Logic* or *Phenomenology of Spirit*. Indeed, the overriding motif in *Phaedrus* concerns the question as to whether or not Typhonic Phaedrus will become identical to, or can become identical to, his opposite, the simple Socrates.

γ) Pre-textual Abbreviation

Finally, *Who Is Phaedrus?* employs what could be called pretexutal abbreviations.

More than most commentaries on *Phaedrus*, *Who Is Phaedrus?* attempts to address, as far as is reasonable, the extraordinary intrigues that

---

8. Owen, "A Proof in the '*peri ideon*,'" 311.

constitute the pretext of *Phaedrus*. To that end, I have followed Ronald Polansky's urging that Plato commentators address in some detail the histories or characters of the persons in the dialogues: "the dialogue [must] be mined as strenuously for the evidence of an interpretation of the character of its participants as for the presuppositions of its arguments."[9] In part, but hardly on the whole, I proceed much as Rhodes who urges and employs a similar hermeneutical principle. For example, regarding the authenticity of *Alcibiades I*, Rhodes reveals that some critics of *Alcibiades I* claim *Alcibiades I* could not have been composed by Plato because of *Alcibiades I*'s alleged "reasoning unworthy of Plato."[10] According to Rhodes, any critic who argues thusly "ignores dramatic context" and fails to notice that "the shoddiness of its [*Alcibiades I*'s] philosophical reasoning" is precisely what to expect in parts of a dialogue in which the confounding Alkibiades figures so prominently. If Rhodes is right in that case, granted, an extreme case, an accounting of the personal character of the historical individual almost entirely trumps the assumed priority of the argumentation. (I will demonstrate how something similar happens in *Phaedrus*; and pointedly in the *PL* in particular.)

So, as the title asks, who is Phaedrus? Phaedrus is an intellectual mediocrity, but he has an unusual personal history, one that intersects with the legendary dyad of scandals in Athens's history: the famous, or infamous, Mutilation of the Herms on the eve of the expedition to Sicily in 415; and the famous, or infamous, Profanation of the Eleusinian mysteries.

The extent to which Phaedrus was actually involved in both the Profanation of the Eleusinian mysteries and the Mutilation of the Herms will probably be an issue of debate as long as Plato is read, barring some remarkable find. Debra Nails is one of the few historians of Plato's texts to claim that Phaedrus was involved in only one of the scandals, the Profanation of the Eleusinian mysteries.[11] Many others, such as Rhodes and Martha Nussbaum, following the work of J. K. Davies, believe that Phaedrus was involved in both the Mutilation of the Herms and the Profanation of the Eleusinian mysteries.[12] My position, that Phaedrus was likely involved in both scandals, will become clear in the course of the commentary. Yet, unlike Rhodes and Nussbaum, I will argue, by connecting some historical dots

9. Polansky, "Reading Plato," 209.
10. Rhodes, *Eros, Wisdom, and Silence*, 381n.
11. Nails, *The People of Plato*, 233–234.
12. Nussbaum, *The Fragility of Goodness*, 212.

Preface

never before connected, that Plato himself is actually the best source by which to infer that Phaedrus was involved in both scandals.

On that point I would add that I make no pretense to adding anything historically original when I refer to the Mutilation of the Herms on the eve of the expedition to Sicily and the Profanation of the Eleusinian mysteries. Indeed, I confess I hardly have a total understanding of the political-religious machinations behind those bizarre scandals. Nobody does, it seems. It is difficult enough to comprehend political scandals of one's own time, to say nothing of religious scandals in another. Moreover, as almost all ancient Greek religion is difficult to fathom in its own right, when the obscurely religious is mixed with political intrigue, it makes for murky going indeed.

So, even as I follow Polansky's urging to Plato commentators to address more history in a dialogue, I realize that doing so invites more speculation than I, *qua* philosopher, would otherwise like to embrace. Yet, maybe the risk will have rewards.

The immediate point is that I shall refer so often to the famous dyad of Athenian scandals, the Mutilation of the Herms on the eve of the expedition to Sicily, and the Profanation of the Eleusinian mysteries, I thought it best to provide abbreviations for them. Thus the following *pretextual* abbreviations:

$MH \equiv$ Mutilation of the Herms on the eve of the expedition to Sicily;

$PEM \equiv$ Profanation of the Eleusinian mysteries

δ) Index of Abbreviations

In sum, the reader should keep in mind the following abbreviations:

Textual
　$L'/P' \equiv$ 230e–234c; Lysias's speech read by Phaedrus
　$P'/S' \equiv$ 237b–241d; Socrates's first speech instigated by Phaedrus
　$HH \equiv$ 241d–243e; Socrates's Half-comical Halting of P'/S'
　$PL \equiv$ 243e–257b; the Palinode to Love

Contextual
　$CO \equiv$ "compresence(s) of opposites"

Pretextual
　$MH \equiv$ Mutilation of the Herms on the eve of the expedition to Sicily
　$PEM \equiv$ Profanation of the Eleusinian mysteries.

Acknowledgments

WITH A KIND OF chronology, I should like to thank the following persons, from different schools and different schools of thought, whose tutelage, or moral and professional support, helped me realize the completion of this work many years in the making.

Dr. Ernest Kalbach, S.J., was mightily encouraging to this overwhelmed undergraduate, as was Dr. John Vielkind, the kindest mentor a young man could ever have. Dr. Gareth Morgan and Dr. David Armstrong were inspiring in their infectious teaching of the Greek language. Dr. John Sallis saw to it I would see Philosophy in various lights; and study and teach it in various countries. Dr. Ronald Polansky confirmed the absolute importance of Ancient Philosophy.

Also, various venues have provided me occasion to air elements of this commentary. As Visiting Professor at the Pennsylvania State University, I had access to professors and graduate students who brought the best of challenges. The North Texas Philosophical Association provided me occasion to read a lengthy portion of this work. Also, Dean John de Castro's Faculty Colloquium Lecture Series at Sam Houston State University provided occasion to present a summary of *Who Is Phaedrus?* to a body of scholars from a variety of disciplines.

In the final tally, however, I am most grateful for the caring support of my wife, Dr. Rochelle Bradley: an inspiration without equal.

Introduction

IN OUR TIME, ANY composer of a commentary on Plato's *Phaedrus* needs a ready apology. Given centuries of so many books on *Phaedrus*, why another?

Of course, a proper apology anticipates interrogatives. Where is the concomitant commentary? Many who address *Phaedrus* also treat the *Symposium*. Indeed two thinkers, William Cobb and James Rhodes, have written separate books on those two dialogues with essentially the same title (or subtitle): *Plato's Erotic Dialogues*.[1] Here, however, I limit my focus, as far as possible, to *Phaedrus*, though it is nigh impossible to write about one Platonic dialogue without reference to another.

As for the compendium of commentaries on *Phaedrus*, David White sees no need for competition among them: "The complexity of the *Phaedrus* is such that it admits many worthwhile interpretations, their value depending on the centrality of the approach taken and the consistency in which these approaches are developed."[2]

Actually, I think the highly competitive Plato would appreciate some wrangling about his work. But White is right. Competition aside, there is sufficient challenge in reading *Phaedrus* well: that is, with a central approach and a consistent development thereof.

Given the complexity of *Phaedrus*, reading *Phaedrus* well, with a central approach and consistent development, is no easy task. Indeed, for centuries it has not been clear what the central theme of *Phaedrus* is. As J. E. Raven writes: "As with the *Republic*, so again with the *Phaedrus*, scholars have always disagreed on its main subject and its main purpose. In ancient times, according to the commentator Hermeias, some thought its central

---

1. Cobb, *Plato's Erotic Dialogues*; Rhodes, *Eros, Wisdom, and Silence*.
2. White, *Rhetoric and Reality in Plato's Phaedrus*, 8.

Introduction

theme was Love, some Rhetoric, some the Good and some Beauty. Each view still seems to have its adherents."[3]

Phaedrus is a challenge on numerous fronts. Many issues found in *Phaedrus* are found elsewhere in Plato's work: the priority of dialectic over rhetoric; philosophy as a divine activity; recognition of the "Forms" (I prefer the term Essences); the three-fold psychology of wisdom-love, honor-love, money-love; etc.

Yet, what, in White's words, is the centrality of approach in *Who Is Phaedrus?*? What overriding motif would I develop as consistently as possible?

Here the centrality of approach concerns the complicated pretext of *Phaedrus*. How did Phaedrus, a rather unremarkable man, become the titular figure of a Platonic dialogue? We need to consider better who Phaedrus is, or was, to appreciate how this intriguing dialogue, that legendarily seems to defy a unified understanding, actually makes consistent sense from beginning to end.

Before I proceed further with the central question *Who Is Phaedrus?* I should address another. Should I have used the term "masterpiece" in the subtitle? Given so much commentary on Plato, perhaps it was ineluctable someone would deem it problematic to call a Platonic dialogue a "masterpiece." In *Descent of Socrates*, with a benign but important qualification, Peter Warnek warns us about the use of the term "masterpiece" relative to Plato. Warnek writes: "if the achievement of the Platonic 'masterpiece' is that it is able to reveal something radically other and strange to its own production, that it is able, like all great poetry, to release something excessive or prior to its own intent or design—without simply contradicting itself—in no way does this then lessen the demand, imposed upon the reader, to take everything in the text, to the most minute detail, as meaningful and necessary . . ."[4]

Warnek expresses my inclination and recommends my method. When I refer to *Phaedrus* as a dyad (or dianoetic) masterpiece, I hardly intend that *Phaedrus* is a formulaic machine the particulars of which can be ignored for the sake of abstracting dogma once removed from the textual details. Rather, I proceed on the premise that even the seemingly little things in *Phaedrus* have great importance. In this vein, I also concur with Cobb: "the Platonic dialogues . . . are complex and convoluted; full of irony

3. Raven, *Plato's Thought in the Making*, 188.
4. Warnek, *Descent of Socrates*, 89–90.

and sophistry, as well as positive philosophical insights and sound logical inferences. As a result their meaning can be discovered only by poring over every detail, including all dramatic elements, and comparing each bit with the total context."[5]

As for the very term "masterpiece," Raven writes: "The *Republic* is generally and rightly acclaimed as Plato's masterpiece."[6] Fair enough. I would argue, however, and no doubt Raven would too, with qualification *per* predication, that Plato was capable of more than one masterpiece.

This obvious point is to aid the reader's anticipation. That is, I also agree with Raven when he argues that Plato's is a "basically religious approach to philosophy."[7] Others have said the same. Paul Natorp expresses the religious nature of Plato's thought thusly, especially relative to the role of love/desire, or ερως, in *Phaedrus*: "*eros* has edged very close to our conception of religion. Religion does indeed signify the 'knotting together again' of the ties that are sundered . . . but through which the finite is, in accordance with the ultimate truth of things, eternally maintained in the super-finite and total."[8]

Phaedrus is, indeed, a very religious dialogue in many senses, not the least of which is that the pretext of the dialogue contains elements of the fact that in *Phaedrus*, unlike the *Symposium*, the very relationship between Phaedrus and Socrates is colored by Phaedrus's involvement in at least one of a dyad of religious scandals: the Mutilation of the Herms on the eve of the expedition to Sicily, and the Profanation of the Eleusinian Mysteries.

This dyad of religious-political issues behind the scenes involving the dyad of interlocutors, Phaedrus and Socrates, is but one of many dyadic phenomena operative in *Phaedrus*. Yet, this dyad of religious-political issues is arguably the most crucial dyad overlooked by most commentators to date; and, more, it holds the keys (hence our subtitle) to an appreciation of the unity of this dialogue that, in the eyes of many, suffers from inoperable convolution.

So, as for hermeneutical centrality, one cannot stress enough the dyadic or dianoetic elements in *Phaedrus*, especially relative to the titular figure. No previous commentary on *Phaedrus* has made centrally thematic that which Socrates tells us, quite pointedly, is Phaedrus's primary problem:

5. Cobb, "Anamnesis," 605n.
6. Raven, *Plato's Thought in the Making*, 187.
7. Ibid., 187.
8. Natorp, *Plato's Theory of Ideas*, 432.

Introduction

Phaedrus επαμφοτερίζει.[9] Phaedrus has a dyadic flaw: he always wants things both ways. Phaedrus, in the moment, is torn between Lysian rhetoric, that is almost always specious, and Socratic discourse, that is profound and revelatory. This being torn in the moment is actually but a symptom of Phaedrus's key flaw of wanting just about everything both ways, as a study of his past and his character will demonstrate. Granted, Phaedrus's state of being torn between Lysian rhetoric and Socratic enchantment is the superlative symptom because the very cure for Phaedrus's flaw lies with Phaedrus choosing, if he can, the Socratic course. Yet, Phaedrus was always torn dyadically in many ways. So, thematically, we have a dialogue with only a dyad of interlocutors presented in two famously distinct halves.

Viewing *Phaedrus* as a dyadic or dianoetic masterpiece has been my operating premise for over twenty years. My inclination toward that hermeneutical orientation was later reinforced by Charles Kahn who, for some reason, left a bit of his best work to a footnote. In *Plato and the Socratic Dialogue: The Philosophic Use of a Literary Form*, Kahn makes the compelling point that the very structure of a Platonic dialogue is a key to understanding that dialogue. Kahn, however, left it to a footnote to observe that the structure of *Phaedrus* is "dyadic."[10]

Why Kahn left this crucial claim about the form of *Phaedrus* to a footnote, I do not know. But I have moved it to the body; this book.

---

9. *Phaedrus*, 257b.
10. Kahn, *Plato and the Socratic Dialogue*, 373n.

1

Situating *Phaedrus*

a) Chronology

DEBATES ABOUT THE CHRONOLOGICAL place of *Phaedrus* in Plato's body of work will likely never cease. There appears to be no way to make a definitive statement on the issue, even after Kahn's outstanding study, "On Platonic Chronology."[1] So, if I refer to *Phaedrus* as a middle dialogue, as distinct from an early or late, I do not aim to belabor the temporal reference.

Summarily, I agree with Charles Griswold: when a dialogue was written is less important than how a dialogue is read: "Our interpretation of a dialogue in its literary and philosophical integrity will include taking into account historical allusions or events made from within its fictional frame; but the chronology of Plato's composition of the dialogue does not seem in and of itself to shed light on the drama, or the argument, or any such allusions or events."[2] In the case of *Phaedrus*, Phaedrus's relationship with Athens and Socrates is more important, and more compelling, than the place of *Phaedrus*, the dialogue, in the Platonic *corpus*.

In brief, Louis Dyer argued long ago, and to my general satisfaction at least, that *Phaedrus* seems characteristic of a so-called middle run of dialogues that includes *Cratylus*, the *Symposium*, *Phaedo*, the *Republic*, *Theaetetus*, and *Parmenides*.[3] That assessment, based in part on a study of style and motif, seems mostly reasonable and has been seconded by many commentators since, even if not defending Dyer in particular. But as no final

---

1. Kahn, "On Platonic Chronology," 93–127.
2. Griswold, "Comments on Kahn," 134.
3. Dyer, "Plato as a Playwright," 174.

Who Is Phaedrus?

statement on Platonic chronology seems necessary, or even possible, we might wish to refer, rather, to dialogue types: a "Definitions" Plato, to situate the shorter, simpler dialogues such as *Lysis*; a "Forms" Plato, to explain the longer, complex dialogues in which Socrates seems so fictive, such as the *Symposium*; and a "Kinds" Plato to explain the long dialogues in which Socrates is not as prominent, such as *Sophist*. C. J. Rowe recommends other terms for such categorization: "'early' roughly equals 'Socratic,' 'middle' is 'constructive' or 'optimistic,' while 'late' is 'critical' or 'pessimistic.'"[4]

These brief comments on Platonic chronology would serve this much: to re-assess what Dyer and others mean by the claim that the "Middle Period" Socrates is a merely dramatic figure, or an entirely dramatic character.

Here I disagree in part with Dyer's claim that in *Phaedrus* (and other middle dialogues) we see a "Platonizing Socrates," a nearly wholly dramatic character. That claim seems to rest on the assumption that there is simply no way a street Socrates, as it were, could speak so well, so quickly, and so profoundly as the *Phaedrus* Socrates or the *Republic* Socrates, etc.

Apparently to Dyer and others, there is more of a blood-and-guts Socrates in the shorter, apparently early dialogues such as *Lysis*, while the extraordinarily subtle conversations in *Phaedrus* or *Cratylus*, etc., are so complex they are implausible as historical reports. True enough. No one thinks every word of *Phaedrus*, or any Platonic dialogue, is offered as precision journalism.

Yet, we should realize, although some would not like to admit as much, that the Plato of whatever period or category, "definitions Plato," "Essences Plato," or "Kinds Plato," was writing what we now call creative non-fiction, albeit arguably the most creative creative non-fiction ever composed. The significant persons in Plato's dialogues are real, but Plato never made any pretense to quotidian commentary. Plato manipulates scenes to present the essences of situations in which the historical persons were involved, and oftentimes the essence of the topic that concerns them. So, Socrates, especially, is always going to come across as fictive; in some works more fictive than in others.

So, there is little reason that Jan Zwicky, for example, should have to belabor the claim, though it is well made, that Socrates was long dead when *Phaedrus* was composed.[5] What matters most about Zwicky's claim that *Phaedrus* was surely composed after Socrates's death is not timing but

---

4. Rowe, "Killing Socrates," 64.
5. Zwicky, "Plato's *Phaedrus*: Philosophy as Dialogue with the Dead," 19–48.

motif. *Phaedrus* may stand alongside the *Apology* as a longer version of the latter in that sense. Similarly, there is little reason Spiro Panagiotou should have to belabor the claim, though it is well made, that Lysias was already dead at the supposed time of the events of *Phaedrus*.[6]

Yet, we might ask: if Plato wrote creative non-fiction, are Plato's dialogues then "true?" Here we should adopt, I argue, the position of Socrates himself when Phaedrus asks Socrates what Socrates thinks about the myth of Boreas associated with the place in which they are talking. Socrates says he deems the myth "true," given the ineluctable import of the message behind it.

A final note, then, on chronology: I would second Dyer's assessment, and that of others, that *Phaedrus* may be called a middle period piece given that so many elements of *Phaedrus* closely relate to the *Republic*, the textual anchor of the middle period. Yet, I am hardly alone when I call attention to intersections between *Phaedrus* and the *Republic*. Natorp, for example, regards the *Republic* a repository of themes of many middle dialogues, especially the *Symposium, Phaedo,* and *Phaedrus*.[7] Natorp stresses the commonality of the function of dialectic in these dialogues (more implied than express in the *Symposium*). Natorp even concludes that there is an emphasis on collection over division in these late-middle dialogues, even though the usually thorough Natorp makes no compelling defense of that very particular claim.

Natorp appears to make that claim based on the impressions left by *Phaedrus*, and the *PL* in particular, in which there is no obvious tie, downward, as it were, to the mundane order from the Essence revolution revealed in the chariot-train myth in the *PL*.[8] Otherwise, relative to Natorp's claim, I see no extraordinary emphasis on collection over division in the middle period. Yet, my linking of *Phaedrus* with the *Republic* certainly does center on the issue of dialectic.[9]

Other connections between *Phaedrus* and the *Republic* have been persuasively posed. For example, G. J. De Vries finds a rather pointed identity of the meaning of ἁπλόος, or "simple," as a sign of genuine character in both *Phaedrus* and the *Republic*.[10]

6. Panagiotou, "Lysias and the Date of Plato's *Phaedrus*," 388–89.
7. Natorp, *Plato's Theory of Ideas*, 204.
8. Cf., "The Line on Dialectic, Part 2."
9. Cf., "The Line on Dialectic, Part 1."
10. De Vries, *A Commentary on the Phaedrus of Plato*, 52.

Who Is Phaedrus?

The most crucial moment in which Socrates emphasizes the idea that Phaedrus is to become ἁπλόος, or "simple," is actually expressed with the adverbial ἁπλῶς, "simply" or "single-mindedly," as Phaedrus is to learn to proceed simply or single-mindedly, via the love of wisdom, in contrast with the way in which Phaedrus proceeds dyadically or duplicitously via the mere love of honor.[11] *Who Is Phaedrus?*, indeed, more than De Vries's commentary, will make much of Socrates's aim to move Phaedrus's soul to the state of "simple."[12]

Otherwise, the many connections I see between *Phaedrus* and the *Republic* will become obvious in due course, but the most important and novel lies with the *dianoetic* intersection I see between the two works. *Phaedrus* is the exceptionally engaging thought-experiment extension of the treatment of *dianoia* central especially to the *Republic*.

β) Reading Plato

Again, the manner in which a Platonic dialogue is read is just as important as when the dialogue was composed, if not more so. Reflections on how Plato has been read are therefore worthy of consideration.

Among others, Gerald Press has provided one of the best inventories of ways Plato has been read, especially pre- and post-Schleirmacher.[13] Press argues that Plato's readers over the centuries, especially pre-Schleirmacher, have operated on at least two problematic assumptions: a) that Plato has a merely doctrinal philosophy that exists entirely independently of the dialogues; and b) that the poetic elements in Plato's dialogues are literary fluff. I try to avoid both assumptions, although I do argue that there is more of a system in Plato than many allow; or, as Kathryn Morgan writes: "Plato challenges us to move from local to systemic readings, but not to do so in a doctrinaire way."[14]

The post-Schleiermacher readers who work upon those previously noted assumptions are usually associated with Analytic philosophy. Stanley Rosen is one of the most famous critics of Analytic studies of Plato that do not reflect what may be called the fullness of the dialogues. Some Analytic studies of Plato are so preoccupied with mechanics of argument they do not

---

11. *Phaedrus*, 257b.
12. Cf., "Phaedrus's Whither."
13. Press, "Principles of Dramatic and Non–Dramatic Plato Interpretation," 107–27.
14. Morgan, "Comments on Gill," 184.

Situating Phaedrus

appreciate that sometimes, as Rosen says, "the unspoken dimension of the dialogues is their most important dimension."[15] I would not say the unspoken dimension of a dialogue is always the most important dimension, as Rosen says; yet, the unspoken in a Platonic dialogue can be as important as the spoken: thus my emphasis on the importance of Socrates's HH, which is just as significant as a deed as it is something spoken.

Yet, as for the spoken word, there is certainly more to a Platonic dialogue than just obvious argument. Hence, further, to quote Mark Moes quoting Rosen: "The dialogues impel readers 'to engage in the act of interpretation, to fill in the missing links, to revise accommodated arguments, to discern the import of hints, and to understand the significance of jokes.'"[16]

Hints, jokes, arguments: Plato employs them all, and for various purposes. *Phaedrus* is no exception. In parts, indeed at crucial moments, *Phaedrus* is just about the silliest of Plato's dialogues. Yet, the occasional silliness has serious implications.[17]

Also, it is a good thing Plato cared little or nothing about political correctness; otherwise Plato would not be Plato; and *Phaedrus* would not be the text we have.

In brief, regarding how to read Plato, I concur with Rosen when he says: "it amounts to the careful and reflective consideration of every aspect of the dialogue under study."[18] That seems to say it all.

Yet, studies as to how to read Plato continue to appear. Drew Hyland's *Questioning Platonism* offers yet another inventory of readings of Plato. Hyland revisits the issue of pre- and post-Schleirmacher assumptions about Plato, but Hyland does not blame Analytic philosophy alone for viewing Plato as a doctrine-monger obsessed with cutesy poetry.[19] In fact, Hyland hardly mentions Analytic philosophy. Hyland's thesis in *Questioning Platonism* is that the most famous Continental thinkers, Heidegger, Derrida, et alia, have also read Plato in a way too reductionist to do the dialogues justice.

---

15. Moes, *Plato's Dialogue Form and the Care of the Soul*, 23.
16. Ibid., 23.
17. Cf. "Phaedrus's Whither."
18. Rosen, "The Non-Lover in Plato's *Phaedrus*," 423.
19. Hyland, *Questioning Platonism*, 1–15.

Who Is Phaedrus?

γ) Reading *Phaedrus*

Given his critique of so many reductionist readings of Plato, Hyland surely knew he could have delved deeper in the history of philosophy for other criticisms of Continental thinkers. For example, despite his own elaborate Aesthetics, Hegel eschewed the poetic elements in Plato, and *Phaedrus* in particular.

One Hegelian line about *Phaedrus* expresses volumes. Hegel has a curt comment about the image of the soul in *Phaedrus*: "This image expresses nothing to us."[20] I argue: quite the contrary. It depends on how one reads the dialogue on the whole. I argue that the image of the soul in *Phaedrus* has ultimate significance and in a way never before appreciated: that the image's very constitution serves as a paradigm of other significant, and ultimately telling, structures in the dialogue. Those structures in the dialogue in turn disclose ultimate points about *Phaedrus* in ways that serve not only to ground the argumentation, but to highlight other keys: who Phaedrus is; what his problems are; what remedies Phaedrus needs; and what remedies Socrates can bring to this particular case.[21]

A word more about Hegel: In Hegel's view, Plato should have abandoned poetry and proceeded toward a coherent definition of dialectic. Hegel was right to criticize the sometimes pedestrian accounts of dialectic found in Plato, especially in the so-called early dialogues. Hegel was not the first or last to be so critical.[22] However, regarding *Phaedrus* at least, Hegel ignored poetic devices that highlight dialectic, not only as Plato more maturely understood it, but even along lines by which Hegel himself construed it. Indeed, I argue that one of the high points of *Phaedrus* is a critique of the Eleatics for not conceiving of a logic that accommodates becoming, to say nothing about development. That theme should have been dear to Hegel, but Hegel missed it because he had little patience with the dialogue's dramatic particulars.

Another reference to Hyland is apposite: *Who Is Phaedrus?* was begun long before the appearance of Hyland's *Questioning Platonism*. So, given Hyland's challenge to commentators to read Plato more thoroughly than most in the past, I am responding to Hyland's charge by default, not by design. Thus my appreciation of Press's summation of the challenges of

---

20. Hegel, *Plato and the Platonists*, 38.
21. Cf. "Images of the Image of the Soul."
22. See Robinson, *Plato's Early Dialectic*.

Situating Phaedrus

reading Plato: I try to account for as many social, political, linguistic, and dramatic elements in the dialogue as possible, without, that is, composing a book of a thousand pages.

In situating *Phaedrus* further, especially relative to the *Republic*, as noted in the Introduction, the very dyadic formatting of *Phaedrus* needs more attention than Kahn offered, especially after Kahn stressed the absolute importance of a Platonic dialogue's format. The dyadic structure of *Phaedrus* is of ultimate importance, along with the ascending/descending motif written into that structure.

As I survey *Phaedrus* and the *Republic*, I observe with Sallis and Rhodes, but especially the former, an ascending/descending motif in *Phaedrus* barely removed from the ascending/descending frame of the *Republic*.[23] Others have found the operation of such motif in both dialogues, and in fact have argued that *Phaedrus* and the *Republic* are sister dialogues in effect, with the action of Phaedrus following immediately after the action of the *Republic*. Richard Rojcewicz argues that Phaedrus encounters Socrates on the morning after the evening Socrates had descended to Piraeus to engage in the action of the *Republic*: "If Lysias had just arrived [in Athens] the evening before, while Socrates was still at the Piraeus, it would explain why, in the *Phaedrus*, Socrates is at first uninformed that Lysias is in town. Socrates, with a reputation as a busybody, is not likely to be unaware that a personage such as Lysias is visiting the city—unless Socrates was not in Athens himself when Lysias arrived."[24] Further: "The mention of Epicrates' house also ties the *Phaedrus* to the *Republic*. This house is said to be located near the Olympieum, i.e., near the temple to Olympian Zeus on the southeast side of Athens. The closest city gate in that direction is the same one that leads down to the Piraeus; just beyond the gate is the Ilissus. If Phaedrus left that house with the intention of going beyond the walls, he would then naturally make for the same gate Socrates would use in returning to the city."[25]

A dyadic format and ascent/descent motif are not all *Phaedrus* and the *Republic* have in common. Granted, we should hesitate to tie dialogues together by "the thinnest of threads," as Jowett says.[26] In such tying, Jowett suggests, there is the temptation to find in Plato a philosophical system

---

23. Sallis, *Being and Logos*, 455.
24. Rojcewicz, "The Festive and the Workady in Plato's *Phaedrus*," 163.
25. Ibid., 163–64.
26. Jowett, *Gorgias and Timaeus*, 1.

where none might exist. And, of course, for the longest time many thinkers of various stripes have argued that Plato has no philosophical system. Emerson says, for example: "he has not a system. The dearest defenders and disciples are at fault. He attempted a theory of the universe, and his theory is not complete or self-evident."[27]

Yet, should we quibble here? How many theories are self-evident? Even assuming Plato has no philosophical system, the sheer complexity of the dialogues forces one to raise questions as to how to read all of the dialogues with an integrity they all but command.

So, if the dialogues are works of creative non-fiction, should we start with the historical? If they are philosophical works of creative non-fiction, should we start with epistemology and metaphysics, or other issues?

As to whether or not concerns with metaphysics or epistemology should be the starting points of a reading of *Phaedrus*, my reading would somewhat qualify the operating premise of Griswold's commentary on *Phaedrus* which states: "a defense of the *Phaedrus'* notion of dialogue might begin not with metaphysical or epistemological doctrines but with an exercise in the art of rhetoric also described in the *Phaedrus*—the effort to lead one's interlocutor to reflect on himself."[28] My approach to *Phaedrus* is perhaps distinct from Griswold's but with not a considerable difference. That is, is not the emphasis on self-reflection or self-knowledge emphasized by Griswold a kind of emphasis on epistemology?

So it is that I begin my reading of *Phaedrus* with an admitted admixture: in part from a consideration of the historical elements surrounding Phaedrus's situation; in part from a systematizing, as far as possible, of the epistemological elements gleaned from the *Republic*; and in part from an appreciation, within boundaries, of Plato's genius for creative non-fiction. I argue that it is entirely legitimate, and exceedingly instructive, to find more than isolated intersections between *Phaedrus* and the *Republic*; and I would carry Sallis's, Rhodes's, and Rojcewicz's linking of the two dialogues even further.

Establishing connections between *Phaedrus* and the *Republic* has been authorized by many others on many grounds; granted, some more compelling than others. One of the less compelling comes from Kahn. Despite his brilliant work on the whole, at one point Kahn offers a rather pedestrian connection between *Phaedrus* and the *Republic* when he notes that in the

---

27. Emerson, "Plato; or The Philosopher," 131.
28. Griswold, *Self-Knowledge in Plato's Phaedrus*, 238.

second sentence of *Phaedrus* there is mention of "Lysias, son of Cephalus," which "recalls the opening scene of the *Republic*."[29] Of course, in *Phaedrus*, Lysias is really a central figure, even if not in the action. Indeed, in Socrates's peculiar way of expression, Socrates claims that Lysias is "present."[30]

Not only is Lysias mentioned early and often in *Phaedrus*, Lysias is also mentioned at one point in a set of comments that includes another name from the *Republic*, Thrasymachus.[31] Yet, Kahn says nothing of that reference; and while Kahn's work on the whole is outstanding, such threads, Jowett is right, are thin indeed.

Ultimately, however, the connections I find between *Phaedrus* and the *Republic* extend beyond such biographical or nominal intersections. But let us rethink for a moment Emerson and his claim that Plato has no system. Griswold is certainly right about Plato's thought not being a system in the modern sense of the word in which the terms from one work carry over mechanically to another (or are supposed to do so): "Plato's dialogues evidence a studious and frustrating avoidance of 'technical' terminology."[32] So, Plato has no philosophical system in the sense in which Kant has a philosophical system, wherein terms in one work must, or should, mean the same in another. Plato is not Kant: agreed.

Yet, surely Plato's whole thought is more than a repository of threads. The absence of strict terminological correspondence between and among dialogues hardly precludes the function signified by a term from one dialogue from actually operating in another. Indeed, in virtually the same place that Emerson claims that Plato has no system, Emerson also writes: "A key to the method and completeness of Plato is his twice bisected line."[33] There is at least, even Emerson allows, some kind of "method" and "completeness" in Plato, with the *Republic* and the Divided Line in particular as the focal point of something akin to a system.

Along that line, as it were, I observe in *Phaedrus* that which is so important in the *Republic*: dialectic, and the function of *dianoia* in particular. Thus my position: in the *Republic*, Plato attributes a fairly precise epistemological function to *dianoia*; and one of the keys to understanding *Phaedrus*

---

29. Kahn, *Plato and the Socratic Dialogue*, 373.
30. *Phaedrus*, 228e.
31. Ibid., 266c.
32. Griswold, "Plato's Metaphilosophy," 148.
33. Emerson, "Plato; or The Philosopher," 130.

Who Is Phaedrus?

is the recognition that *dianoia*'s function in the *Republic* still operates in *Phaedrus sans* an obvious declaration thereof.

In *Phaedrus*, as in other dialogues, Plato uses the term *dianoia* desultorily. Plato uses the term *dianoia* early, and has the superficial Phaedrus say it. Phaedrus acknowledges he cannot recall *L'/P'* verbatim. So, were he not actually to read *L'/P'* aloud, Phaedrus confesses, he could do no more than merely impart the "general sense," or *dianoia*, of it.[34] This is telling. Even if *dianoia*, there, has no explicitly technical meaning in *Phaedrus*, later in the dialogue *dianoia* bears at least more epistemological significance than the mere "general sense" of something. Later in the dialogue, that is, Socrates employs the term *dianoia* in a more specific way; i.e., to signify the operation of "intellection."[35] Although that use of *dianoia* may not recall precisely the dyadic power of intellection in the *Republic*, it means certainly more than a mere "general sense."

Finally, the term *dianoia* appears near the end of *Phaedrus* when Socrates refers to the *dianoia*, or "mind," of Isocrates.[36] In this final use, *dianoia* suggests a more obviously epistemological function, as Socrates is referring specifically to Isocrates's philosophy in that context. Thus the subtle, near conflation of the two prior uses of *dianoia* in *Phaedrus*: "general sense" and "intellection." For Socrates, Isocrates is a philosopher to some extent, because Isocrates's *dianoia* shows that Isocrates is not just a rank rhetorician. But Isocrates is little more than a rhetorician-pragmatist for whom life reduces to "speaking well, persuading others, and seeking advantages."[37] Isocrates derives his wisdom from the way humans operate conventionally with the "things" (πραγμα) in their world. Hence, Isocrates only provides a "general sense" of the good derived mostly from custom and manners. Isocrates does not systematize in the sense in which he traces accords between mind and thing, as Plato does with the Divided Line. Yet, Isocrates achieved something more properly dianoetic (in the Platonic meaning) than other thinkers, even if Isocrates did not make *dianoia*, or something like it, expressly thematic. That is, Isocrates had to achieve some epistemological height to be in a position to criticize rhetoricians who did not even appeal to habit or custom, signs of consistency reasonably associated with

34. *Phaedrus*, 228d.
35. Ibid., 244c.
36. Ibid., 279b.
37. McAdon, "Plato's Denunciation of Rhetoric in the *Phaedrus*," 31.

Situating Phaedrus

rationality itself. In that sense at least, Isocrates is superior, in principle, to Lysias, who is pleased to appear a non-philosopher altogether.

Yet, Socrates realizes that, in reality, Lysias is cleverer than Isocrates and therefore more dangerous; that Lysias is aware of the functions of dialectic even if Lysias does not advertise as much. Lysias could not write such clever speeches were he not somehow attuned to the functions of dialectic. Yet, Lysias is, at best, yet another antilogician who can generate speeches that employ some of the basics of dialectic but only to conceal the truth, not reveal it.

That is why, between the early and the late uses of the term *dianoia* in *Phaedrus*, Plato refers to the most pointed uses of the term. Socrates refers to "the *dianoia* of the philosopher" (ἡ τοῦ φιλοσόφου διάνοια)[38] that best reflects the "divine *dianoia*" (θεοῦ διάνοια) that is nurtured on mind and the knowledge of Essences.[39] In the Zeus myth in the Palinode, even the god "goes home" after beholding pure Essences.[40] Yet, the gods never have to sort their way through idle opinions the way humans must via *dianoia*, given the human condition that is steeped in particulars. Therein is, arguably, the truly central motif among many motifs in *Phaedrus*: homecoming. Until a human has returned again to the Essence revolution, to the knowledge of Essences, he is lost.

The main problem (among many) with Lysias is that Lysias is pleased to sow confusion in the minds of his hearers by mingling truth with opinion. Isocrates, at least, is nobler in intent than Lysias; but Isocrates is not an exceptional lover of wisdom due to the fact that Isocrates reduces wisdom to the rather routine truths that accrue from the ways humans habitually deal with particulars. Socrates, of course, the true philosopher, always has something higher in mind as the ground of those particulars; and what Socrates has most in mind in *Phaedrus* is the recognition that the once-exiled Phaedrus, who had come home to Athens, had actually not made a proper return. The necessary condition for Phaedrus's proper return to Athens was Phaedrus's proper return to the Essence Wheel.

So, given the issue of *dianoia* in the *Republic*, *Phaedrus* allows for multifarious, extended, yet consistent use of *dianoia*-driven discernment on display *per* the Divided Line. I refer to the employment of *dianoia* in *Phaedrus* as extended because the many *CO* for consideration in *Phaedrus*

---

38. *Phaedrus*, 249c.
39. Ibid., 247d.
40. Ibid., 247e.

do not involve mere fingers, as in the *Republic*, but whole persons, speeches, etc. If Owen and Sallis are correct to say that triadic/dyadic confusion in the sensuous is what led Plato to "invent" or hypothesize the Forms for clarification, one may say that in *Phaedrus* we see the creative-non-fiction-writing Plato "inventing" triad/dyad relations that call for various clarifications in various situations in the lived world, in Phaedrus's world in particular. Plato "invented" the scenario in which Socrates exits the city with Phaedrus to discuss Phaedrus's rather complicated situation. Yet, Plato did not invent Phaedrus; or Phaedrus's involvement in the *MH* or the *PEM*; or Phaedrus's banishment from Athens; or Phaedrus's return from exile; or Phaedrus's return to an Athens dominated by democrats like Lysias, etc.

What Plato gives us in *Phaedrus*, then, is an ingenious experiment in psychological and historical analysis that seamlessly suits the epistemological premises offered in the *Republic*. The *Republic* offers a proto-methodology that *Phaedrus* applies.

After the fashion of the Divided Line in the *Republic*, in *Phaedrus* Plato places before us many occasions for the task of comparing-and-contrasting among and between various triads and dyads: Lysias-Phaedrus-Socrates; Morychus-Epicrates-Lysias; L'/P'-P'/S'-PL; and even Homer-Solon-Lysias at the end. All of these triads reduce to telling dyads, the analysis of which is indispensible for a full understanding of *Phaedrus* from beginning to end: hence the subtitle, *Keys to Plato's Dyad Masterpiece*. If Emerson is right that the key to understanding Plato best lies with understanding the Divided Line, there are keys derivative from that key. So, another key to understanding *Phaedrus* is the appreciation of triad/dyad, compare-and-contrast thinking promoted in Plato's *Republic*.

Finally, the intersections between *Phaedrus* and the *Republic* highlighted in *Who Is Phaedrus?* are more grounded in the particulars of the texts than many intersections found by other commentators. For example, G. R. F. Ferrari finds a very tenuous tie between the *Republic* and *Phaedrus* on the topic of psychological internalization. I shall elaborate on this tie here because, while I find Ferrari's textual ties between the dialogues tenuous at times, the spirit with which Ferrari writes about *Phaedrus* verifies what I find in *Phaedrus*: hardly just a fictionalized Socrates, but a flesh-and-blood man; yes, more than a tad fictive, but one who is trying hard to help a struggling soul in the person of Phaedrus in a very trying time.

In his excellent commentary on *Phaedrus*, Ferrari analyzes the problem of the embodiment of the philosopher in light of the issue of love. The

Situating Phaedrus

philosopher's very embodiment challenges the philosopher to deal with the question of contingency. Ferrari cleverly shows that the question of contingency and necessity is not an abstract one when properly recognized in complex, lived situations, like we see in *Phaedrus*.

Regarding the basic dynamics of the lover/non-lover debate in the first half of *Phaedrus*, Ferrari argues that the very act of falling in love can throw a philosopher into a serious conundrum. If part of *Phaedrus* is correct, the phenomenon of falling in love can move the lover of wisdom to pursue wisdom all the more in light of the contingent emergence of another person in one's life; presumably a physically appealing person. Yet, Ferrari suggests that when such a contingent encounter occurs, the especially attractive beloved might become aware that he or she might not be loved as a matter of eternal devotion, or from a principle of necessity. So, Ferrari's philosopher, who is supposed to operate from a principle of necessity, might be revealed as a bad lover attracted to the beloved due to mere appearance, a signature of the contingent, an accident of birth.

Ferrari feels, as it were, for the beloved in such a circumstance. Such a beloved, despite the beauty, is usually spurned in the end, especially when the beauty fades. And more, the very attractive beloved is usually plagued over the course of the relationship. Such a sad beloved is in essence always asking the lover, if only silently: "Why do you not love me for myself?"[41]

Ferrari notes the alternate effect when the genuine philosopher falls in love. The genuine philosopher, or genuine lover, internalizes the opposite of the question posed by the attractive beloved who asks the lover (essentially continually) why the beloved is not loved for herself. That is, the philosopher who falls in love asks himself (essentially continually): "Now that this relationship has happened, how can I find a way to love this person continually in a way that supersedes the contingencies of appearance, time, place, etc.?" That is, the genuine philosopher asks: "How can I now love this individual, within this sea of contingencies that brought this beloved to me, with a sense of necessity?"

Ferrari proceeds to claim that this profound internalization of the question of contingency and necessity, an internalization that Ferrari thinks constitutes the essence of *Phaedrus*, finds a parallel in the internalization of the definition of justice in the *Republic*.

In the *Republic*, it is as though Socrates has to remind his audience that Justice is not only, and not first and foremost, an instrument of the

---

41. Ferrari, *Listening to the Cicadas*, 160.

Who Is Phaedrus?

state. Justice is rather first and foremost, along with wisdom, courage, and moderation, a part of individual virtue. Accordingly, Ferrari argues that in the *Republic* Plato: "analyzes a virtue which pertains to our relations with other people in terms pertaining only to ourselves; for the psychic harmony which justice turns out to be is a condition of the individual soul. Similarly, here in the *Phaedrus*, the supremely other-directed feelings of love are assessed primarily in terms of what takes place within the individual souls of lovers rather than with reference to the structure of the relationship between them."[42]

Ferrari's analysis of the internalization of love and justice in *Phaedrus* and the *Republic* respectively is quite compelling, and daily applicable. Yet, it is based on a tenuous textual tie. I shall draw stricter, more methodological comparisons between the two dialogues, and with tighter textual orientations; but those references, I hope the reader will see, deal with real blood-and-guts persons struggling with real difficulties for which Socrates might have some remedy.

---

42. Ferrari, *Listening to the Cicadas*, 161.

2

The Line on Dialectic, Part 1

a) "... as if he were a god"

DESPITE THE OBVIOUS ATTENTION paid to rhetoric in *Phaedrus*, *Phaedrus* is ultimately about dialectic. Socrates refers to dialectic on more than one occasion, and especially in what may be regarded the dialogue's most telling line.

Socrates proclaims provocatively that if anyone could teach him dialectic he would "walk in his footsteps as if he were a god."[1] This line is seminal for many reasons:

1) it suggests that dialectic is a kind of divine knowledge or the key to the most divine understanding a human might attain.

2) it is a paraphrase of a line from Homer. It therefore intentionally evokes the poetic. In *Phaedrus*, Plato the philosophical poet, or poetic philosopher, is, as always, engaging in open competition with the poets; and he beats them at the game, especially those who had already begun to develop the dialogue as an art form.[2]

3) it broaches a core question of the dialogue: whether or not dialectic itself, which Plato thinks is presupposed in the teaching of all particular arts or sciences, is itself teachable. If dialectic is teachable, is it teachable as other arts and sciences are? After all, Socrates's line suggests that only a god could teach dialectic; and how many gods are available? If dialectic is the very means by which one speaks and thinks well and systematically, how does one become attuned to something so basic, so archaic in the most

---

1. *Phaedrus*, 266b.
2. See Kahn, *Plato and the Socratic Dialogue*, 1–35.

profound sense of the word? Moreover, if dialectic is really so fundamental, important, and universal, how is it so many persons, including Phaedrus, are either unaware of it, forgetful of it, or indifferent to it?

4) can Socrates "teach" dialectic to Phaedrus; and if so, to what extent; and how? Also, especially as Phaedrus is preoccupied with rhetoric, how might Socrates deliver speeches in such manner that the function of dialectic filters through the speeches for Phaedrus's consciousness of it? Thus another question implied in that consequential question:

5) to what extent is Socrates a god or like a god? More, on the receiving end, does Phaedrus have any divine element in him such that he is teachable regarding the divine science, dialectic? Plato's basic and ultimate pedagogical principle lies precisely in this dynamic: a person cannot learn anything divine without a spark of divinity in the person in the first place.[3]

The line about walking in the footsteps of a teacher of dialectic "as if he were a god" is echoed by another crucial line in *Phaedrus*. In the *PL*, when Socrates is describing the Zeus-like lover, the true lover, Socrates says the Zeus-like lover leads the beloved to the highest of heights and tries to make his beloved, as far as possible, like the god. The Zeus-like lover stands in stark contrast with the all-too-human lover who does not lead but merely dominates.

Further, the line on dialectic offers some subtle comedy. Socrates's line about following the teacher of dialectic "as if he were a god" is posed in a way that is almost as silly as the premise of a satyr play. Phaedrus led Socrates out of the city. Socrates would lead, by following, to "teach" an unteachable subject, dialectic, the divine science, to a man who had become a virtual atheist. Here, as so often in Plato, much of the message is in the drama itself.

Accordingly, it is the discernment afforded by dialectic that allows for recognition of the significance of so many *CO* in *Phaedrus*'s dramatic setting. Such is the nature of dialectic that once attuned to it one can see, and duly note, so many plays between the similar and dissimilar, being and seeming, truth and error, divine and mortal, etc. This dialectically charged reflexivity in the drama is what separates Plato's philosophical poetry from typical poetry. The latter is often flatly narrative by comparison.

---

3. Cf., "Phaedrus's Whither."

The Line on Dialectic, Part 1

β) Dialectic and Rhetoric

Thus a major challenge: how to communicate dialectic, the divine science, to Phaedrus, a man who had grown indifferent to the divine. Dialectic is the very font of philosophy as Socrates understands it. But how can Socrates convert Phaedrus to true philosophy when Phaedrus, foremost a fan of rhetoric, does not acknowledge any truth to be cherished?

Further, can Socrates present the nature and function of dialectic in terms that suit Phaedrus's rather prurient interests? Phaedrus likes cleverness and, apparently, sex; prefers entertainment in speech to genuine dialogue. As Kathryn Morgan writes, not necessarily about Phaedrus although the words apply to him: "Conversation gives us the power to refine our thought, but we have to be aware that refinement is a desideratum before we can achieve it."[4]

Phaedrus does not know what true refinement is. Ironically, the state of soul to which Socrates would move Phaedrus is that of "simple" (ἁπλόος) yet by some of the most complicated conversation imaginable, superseding in cleverness the clever Lysias along the way.

Hence another crucial question: can Socrates present dialectic to Phaedrus in a way befitting Phaedrus's complicated past? Even though Socrates knows his audience well in this case, an audience of one, his task is still daunting. Socrates has to teach dialectic, as far as possible, to a man who has been, as long as Socrates has known him, obsessed with three things: speeches, mere appearance, and male homosexuality as a kind of civic religion. Can Socrates make dialectic intelligible, and quickly, in conversation about all of these phenomena? Can Socrates do this while also hinting, at least, that had Phaedrus heeded dialectic as a younger man, Phaedrus would not have been embroiled in scandals that led to Phaedrus's exile?

In the *Symposium*, Phaedrus was called "the father of speeches."[5] That title was given not only because Phaedrus was the first to speak at the banquet. Phaedrus had been an acknowledged lover of speeches for as long as anyone could remember. *Phaedrus* Phaedrus is no different from *Symposium* Phaedrus, except for one thing. Phaedrus has a new lover, Lysias, the most influential speech-writer in or about Athens. So, Phaedrus in *Phaedrus* seems to maintain by default that rhetoric is a τέχνη, an "art," even if Phaedrus cannot define rhetoric. If rhetoric is not an art, then Lysias is just

---

4. Morgan, "Comments on Gill," 182.
5. *Symposium*, 177d.

Who Is Phaedrus?

a literary, or logographical, hack; and if Lysias is a literary hack, Phaedrus is little more than a kind of speech fan and associate of a fraud.

It is not historically evident that Lysias and Phaedrus were lovers; but when Socrates says something is the case in a dialogue, the reader has to proceed on that assumption, especially when Phaedrus offers no denial. After the *PL*, when Socrates prays for an apology for denigrating love, Socrates refers to Lysias and "his lover here" (ὁ ἐραστης ὅδε αὐτου), Phaedrus.[6] In this case, it is not that Socrates means that Phaedrus is actually functioning as *erastes* to Lysias as *pais*; rather, however, but not far removed from that intention, Socrates is prodding Phaedrus to realize that Phaedrus, going by the strict terminology of the pederasty relationship, if anyone, ought to be the *erastes* in his relationship with Lysias because Phaedrus is likely older than Lysias, if only slightly.

Also, in essentially the very next moment, when Phaedrus says that Lysias might be afraid to be called a speech-writer, Socrates thinks Phaedrus is wrong; and in that context Socrates refers to Lysias as Phaedrus's "other" (ἑταίρου), a term that is loaded indeed.[7] When Socrates refers to Lysias as Phaedrus's εταιρου, he could mean either "comrade," as in those of the same political persuasion, in this case, democrat; or "lover," as in Typhonic, honor-love-based lover; or even something surly, as in quasi-illicit lover, as εταιρου could mean "courtesan" (at least in heterosexual circles).

Further, Socrates's claim about love between Phaedrus and Lysias allows for another indirect allusion to dialectic. For Socrates, dialectic is prior in principle to all of the arts. So, even if rhetoric is an art, Phaedrus is supposed to realize that he is to choose Socrates's sublime philosophical speaking over Lysias's merely clever rhetoric, especially as the former is the very font of rhetoric as a τέχνη in the first place.

This would be a difficult choice, and even realization, for Phaedrus, as Phaedrus was not astute enough to realize quickly that dialectic is artistically prior, at least in principle, to rhetoric; and, besides, Lysias had his attractions. Lysias became a wealthy businessman, and augmented his wealth with his writing ability. As a clever logographer, Lysias became the equivalent of a successful modern lawyer, and achieved remarkable social status as a prosecutor. In this light, given Phaedrus's criminal past, Socrates had to intimate, somehow, that Phaedrus needed to see that Phaedrus's very relationship with Lysias required some serious discernment that could only

6. *Phaedrus*, 257b.
7. Ibid., 257d.

The Line on Dialectic, Part 1

be achieved by dialectic. That is, as the machinations of Athenian law were complex, Phaedrus could easily be accused, as a former exile, of something again someday (as the famous case of Andokides proves); and accused, perhaps, by none other than his new lover, Lysias.

γ) Dialectic and Discernment

Socrates had to move Phaedrus to realize that rhetoric, even if it is not an art, operates on a stunning scope. Feats of persuasion are attempted in all areas of life, public and private; from debates about war in the agora, to negotiations of sexual favors in the bedroom. If rhetoric extends so far, so must dialectic in principle, either as the intellectual ground of rhetoric as an art, or as the means to recognize various forms of similarity and dissimilarity, identity and difference, to say nothing of definitions for the sake of sciences or stipulations.

So, after noting the two basic operations in dialectic, collection and division, Socrates states: "Can there be anything of importance which is not included in these processes . . . ?"[8] Every facet of Phaedrus's or anyone's life requires, according to Socrates, dialectical discernment. Phaedrus especially needed lessons in dialectic, the better to see into the basics of his situation.

As Phaedrus had returned to Athens from exile, it is likely several negative circumstances moved Phaedrus to embrace Lysias as a lover. Mainly, *qua* former exile, Phaedrus had become impoverished. Regarding many who were banished from Athens for whatever reason, Athens published the records of the sale of their confiscated properties, and it was surely no secret that the locally famous Phaedrus had become a pauper. No less than Lysias himself once publicly noted that Phaedrus had become impoverished, but "οὐ διὰ κακίας," that is, "not from evil"; or, paraphrasing, "through no fault of his own"; or, more in terms of an Athens in which shame and honor played such major roles, "not from something dishonorable."[9]

Of course, Lysias's choice of terms here could be qualified. If Lysias did not see Phaedrus's loss of property due to any particular evil of Phaedrus's own, it is because either: a) Lysias, *qua* democrat, did not find the *PEM*, that was designed to offend aristocrats, particularly offensive; and/or b) it was clear that Phaedrus, a man of little initiative, was merely caught

---

8. *Phaedrus*, 266d.
9. Lysias, *The Orations of Lysias*, 42; Hackforth, *Plato's Phaedrus*, 8.

Who Is Phaedrus?

up in an uncivil act for which he, as unthinking joiner, bore little or no responsibility.

The key point is this: Phaedrus had likely become dependent upon Lysias financially. So, even though Lysias was possibly younger than Phaedrus, Lysias nonetheless assumed the role of *erastes* to Phaedrus as *pais*, or boy, in a most unusual version of the pederasty relationship. Marian Demos has noted that "both figures [Lysias and Socrates] can be viewed as potential *erastai*" relative to Phaedrus.[10] Indeed. One of the keys to understanding *Phaedrus* is the recognition that, oddly, Phaedrus had become little more than a pederasty "boy" to Lysias as *erastes*. That is why Socrates playacts the role of would-be *erastes* to Phaedrus, basically in the guise of Lysias, especially in *P'/S'*. In subtle ways, and one way not so subtle, Socrates tries to reveal just how problematic Phaedrus's relationship with Lysias is. Phaedrus might come to see his own pathetic status relative to Lysias, but only after some discernment borne of dialectical thinking.

As a long-corrupted youth of Athens, Phaedrus was indeed somewhat a boy mentally, but hardly physically. Nails puts Phaedrus's age at the "midtwenties" at the supposed time of *Phaedrus*.[11] Rhodes suggests, inferring from historical hints in the text of *Phaedrus*, that Phaedrus was forty-three or so at the alleged time of *Phaedrus*.[12] Hackforth, prior to Rhodes, put Phaedrus's age at about forty at the alleged time of *Phaedrus*: age eighteen in *Protagoras*; age thirty-four in *Symposium*; age forty in *Phaedrus*.[13] Whatever his precise age, Phaedrus is old enough to know better about many things; and one thing Phaedrus is supposed to know, finally, is dialectic, the means by which he might discern that he is being treated like a mere "boy," basically his opposite, in a perverse version of an already problematic type of relationship, pederasty.

Yet, Socrates's task of disabusing Phaedrus as to Phaedrus's status as Lysias's boy would not be easy. It seems Phaedrus would approve of pederasty no matter the age of the parties involved. Victoria Wohl reminds us how "Phaedrus . . . waxes lyrical upon this theme [pederasty] in Plato's *Symposium* when he pictures an army of lovers and beloveds, a productive, happy polity composed entirely of *erastai* and *eromenoi* (178e3–179b3)."[14]

10. Demos, "Stesichorus' Palinode in the *Phaedrus*," 236.
11. Nails, *The People of Plato*, 232.
12. Rhodes, *Eros, Wisdom, and Silence*, 424.
13. Hackforth, *Platto's Phaedrus*, 8.
14. Wohl, "The *Eros* of Alcibiades," 356.

The Line on Dialectic, Part 1

In *Phaedrus* we see a Phaedrus who seems to think he has no other role to assume than that of Lysias's boy, even though all this time Phaedrus thinks he is a Typhonic, honor-love lover: Lysias's social equal.

Aside from financial need or desire, there is another reason Phaedrus might have problematically embraced Lysias as a lover, if, in fact, Phaedrus were that aware of his circumstance: fear of prosecution, again. Lysias had successfully led or participated in the prosecution of many men involved in the *MH* and the *PEM*, even the famous Andokides.[15] Indeed, Andokides was tried arbitrarily in a kind of double-jeopardy relative to the *MH* in particular, and many years after the events.

While Phaedrus had been found guilty in the *PEM* only, others were suspected of participation in both the *MH* and the *PEM*; and there was reasonable speculation that Phaedrus had been involved in both scandals. Rhodes, with whose argumentative strategy I often agree, relies on K. J. Dover's "The Date of Plato's *Symposium*" and J. K. Davies's *Athenian Propertied Families, 600–300* to conclude that Phaedrus was very likely involved in both the *MH* and the *PEM*.[16] That reasonable speculation as to Phaedrus's involvement in both also applied to Alkibiades; and it is reasonable to speculate that Phaedrus was a joiner in all things Alkibiades. It would be relatively easy for someone to charge Phaedrus for involvement in both the *MH* and the *PEM*, even years after the events. That someone, someday, could be Lysias.

So, was Phaedrus astute enough to realize the perils of his relationship with Lysias? Apparently not. Phaedrus had surely embraced Lysias for Lysias's social status, money, and the fact that the speech-addict in Phaedrus could not resist association with a logographer as successful as Lysias. Even if Phaedrus did not love Lysias, Phaedrus had reason not to cross Lysias, lest Phaedrus find himself prosecuted by his "lover." So, according to Socrates, perhaps Phaedrus should learn to construe an anticipatory defense against charges anyone like Lysias, or Lysias himself, might bring.[17]

Yet, to formulate such a future defense, Phaedrus would need dialectic. It is only by dialectic that Phaedrus would be able to supersede in cleverness the clever Lysias. Indeed, it is only by dialectic that Phaedrus would come to realize he was not in a Typhonic, honor-love relationship with Lysias, but was little more than a boy to Lysias as *erastes*.

15. Furley, "A Note on [Lysias] 6, against Andokides," 550.
16. See Rhodes, *Eros, Wisdom, and Silence*, 414.
17. Cf., "An *Apologia* for Phaedrus."

Who Is Phaedrus?

Phaedrus's freedom could be in peril were he not to embrace all things Lysias: Lysias's rhetoric; Lysias's business; and Lysias's democrat agenda. Thus another challenge for Socrates the dirt-poor aristocrat: to try to help Phaedrus find some courage, moral and intellectual, by which Phaedrus might someday liberate himself from what Socrates considered a demeaning and actually precarious relationship with the prosecutorial master, Lysias.

There could have been another very specific reason for Phaedrus's embrace of Lysias. Rhetoric was a preoccupation Phaedrus might make an occupation. That is why Socrates says to Phaedrus early: "Don't you believe that I consider hearing your conversation with Lysias 'a greater thing even than business,' as Pindar says?"[18]

Indeed, Socrates signifies Phaedrus had begun to consider Lysias not just a lover but a business partner; a partner in the business of rhetoric. When Socrates claims at one point not to know what to call the "dialectician," he also playfully suggests that rhetoric is a dubious name for a dubious art. That is why Socrates asks Phaedrus provocatively what name he should give "to those who are taught by you and Lysias."[19] In brief, even if Phaedrus wished to learn the art of rhetoric, if it be an art, he would do so properly, and with more facility, if he knew dialectic first. Yet, it is hard for Phaedrus to understand how it would be in his own best interests, professionally and in the sum of his personal life, to attend to dialectic first and rhetoric second.

In this light, *Phaedrus* is almost a study in contrast with *Gorgias*. In *Gorgias*, Socrates is caustic and rather aggressive with actual rhetoricians, Polus, Callicles, and Gorgias. In *Phaedrus*, regarding the foibles of rhetoric, Socrates tries to disabuse Phaedrus rather gently by comparison. Socrates tries to intimate, if only between the lines, that the problematic nature of rhetoric finds a kind of figure in nothing less than Phaedrus's problematic relationship with Lysias himself. That is, if Lysias really loved Phaedrus, and if rhetoric is an art, Lysias would teach Phaedrus rhetoric properly by introducing Phaedrus first to dialectic, as only by dialectic might Phaedrus disclose the truth of any subject rhetoric would address.

Yet, only a god, or one possessed by a god, could teach dialectic; and Lysias was no divine. If Lysias did not at least attempt to teach Phaedrus dialectic, the condition for the possibility of the mastery of rhetoric, then

---

18. *Phaedrus*, 227c.
19. Ibid., 266c.

that was evidence Lysias did not love Phaedrus. The inference Phaedrus could draw is clear: if Lysias had tried first to impart to Phaedrus knowledge of dialectic, that very effort would prove Lysias was a genuine lover, as his love of Phaedrus would prove grounded in the love of wisdom.

This is why Socrates says summarily at one point: "Neither human wisdom (σωφροσυνη ανθρωπινη) nor divine inspiration can confer upon man any greater blessing than [the encounter with the Essence Wheel in the *PL*]."[20] The "human wisdom" or "human moderation" to which Socrates refers here is represented in *Phaedrus* by Lysias's speech in praise of the non-lover that promotes calculating prudence as the highest virtue. Also, as by Phaedrus's own language from the *Symposium*, Phaedrus thinks the lover in pederasty is "divinely inspired";[21] yet, even if that were true, Socrates's point is that the truths revealed in the love of wisdom are categorically superior to all forms of honor-love and money-love, especially Typhonic *eros* and pederasty.

Lysias did not educate Phaedrus in dialectic. So, Socrates has to do so, that Phaedrus might realize, by the discernment borne of that very instruction, the truth of Phaedrus's situation: Lysias is treating the famously handsome yet desperate Phaedrus as little more than a boy in a weird version of pederasty. Thus the ultimate significance of *L'/P'*: *L'/P'* itself, in praise of the non-lover, actually applied to the situation between Lysias and Phaedrus themselves. With some dialectical discernment, Phaedrus would realize that Lysias was a non-lover and was not at all treating Phaedrus "as if here were a god." So, again, how can Socrates teach Phaedrus dialectic?

Socrates knew that the priority of dialectic over rhetoric, or any other discipline, is not easy to present. One difficulty in presenting dialectic as the divine and ultimately prior science lies in the fact that dialectic is not easy to objectify. Such perplexity over the seemingly simple provides occasion for the famous, or infamous, Socratic irony, especially what Karl Jaspers calls second order Socratic irony: that "by which Socrates seeks to provoke the knowledge of nonknowledge."[22]

Socrates, somehow, has to make Phaedrus aware of Phaedrus's ignorance. This is why *Phaedrus* is often so silly; why Socrates challenges Phaedrus at times about some very simple things, which, all told, might not be so simple after all. For example, Socrates says the real philosopher

---

20. *Phaedrus*, 256b.
21. *Symposium*, 180b.
22. Jaspers, *Plato and Augustine*, 27.

Who Is Phaedrus?

is a dialectician, and the dialectician is capable of definition: "One must know the truth about all the particular things of which he speaks or writes, and must be able to define everything separately; then when he has defined them, he must be able to know how to divide them by classes until further division is impossible."[23] Yet, Socrates balks a bit at even naming the person who can determine names or definitions when he says: "[only] God knows if it is right to call those persons who have the capacity of division and collection as aids to speech and thought . . . dialecticians."[24] One would think the very key to definition, dialectic, would be easy to define, or at least to name.

When Socrates hesitates to give a name to the dialectician, he is putting Phaedrus on guard about obsession with words. Here an account from Natorp, not specifically related to *Phaedrus*, nonetheless applies:

> But *dialektos* also points in another direction: to the role of words and their place in the system of fundamental philosophical concepts. Plato has never been anything but clear about this: words are not something ultimate, but always remain subject to something else, the "thing itself" (*auto to pragma*); words do not give meaning to things, but rather receive meaning from things alone. One does not know things in the first instance from the way that words are formed, but only from the things themselves. This holds good right up to the ultimate intensification of *logos*: the *episteme* that stands close to, and is in fact practically on the threshold of the eternally inexpressible, ultimate "thing."[25]

It should occur to Phaedrus that Socrates's questions about some seemingly simple things may not be so simple or insignificant. Socrates also balked at the hasty use of the term dialectic because, since Zeno, the term apparently had some currency bearing a meaning Socrates would not maintain.[26]

As for the issue of definition, going back as far as the *Symposium*, Socrates knew the capacity for definition was not Phaedrus's strength. In the series of speeches in honor of *eros* in the *Symposium*, Phaedrus delivered the first encomium. Yet, Phaedrus simply proceeded by citing some problematic attributes of love without defining it.

---

23. *Phaedrus*, 277b.
24. Ibid., 266b.
25. Natorp, *Plato's Theory of Ideas*, 431.
26. Cf., "Countering Zeno and Lysias."

The Line on Dialectic, Part 1

Given Phaedrus's problematic relationship with Lysias, some kind of definition of love was crucial. The personal stakes for Phaedrus were high. Indeed, if Phaedrus was wrong about love, and therefore wrong about Lysias, Phaedrus's personal freedom and his soul's integrity, both, could be at risk.

Phaedrus had already made one bad return to Athens after his exile. Socrates was trying to prevent another. In Socrates's view, Phaedrus must return to Phaedrus's own proper nature as an intelligent human being. That means Phaedrus must return to the root science, dialectic, to discern the interconnections between and among the Good, the common good, and the good in, and for, the individual.

3

The Line on Dialectic, Part 2

a) *Dianoia* and the Good: The *Republic*

PLATO'S MOST COMPELLING ACCOUNT of dialectic appears in the discussion of the Divided Line in the *Republic*. A crucial element of that discussion concerns the function of *dianoia*.

The function of *dianoia* in the *Republic*, I maintain, is an operative assumption in *Phaedrus*. Plato may not have had a philosophical system such as Kant's wherein, for example, a fair comprehension of the *Critique of Judgment* requires a good understanding of the *Critique of Pure Reason*. Yet, the function of *dianoia* in the *Republic* is operative in *Phaedrus* in the sense in which the metaphors and motifs in *Phaedrus* urge an epistemology virtually identical to that made obvious in the *Republic*.

In the *Republic*, when Socrates offers the very idea of a philosopher-king, Socrates is compelled to address the very nature of thinking as, somewhat collectively, Glaucon, Adeimantus, Polemarchus, and Thrasymachus demand that Socrates explain what it is the philosopher knows that others do not. In effect, Socrates's answer is that the philosopher does not know, ultimately, anything different from what any other human knows; but the philosopher cherishes truth, the way it is realized, and the employment of Essences in the sensuous order via *dianoia*.

So, what summons thinking? This is basically Socrates's own question that he answers in the *Republic*: "some things are apt to summon thought, while others are not, defining as apt to summon it those that strike the sense at the same time as their opposites . . ."[1]

---

1. *Republic*, 524d.

The Line on Dialectic, Part 2

In the *Republic* this emphasis on the mind's encounter with any CO in the sensuous order is the central motif in Plato's presentation of *dianoia*. *Dianoia*, activated by the confrontation with a CO in the sensuous order, is the necessary function for embodied thinkers to exercise dialectic on the whole. In *Phaedrus*, many CO are comprised of more than merely sensuous particulars. Indeed, there are many and various triads for dyadic, compare-contrast reduction in *Phaedrus*, as *Phaedrus* operates as a sophisticated extension of the dynamics of *dianoia* as displayed in the *Republic*. But how, more precisely, is *dianoia* a function of dialectic?

In the *Republic*, when the topic of *dianoia* is introduced, we recall Socrates's seemingly ridiculous example of the three fingers. When index, middle, and smallest fingers are considered merely as fingers, *dianoia* is not initiated; no compelling thought is provoked. However, upon consideration of the contrast between and among the fingers, thinking is summoned; *dianoia* is instigated. R. E. Allen and John Sallis, separately, call special attention to the three-finger example of *dianoia* in the *Republic*. Allen states the Platonic position on the instigation of thinking *per* encounters with CO thusly:

> reflection is provoked when the same object produces two opposite impressions, and not provoked when such opposition does not occur[;] . . . for sight presents two opposite qualities with equal clearness, declaring that the third finger is both large and small. When this happens, the mind is driven to question what the senses mean, and so comes to regard largeness and smallness as distinct things, confusingly mingled in the thing seen. In asking what is meant by large and small, the mind is led to distinguish objects of intelligence from objects of sight.[2]

Sallis writes of the issue of *dianoia* as follows: "[More precisely,] the kind of situation which provokes *dianoia* is that in which one of the fingers appears as a member in two pairs and such that it has one or the other of opposite qualities depending upon which pair it appears in. So, the kind of situation that provokes *dianoia* is that in which things appear in pairs, in dyads."[3]

Dianoia is prompted by a confrontation with differences, more particularly, a CO, or a dyad of opposites; at least a dyad. Sallis writes further: "*Dianoia* involves the posing of an order of total distinctness over against

---

2. Allen, "The Argument from Opposites in *Republic* V," 167–68.
3. Sallis, *Being and Logos*, 430.

the visible order or indeterminate duality."[4] Faced with an indefinite dyad, *dianoia* supplies instances of distinctness within the order of the sensuous so as to move the soul to even higher thought, to Mind Proper which can then realize more proper "ones," Essences, and their relation to one another.

Socrates's seemingly simple example of the three fingers proves to be complex. Not only does *dianoia* work with triads/dyads of objects, *dianoia* itself is dyadic. As Sallis's account of *dianoia* notes, there is descensional *dianoia* and ascensional *dianoia*.[5] In my extension of Sallis's treatment, *dianoia* is ascensional when the soul moves entirely beyond the sensuous and conditional to arrive at definitive knowledge, *episteme*. This knowledge of the unconditional, the imageless unity of an Essence (or "Form") is the function of ascensional *dianoia* in the process of definition. Even in the accomplishment of a definition, there is a unity that is yet dyadic. A definition is a bi-conditional presentation of the identity and difference of *definiendum* and *definiens*: e.g., a triangle is a triangle *if and only if* it is a three-sided enclosed plane figure with three angles the sum of which is 180°.

The function of Mind Proper in dialectic is to maintain steadfast knowledge of the imageless Essence, while *dianoia*, once ascended, cooperates with Mind Proper so as to grasp those imageless Essences in species types that do or can appear in images. Triangleness, known by Mind Proper, is imageless, while isosceles is known, as imageable, by *dianoia* in conjunction with Mind Proper. In this sense triangleness is the "hypo-thesis" of, (i.e., that which "under-lies") isosceles. Descending *dianoia* then provides derivative "hypo-theses." As imageless triangleness "under-lies" imageable isosceles, isosceles is the "hypo-thesis" of, or "under-lies," isosceles-shaped extended things that must appear in images because they appear in matter (even "intelligible matter," as Aristotle later calls it).

So, *dianoia* is descensional when the soul is engaged in applying the knowledge of an Essence to an admixture of *CO* in the sensuous realm, to things with extension that therefore can be manifested in images. Accordingly, the Divided Line might better be called the Imaging Line. What is foundational for Plato, as poetic philosopher, is the dynamic between the unities *par excellence* that have no image—the Divine, the Good, Beauty—and imageless Essences that are yet, in a sense, "images" of those supreme unities.

---

4. Ibid, 432.
5. Ibid, 433.

The Line on Dialectic, Part 2

Dialectic requires *dianoia*, and *dianoia* necessarily involves the capacity to work with and without images simultaneously. Hence, the highest functions of dialectic are difficult to objectify because the "objects" of contemplation—the Divine, the Good, and Beauty—are imageless, as are "lesser" Essences, which are nonetheless, in a sense, "images" of the highest, imageless Ones. In *Phaedrus*, so rich in imagery, Plato all but volunteers himself as the master, because inventor, of dianoetic poetics.

Engagement in ascending *dianoia* is a kind of homecoming for the soul. When the soul returns to the domain of non-imaged Ones, it has returned to the domain of its true nature, the domain associated with the Divine, the Good, and Beauty. This is the point of the defense of the philosopher-king in the *Republic*, and the point of the presentation of the soul's contemplation of Essences in the Essence Wheel in the *PL* in *Phaedrus*. The philosopher-king, or the philosopher period, does not know some arcane something others cannot. The philosopher simply pays extreme attention to Essences and definitions, and recalls regularly discernments achieved and confirmed by the exercises of division and collection and the concomitant reckonings of similarity and dissimilarity, identity and difference. Or, as Catherine Pickstock writes: "for Socrates it is only by means of the dialogic art of differentiation (dialectic) that it is possible to transcend the confusion of mere opinions and prejudices, and only the dialectician, who holds steadfastly to the good, is in a position to differentiate and to discern the true from the false."[6]

Socratic philosophy also appreciates the mysterious way the supreme Ones, especially Beauty, originate truth and unity in Essences, a way that defies representation *per* division, as in descending *dianoia* in particular. This is apparently why Natorp makes the claim about *Phaedrus* that, at a certain level, and at a certain point, presumably the *PL* and its display of the Essence Wheel, *Phaedrus* is the dialogue in which Plato has "left all division behind."[7]

Those who treat the images and dramatic elements in *Phaedrus* lightly or not at all cannot help but be frustrated at this point. Here is where Natorp, for one, retreats in his praise of *Phaedrus*. Natorp argues that, overall, *Phaedrus* is mostly a confused, epistemological mess of a dialogue written before the *Republic*. According to Natorp, there was a confusion wrought in

---

6 Pickstock, *After Writing*, 17.
7. Natorp, *Plato's Theory of Ideas*, 415–16.

Who Is Phaedrus?

Plato's mind just prior to, or during, the composition of *Phaedrus*.[8] Natorp surmises that the beginning of the so-called middle period in Plato's intellectual life was marked by a kind of bewilderment. In that period, Natorp's Plato was defenseless against a stupefying epiphany of the "Forms." Natorp's Plato, despite apparently being halfway out of his wits, nonetheless managed doggedly to compose the mish-mash of near nonsense that came to be called *Phaedrus*. *Phaedrus*, according to Natorp, at least tells a good story; but Plato was consequently embarrassed by it. Yet, according to Natorp, Plato could not or would not disown *Phaedrus* after so much effort. So, in the final analysis, Natorp's Plato, as the cleverest author of all time, simply labeled the whole of *Phaedrus* a "joke" or mere "sportive jest." *Phaedrus* would have to find philosophical justification externally in the *Republic*.[9]

For all of Natorp's excellent scholarship, it seems that on this point he was engaged more in psychological speculation about Plato than in serious engagement with the way Plato communicates *via* the text on the whole, to say nothing of the pre- or post-text. The nub of Natorp's complaint about *Phaedrus* is that Plato was not Kant; that Plato never volunteered a philosophical system founded on something like three separate but roughly equal critiques, all with a wickedly difficult yet consistent vocabulary. Yet, when read properly, *Phaedrus* is not a hopeless mish-mash of nonsense as Natorp more than suggests. Moreover, *Phaedrus* does not say of itself what Natorp says *Phaedrus* says: that the entire dialogue is a joke. Parts of *Phaedrus* are funny, yes. But even those funny parts are purposive. More, if *Phaedrus* is a joke, or is founded on jest of a sort, it may be understood to be playful in a way even more profound than the way Friedrich Schiller states that one "shall *only play* with Beauty, and he shall play *only with Beauty*."[10]

Here I might qualify further my claim that Plato is the philosopher of the image *par excellence*. By the phrase "philosopher of the image" I am not merely seconding the literary-critical praise heaped upon Plato by Walter Pater: "Like all masters of literature, Plato has of course varied excellences; but perhaps none of them has won for him a larger number of friendly readers than this impress of visible reality."[11] Rather, by emphasizing that Plato is the philosopher of the image *par excellence*, I stress that, while the Divine, the Good, and Beauty do not reduce to images, neither do

---

8. Ibid., 110.
9. Ibid., 109–10.
10. Schiller, *On the Aesthetic Education of Man*, 439.
11. Pater, "The Artistry in Plato's Work," 207.

more "typical" Essences. Yet, even then, when the soul is operating in the imageless domain of Essences, beyond descending *dianoia* that does apply to images, the soul is still thinking in terms of images in some sense of the word. This principle bears repeating. Sallis states it thus: "Even an *eidos*, by which *episteme* would proceed, is an image in a certain respect: it is an image of *the one*."[12] Or, to phrase the dyamic another way, Erich Frank writes: "The single *eide* . . . revealed to dialectic in their relation to each other and to the *agathon*, begin to shift and to become only grades of the dialectical process which leads to the *agathon*."[13]

Of course, Frank's reference to the *agathon*, the Good, more obviously refers to the *Republic*. Moreover, Frank's phrase "which leads to the *agathon*" needs qualification. More properly, as an embodied being, one can only be led up to the *agathon* but one cannot obtain the *agathon* as such once and for all. There is a mysterious chasm between the plateau of "typical" Essences (whence one proceeds with the exercise of division in descending *dianoia*) and the Divine, the Good, and Beauty. Rhodes addresses very well the nature of that chasm between Plato's trinity of Ones and Essences. That is why the term "silence" is in the very title of Rhodes's book on the *Symposium* and *Phaedrus*. In view of the chasm between the "lesser" imageless ones, and the Good, the Divine, and Beauty, one can only be silent, if attentive. In *Phaedrus* the attention is directed to the way one of those supreme Ones, Beauty, serves to supervene the mystery chasm by shining Truth through each and every Essence or One.

β) Dianoia and the Beautiful: Phaedrus

As the Good is the principle of unity *par excellence* in the *Republic*, in *Phaedrus* it is Beauty: hence the subtitle: Η ΠΕΡΙ ΚΑΛΟΥ ΗΘΙΚΟΣ: *On the Beautiful, Ethical*. With the term *ethikos*, suggesting the habitual or the virtually constant, *Phaedrus* reveals that Beauty is what constantly shines Truth through Essences. That shining is what is beheld in the wondrous contemplation of the revolution of Essences in the Zeus myth in the *PL*. For Socrates, the revelation of that imageless shining of Essences could only come in a myth in which a god takes the lead. Only a god could so easily cover the chasm between the realm of Essences and the trinity of Ones *par excellence*, and the mundane order.

12. Sallis, *Being and Logos*, 426.
13. Frank, "The Fundamental Opposition of Plato and Aristotle," 167.

Who Is Phaedrus?

In *Phaedrus*, the most profound praise is bestowed upon Beauty. Beauty is revealed to be nothing less than "that which causes the divine to be divine."[14] This claim is at least as extreme as Plotinus's later claim, as noted by Suzanne Stern-Gillet, that: "Beauty is nothing other than beauty because there is nothing in it that is not beautiful."[15] Were Plato cognizant of Christian language, he would apparently say Beauty begets the divine. In the myth in the *PL*, Beauty reveals itself in every other Essence by shining the Truth of each through each.

Here David Timmerman's statement about Plato's sense of *philosophia* as distinct from Isocrates's sense of *philosophia*, presupposed in *Phaedrus*, is fit. Timmerman writes that, for Plato, "*Philosophia* involves the practice of dialectical reasoning."[16] And, indeed, to quote Plato himself, dialectical reasoning "does not consider [these] hypotheses as first principles but as stepping stones to take off from, enabling it to reach the unhypothetical first principle of everything. Having grasped this principle, it reverses itself and, keeping hold of what follows from it, comes down to a conclusion without making use of anything visible at all, but only of forms themselves, moving on from forms to forms, and ending in forms."[17] For Isocrates, whom we would now call a pragmatist, the very notion of a "first principle of everything" would be absurd.

Yet, Timmerman does not analyze in detail Plato's use of *dianoia*. If he had, he would realize that what Plato is referring to here is the phenomenon of ascending *dianoia* more than descending *dianoia* (which are not to be confused with what M. Gueroult calls *dialectique ascendante* and *dialectique constructive*, which are much broader notions in the alleged "evolution" of Plato's theory of Forms[18]). The more important, narrow point here is that Plato uses the loaded term *dianoia* in reference to Isocrates at the end of *Phaedrus*; and I argue that when Socrates grants Isocrates the compliment, albeit faint, that there is "something of philosophy" in the "mind" (*dianoia*) of Isocrates, Socrates is saying that Isocrates's thought does employ, in a limited way, ascending *dianoia*, even if it does not embrace the notion there is something there to contemplate. If Isocrates's thought did not at least employ some ascending *dianoia*, it could not be so properly critical of idle

---

14. *Phaedrus*, 249d.
15. Stern-Gillet, "Le Principe Du Beau Chez Plotin," 44n.
16. Timmerman, "Isocrates' Competing Conceptualization of Philosophy," 147.
17. *Republic*, 511b.
18. Gaudin, "*Lectio Difficilior*," 48.

The Line on Dialectic, Part 2

rhetoric and sophistry. Yet, in the final tally, Isocrates is clearly different from Socrates. To Socrates, Isocrates is a rather dull pragmatist unappreciative of the means by which he achieves the heights he does achieve, while Socrates, the dialectician, is both discerner and contemplator.

Isocrates's *dianoia*, technicalities aside, does not move the mind higher to the contemplation of the marvelous reconciliation in which imageless Essences are, while non-imaged, yet "images" of higher non-imaged Ones: the Good, the Divine, and Beauty. For Socrates, this awareness is the highest achievement of dialectic and is the condition for the possibility of discernment in manifold cases of identity and difference, similarity and dissimilarity, and truth and appearance in the everyday world. The true philosopher, for Socrates, tries to be vigilant in this hyperawareness. Or, as Pater puts it: for Plato "*Real* notions are to be ingrained by persistent thoroughness of the 'dialectic' method, as if by conscientious dyers."[19]

In *Phaedrus* even the gods engage in a kind of ascending/descending activity similar to the dianoetic traversal of the levels of the Divided Line by the human soul:

> Now the "divine intelligence" [θεου διάνοια], since it is nurtured on mind and pure knowledge, and the intelligence of every soul which is capable of receiving that which befits it, rejoices in seeing reality for a space of time and by gazing upon truth is nourished and made happy until the revolution brings it again to the same place. In the revolution it beholds justice, temperance, and knowledge, not such knowledge as has a beginning and varies as it is associated with one or another of the things we call realities, but that which abides in the real eternal absolute; and in the same way it beholds and feeds upon the other eternal verities, after which, passing down again within the heaven, it goes home, and there the charioteer puts up the horses at the manger and feeds them with ambrosia and then gives them nectar to drink.[20]

Ingeniously, Plato uses the image of the activities of the gods as an image of the activity of ascending and descending *dianoia* in humans, the very activity by which humans discern the imageless as derived from the imageless. Phaedrus has more to learn than he realizes. So, Socrates tries to impart to Phaedrus at least an ongoing use of *dianoia* by the almost constant posing of one *CO* after another to elevate Phaedrus's mind. Some of these

---

19. Pater, "The Artistry in Plato's Work," 210.
20. *Phaedrus*, 247d–e.

Who Is Phaedrus?

CO Socrates contrives; but many are part of the circumstance. Thus again the similar yet dissimilar nature and appearance of Socrates and Phaedrus themselves: wise-shallow; ugly-handsome; aristocrat-democrat; yet both lovers of speeches, though in very different senses.

Of course, what Socrates is doing for Phaedrus in the internals of the dialogue, Plato is doing on behalf of the reader outside it: making the reader think by challenging the reader with one *CO* after another, from the opening "whence and whither" question to the concluding moments when Socrates suggests that Phaedrus compare Athens's opposing schools of rhetoric. That final *CO*, the analysis of which would reveal that Lysias is not a true lover, concerns the most compelling *CO* of all: the living and the dead.

4

Phaedrus's Ultimate Whence
A Mystery Triad

α) The Orphic Mysteries

BEYOND HIS PERSONAL PAST in Athens, Phaedrus had an ultimate whence; an origin he shared with the rest of humanity. But what did Phaedrus think his ultimate whence was? Did Phaedrus even think he shared an ultimate whence with the rest of humanity? Or did Phaedrus, in fact, think he and his friends were different from, and better than, the rest of humanity?

In the context of *Phaedrus*, there were competing views of an ultimate whence, some of which came from mystery-cults, otherwise known as mysteries. Some of those mysteries, such as the Eleusinian, were authorized by the city. Some, such as the Orphic, were not. Given that Phaedrus was once banished from Athens for participation in the *PEM*, it is surprising Plato does not refer more directly to the mysteries in *Phaedrus*, especially given how often in *Phaedo*, for example, Socrates speaks approvingly of the mysteries, where he almost certainly means the Eleusinian.[1]

Yet, there are allusions to the Eleusinian mysteries in *Phaedrus*, albeit subtle. Michael Rinella demonstrates that *Phaedrus* offers a kind of "supplementation of the language and experience of mystery initiation, particularly the form of initiation found at Eleusis."[2] For example, "the conversation of the *Phaedrus* takes place not far from Agrai, the scene of the

---

1. *Phaedo*, 67c; 69c–d; 81a.
2. Rinella, "Supplementing the Ecstatic," 62.

Lesser Mysteries."³ Also, "Plato's juxtaposition of philosophy's version of mystic vision to that of Eleusis is assured by 'his use . . . of the words for the two levels of [Eleusinian] initiation, *myesis* and *epopteia*.'"⁴

The thesis of *Who Is Phaedrus?*, with its emphasis on the pretext of *Phaedrus* and the consequences of Phaedrus's involvement in the *PEM*, justifies especially Rinella's use of the term "supplementation" relative to the mysteries, and to the Eleusinian mysteries in particular. In *Phaedrus*, even though Phaedrus had known Socrates for many years, more than a score most likely, Phaedrus is being initiated into Socrates's mystery philosophy really for the first time as the means for Phaedrus's de-corruption. When John Moore claims that Phaedrus was a "man of . . . intelligence and discernment" and that Phaedrus's "knowledge of Socratic philosophy is sometimes impressive," Moore simply does not supply sufficient evidence to support either claim.⁵ Phaedrus is really rather clueless about Socratic thought; and Socrates is really speaking to Phaedrus himself when Socrates ostensibly refers indirectly to those who are either "corrupted" or "not newly initiated."⁶ It was the corrupted youth in Phaedrus who had allowed himself, later in life, to be involved in the scandalous *PEM*. Socrates sees Phaedrus in need of a good return to Athens, his civic whence, and for that Phaedrus needs to return to Phaedrus's ultimate whence, the Essence revolution, or Essence Wheel, all humanity once contemplated in the recognition of truth.

This occasion of Socrates meeting Phaedrus again, after many years, provides the opportunity for Phaedrus to compare and contrast his own view of an ultimate whence with the mysteries of the city and with Socrates's mystery philosophy. Even if Moore could persuade us Phaedrus is not as ignorant as he seems, Phaedrus would still have to demonstrate the realization that Socratic philosophy requires a kind of perpetual initiation as Socrates himself says: "Now a man who employs such memories [of the Essence Wheel] rightly is always being initiated into perfect mysteries and he alone becomes truly perfect . . ."⁷

Relative to the issue of the mysteries, between the lines at least, Plato is offering yet another triad for dyadic reduction and therefore fodder for

---

3. Ibid., 66.
4. Rinella, "Supplementing the Ecstatic," 70.
5. Moore, "The Relation between *Symposium* and *Phaedrus*," 67.
6. *Phaedrus*, 250e.
7. Ibid., 249c.

Phaedrus's Ultimate Whence

dialectical discernment. Aside from the Orphic and Eleusinian mysteries, Socrates's mystery philosophy is a third system that offers a vision of an ultimate whence, at least an intellectual whence, of the human person. Most importantly, given the immediate circumstance, Socrates's mystery philosophy provides not only a compare-and-contrast alternative to both the Eleusinian and Orphic mysteries; Socrates's philosophy, "the most blessed of mysteries," is the very means to achieve the compare-and-contrast discernment by which Phaedrus might realize the problematic nature of Phaedrus's own worldview.[8]

In *Phaedrus*, Socrates more than implies that a better alternative to Phaedrus's unusual worldview, the very cause of much that plagues Phaedrus, would lie in the Eleusinian mysteries at least; mysteries in which Phaedrus had surely been initiated in his youth but abandoned. Of course, better yet would be Phaedrus's embrace of Socrates's mystery philosophy that supersedes the Eleusinian mysteries, and is also a clear counter to the worldview made manifest in Phaedrus's speech on *eros* in the *Symposium*.

Indeed, Phaedrus's life was in such disrepair, Socrates even seems to suggest that Phaedrus would do well to embrace even the Orphic mysteries as an alternative to the weird worldview the corrupted Phaedrus had adopted to his peril. Of course, Socrates's mystery philosophy would surpass the Orphic mysteries in excellence, too. For the sake of briefly comparing Socrates's and Phaedrus's worldviews to the Orphic mysteries, one might entertain Nicholson's summary analysis of Orphism (drawn from the consideration of the voluminous work of W. K. C. Guthrie and Walter Burkert):

> Whereas the official cults of Athens and other cities promoted festivals, "mysteries," and rituals that were corporate in character, embracing the whole city, Orphism was a religion of individuals joined in a semisecret society, who learned it out of books and out of a musical tradition of hymns. They learned a doctrine about the preexistence of the soul of each person and a fate that had been ordained for each. Owing to a primordial sin, each of us was fallen out of our true place of being—the starry heavens—ordained to fall into a body and to live there through many trials and pains, with the hope that through the purification of our life we might be saved again and return to our true home. For the soul is a fragment of divinity.[9]

---

8. Ibid., 249c; 250c.
9. Nicholson, *Plato's Phaedrus*, 131.

Who Is Phaedrus?

Phaedrus, essentially a naturalist, did not take the Orphic Mysteries seriously; and, in a sense, neither did Socrates, if for different reasons.

Yet, one can compare Socratic philosophy to Orphism on several fronts. Somewhat like the Orphic mysteries, there was a sense of purification in Socratic philosophy. Given the rather obvious purification motif in *Phaedo*, we see something similar in *Phaedrus*. Socrates tries to aid in the transformation of Phaedrus's soul, from Typhonically deranged and *epamphoterious* to "simple." In Socrates's view, Phaedrus cannot, or should not, remain his Typhonic self; artificially complex and rebellious to the point of self-destruction. Indeed, Phaedrus is either to disown Lysias, because Lysias is actually a non-lover, or Phaedrus is to convert Lysias to true philosophy as Lysias's brother Polemarchus had been converted.[10] Of course, if Phaedrus is to convert Lysias, Phaedrus himself must be initiated in Socrates's mystery philosophy to be de-corrupted. The Orphic mysteries may have been superficial according to Socrates, but they were certainly no worse for Phaedrus than the worldview Phaedrus had maintained most of his life to his own detriment.

To many who did not know him, Socrates probably seemed to be an Orphic freak. Like Orphism, Socrates's mystery philosophy was not sanctioned by the city; and, as in Orphism, there was no obvious corporate involvement in Socrates's philosophy, none that was obvious at least. This issue of a mystery's relationship to the city offers another point of comparison of Socratic philosophy with the Orphic mysteries. Socratic philosophy is inherently tragic. Like the Orphic mysteries, Socratic philosophy is not sanctioned by the city; quite the contrary. Yet, Socratic philosophy has little *raison d'être* apart from the city. Indeed, the Socratic mystery philosophy, while not originating from the city as such, is the basic and only means by which the city will improve. Recall Socrates's rather outrageous claim in *Gorgias*: he is the only truly political person in all of Athens.[11]

In *Phaedrus*, Socrates, outside the city, was displaying in essence what he meant by that extreme claim in *Gorgias*. The sublimity operative in Socratic philosophy gives the person engaged in that philosophy sufficient distance from the mundane functions of the city while that person is yet engaged in the city. In this unique case in *Phaedrus*, Socrates leaves the bounds of the city with Phaedrus to provide Phaedrus distance and perspective; indeed, the ultimate perspective as far as Socrates can see.

10. *Phaedrus*, 257b.
11. *Gorgias*, 521d.

Phaedrus's Ultimate Whence

Here the pretext of *Phaedrus* is all-important. Phaedrus, the former exile, unlike others, needed yet another exit from the city so as to understand better the elements in the city which had corrupted him in the first place. Indeed, the idea of accompanying Phaedrus outside the city in *Phaedrus* is to assure, or at least attempt to assure, that Phaedrus makes, finally, a good return to the city. By contrast with Socrates's mystery philosophy, the Orphic mysteries, with their extreme emphasis on individual salvation from the corrupted world, offered a kind of idiotic escapism from the city.

Yet, on the whole, Socrates's philosophy is similar in one way to the Orphic mysteries. As neither the Orphic nor the Socratic was sanctioned by the city, outside the city was just about the only safe place to engage in either. Yet, unlike Orphic initiates, those initiated into Socratic philosophy must engage the city, always at their peril. Were Socrates a priest in the order of the Orphic, Socrates would likely recommend that Phaedrus leave the city as often as possible. Yet, unlike the Orphic, Socrates will be sending Phaedrus back to the city, this time, unlike in the case of Phaedrus's return from exile, to make a good return to the city once and for all: that is, to see the city for the decadent mess it is, and to improve it, starting with himself.

Finally, as if competing manifestly with the Orphic emphasis on hymns, Socrates in *Phaedrus* does a lot of praying and some obvious hymn-making. Socrates's *PL* is a hymn the likes of which no one had ever sung before. Nothing in Orphism can compare with the *PL*, or compete with Socrates.

β) The Eleusinian Mysteries

No mystery in the city, sanctioned or not, could compete with Socrates's mystery philosophy. Socrates, the prodigy, offered the best, most systematic, and most mysterious access to a true origin. Yet Socrates, as citizen, had little hesitation giving voice to appreciation of the Eleusinian mysteries into which Phaedrus, as a boy, had almost certainly been initiated. Gregory Vlastos reminds us how seriously Socrates regarded some of the religions of the city. There is "a fact about Socrates which has been so embarrassing to modern readers that a long line of Platonic scholarship has sought . . . to explain it away: Socrates's acceptance of the supernatural."[12]

We hear Socrates say, for example, glowingly in *Phaedo*: "And it looks as if these people who instituted our mystic rites weren't a bunch of bunglers

---

12. Vlastos, "Socratic Piety," 214.

Who Is Phaedrus?

but spoke with a genuine hidden meaning when they said long ago that whoever arrives in Hades ignorant of the mysteries and uninitiated will lie in Muck, but that he who arrives there purified and initiated will dwell with the gods. For as they say about the mysteries: 'The thyrsus-bearers are many, but the mystics few'; and these mystics are, I believe, those who have been true philosophers."[13]

What we see in *Phaedrus* is Socrates's unhesitating embrace of mystery and, accordingly, Phaedrus's initiation into Socratic philosophy. Many lines in *Phaedrus* bear repeating, and one in particular is Socrates's reference to those who have been either "corrupted" or who are "not newly initiated." Both descriptions apply to Phaedrus, especially the latter if Socrates's philosophy is such as to require perpetual initiation.

Phaedrus had certainly been corrupted. In his youth, as already mentioned, Phaedrus had almost certainly been initiated, for the good as Socrates saw it, in the Eleusinian mysteries. So, when Socrates was referring to a "new" initiation, it was not a "new" initiation into the Eleusinian mysteries that Phaedrus needed, except incidentally. That is, Socrates had an appreciation of the Eleusinian mysteries to the extent to which the Eleusinian mysteries had points of intersection with much of Socratic philosophy: belief in eternal goods; belief in an afterlife; and an ethic that maintained a sense of aristocratic origin and carriage. The Eleusinian mysteries, by comparison, could not deliver epistemological grounding of those and similar truths provided by Socratic philosophy. So, the "new" initiation Phaedrus was to undergo was a proper initiation into Socrates's mystery philosophy, which initiation, incidentally, might make Phaedrus re-appreciate, or appreciate for the first time, the nobility of the Eleusinian mysteries into which Phaedrus had been initiated as a youth, and against which he rebelled.

At times Socrates suggests that Phaedrus consider the extent to which Phaedrus is enmeshed in personal difficulties for which there is no remedy other than a mystery: thus Socrates's references to the types of divine madness that elevate a person beyond the mundane.

In his treatment of the four types of divine madness in the *PL*, Socrates refers to an "ancient guilt" that seems to have afflicted "certain families" with "diseases and the greatest troubles."[14] By referring to families, the corporate, Socrates is certainly referring to the Eleusinian mysteries, not the more freelancing Orphic. According to a tradition Socrates appreciates, a

13. *Phaedo*, 69c–d.
14. *Phaedrus*, 244c.

divine gift, prophecy and participation in "purifications and sacred rites," had saved some families from the ill effects of an ancient guilt.[15] Phaedrus was likely from one of those once-cursed, but eventually blessed, families that saw their salvation in the Eleusinian mysteries. Phaedrus's family was likely crestfallen when they witnessed, later, the profanation of those same mysteries by one of their own: the rebellious, because corrupted, Phaedrus.

Socrates's allusions to the Eleusinian mysteries were to force Phaedrus into some self-reflection. Phaedrus was supposed to entertain the possibility there may have been something crucial about the Eleusinian mysteries, something necessary for the good life. Phaedrus was supposed to entertain the question as to why, in his youth, he profaned the mystery that otherwise might protect him and whole generations of his family.

It is easy to see that Phaedrus, even as a man, has juvenile tendencies. In his younger years, Phaedrus was surely a somewhat spoiled, rebellious person.[16] Phaedrus, the rebellious naturalist, may have participated in the *PEM* to offend not only aristocrats at large but also his own household.

The least Phaedrus could do was reconsider the virtues the mysteries offered as now, in Socrates's presence, Phaedrus had no excuse for ignoring the mysterious. Socrates had always praised the Eleusinian mysteries even as he viewed his philosophy as something that superseded them. Had Phaedrus embraced Socrates's mystery philosophy early, Phaedrus would have realized not only the noble nature of Socrates's philosophy, but even the ennobling elements of the Eleusinian mysteries. From that magnanimous position borne of the discernment of the intersections of the two mysteries, Phaedrus might have risen above his adolescent resentment toward, and rebellion against, the mystery religion embraced by his family and sanctioned by the city.

In *Phaedrus*, the former exile and early aristocrat, Phaedrus, had returned to Athens from exile and, from desperation, had embraced Lysias and Lysian democracy, symptoms of Athenian decadence. Socrates was trying to make Phaedrus aware of the nobler air behind both the Eleusinian mysteries and Socrates's philosophy. Socrates knew the Eleusinian mysteries were "supervised by the *archon basileus* and two old Athenian families, the Eumolpidae and Kerykes."[17] More, while the mysteries were supervised by aristocrats, the mysteries offered a way, apparently, to bridge some of the

---

15. Ibid., 244c.
16. Cf., "Phaedrus's Middle Whence: Was Phaedrus Bi-Rebellious?"
17. McGlew, "Politics on the Margins," 8.

Who Is Phaedrus?

differences between the aristocrats and *hoi polloi*. Some women even held a position of honor, priestess, in the Eleusinian mysteries. Thomas Martin says the Eleusinian mysteries were "a safety valve for the pressures created by the remaining inequalities of life."[18] Yet, as much as Socrates was suspicious of all things democrat, he seemed to realize Athens would always be cursed with some democrat taint; and the Eleusinian mysteries, available to rich and poor alike, seemed to be one way in which the chasm between rich and poor could engage in a nobler "current friendship" not always available in civil society itself.

Some have argued that Plato, more than Socrates, was somewhat suspicious of the so-called "current friendship" allegedly enjoyed by those initiated into the Eleusinian mysteries.[19] Part of Plato's suspicion of the mysteries appears to be of the possibly naïve or superficial sense of equality and friendship that arose from engagement in them. To attempt a modern parallel, there have always been Christians of all classes and types, rich and poor, who, despite their social status, see themselves nonetheless as "friends" in Christ or "fellow travelers." Yet, few of those persons are the deepest of friends even in that serious regard that brought them together, their faith, since many do not understand the depth, principles, and philosophy underlying the faith. In Plato's domain, a similar dynamic appears to have been operative in the Eleusinian mysteries, and Plato, almost certainly more than Socrates, was somewhat suspicious. It was fellow Eleusinian "friends," after all, who would eventually murder one of their own, Dion, one of Plato's favorites.

It is probably fair to infer that Socrates saw more virtues in the Eleusinian mysteries than Plato did, especially as those mysteries, among other kinds of "divine madness," provided "a divine release from the customary habits" of humans. Customary habits, if not sublimely altered once in a while, might accrue to human madness.[20] It is not an aside when Socrates praises the Eleusinian mysteries with much more enthusiasm than he does the pragmatism of Isocrates.

When Socrates praises the Eleusinian mysteries for offering insight into extra-mundane truths, he is also *de facto* delivering, via his claims about "customary habits," a criticism of Isocrates. Isocrates's pragmatism, which derives its view of the good almost entirely from custom, and custom

---

18. Martin, *Ancient Greece*, 62.
19. McGlew, "Politics on the Margins," 9.
20. *Phaedrus*, 265a.

that even has a lot of good in it, is not only borderline banal, it might even lead to a form of madness borne of boredom.

Indeed, Socrates's terms in *Phaedrus* rather remarkably anticipate Nietzsche's praise of the Apollonian in the *Birth of Tragedy*, as the Apollonian allows for a release from "waking reality and its ominous obtrusiveness."[21] Clearly Socrates would have more patience with the Eleusinian mysteries than someone like Nietzsche, especially as the mysteries provided a sense of optimism in another life. Also, Socrates would have more appreciation of the Eleusinian mysteries than someone like Marx for whom religion is the opiate of the masses. Socrates seems to have acknowledged that the Eleusinian mysteries did indeed serve as a kind of glue that maintained a considerable amount of civil harmony. This civic function offered by the Eleusinian mysteries was all the more remarkable because that civic spirit was achieved without the obligation of otherwise onerous duties.

By comparison further, the egalitarian friendships borne of the Eleusinian mysteries were superior to democrat friendships ostensibly offered by the likes of Lysias. The democrat, Lysias, like the Marxist who criticizes Christianity as a front for the maintenance of class differences, would apparently denigrate the Eleusinian mysteries for offering a pseudo-equality. While many of different social strata were initiated into the Eleusinian mysteries, in Lysias's view no true democracy was offered by the mysteries because class differences remained.

Yet, Socrates saw through the democrat ruse. While babbling about equality among (other) persons, Lysias was happy to maintain his fortune and status.[22] That is why Plato informs us that Phaedrus had just come from a session with Lysias at the house of Epicrates, the democrat who was so wealthy he could purchase the house once owned by the famous sybarite, Morychus.

γ) Socrates Defeats Triptolemus

It is supposed to occur to Phaedrus, however, that, for all of their virtues, the Eleusinian mysteries could not really compete with Socrates's "divine philosophy."[23] Phaedrus is also supposed to see Socrates competing with the secular, too. Lysias's rhetoric could not compete with Socrates's sublime

21. Nietzsche, *The Birth of Tragedy*, §4.
22. *Phaedrus*, 279c.
23. Ibid., 239b.

rhetoric. Socrates's mystery philosophy offered the highest kind of insight and the highest kind of friendship.

Those who find their friendship in Zeus, the signature god of *Phaedrus*, are true friends because they are lovers of wisdom fully aware of the object(s) of their attention, the Divine, the Good, Beauty, and Essences. Accordingly, Socratic friends are true friends because they remain as attentive as possible to those "Ones." The friendships borne of the Eleusinian mysteries are significant because they are grounded at least in something not merely mundane; but they are inferior to friendships in Zeus, as rehabilitated in *Phaedrus*, because they are not grounded in anything as profoundly archaic as the Essence Revolution revealed in the *PL*.

The very imagery in the Zeus myth in the *PL* displays that and how Socrates's philosophy supersedes the Eleusinian mysteries. Eleusis was famous for being the place to which Demeter descended from Olympus to live temporarily with humans: "she permitted the fields of the Thriasian Plain to bear fruit once more."[24] Given that agrarian scene, one of the figures associated with the Eleusinian mysteries was Triptolemos, an Eleusinian prince famously depicted distributing corn from a winged chariot. Thus the chariot train image in Socrates's *PL*: Socrates's philosophy, inspired by the chariot-flying Zeus in the Zeus-rehabilitation theology in *Phaedrus*, promises and delivers more than the chariot-flying Triptolemus and the Eleusinian mysteries Triptolemus represents. Triptolemus never revealed anything like the Essence Wheel.

To compare further Socrates's mystery philosophy with the Eleusinian mysteries, which were embraced by the few, Socrates says explicitly of *anamnesis*, arguably the key to Socratic thought, that "few" are capable of it.[25] Surely these "few" are the best: hence Socrates's sense of aristocracy. Yet, Socrates's philosophy is not an exercise in occult escapism, as Orphism seems to be. Socrates's philosophy, in principle, is universal. Socrates says "every soul" has experienced the wondrous contemplation of the Essence Wheel as posed in the *PL*. Indeed, as Michael Leff writes, the passages in *Phaedrus* that stress that loftiest state of contemplation virtually "define man as a Form comprehending animal."[26] Yet, again, only few souls recollect that original whence which is the Essence Wheel.

---

24. Furley, *Andocides and the Herms*, 35.
25. *Phaedrus*, 250a.
26. Leff, "The Forms of Reality in Plato's *Phaedrus*," 22.

From Socrates's standpoint as someone who had a mystery philosophy that intersected with much of the Eleusinian mysteries but superseded them, Socrates could understand that Phaedrus's participation in the *PEM* was not the highest of crimes. Yet, Socrates's reminders of the elements of divine madness even in the city-sanctioned Eleusinian mysteries were ways to chide Phaedrus. Phaedrus might reconsider that embracing the city-sanctioned mystery associated with aristocrats could not be worse than having a criminal past due to juvenile rebellion against those mysteries.

Moreover, allegiance to the aristocratic Eleusinian mysteries certainly offered more for the soul than Lysias's sophistical, democrat-oriented rhetoric and everything associated with it. Socrates viewed Lysias and Lysias's comrades as pseudo-egalitarians competing with the best religion in the city. The democrat pseudo-egalitarians promoted demythologizing while offering no alternative to the mysteries other than superficial rhetoric and vapid plays in the theatre.

So as neither the mysteries nor democrat-influenced sophistry could be extricated from the city, Socratic philosophy had to proceed by being, or seeming to be, similar, in no minor measure, to both to supersede both. Socrates's *PL* supersedes the image of Triptolemus and Socrates's *P'/S'* supersedes Lysian cleverness. Socratic philosophy in *Phaedrus*, with its law of return to an ultimate whence in the Essence Wheel, would establish the basis of Phaedrus's good return to Athens. With his new insights, assuming Phaedrus could retain them, Phaedrus was to return to Athens this time with a new appreciation of the old mysteries, while at the same time prepared either to convert Lysias to philosophy or disown him altogether.

δ) Phaedrus and *Schadenverbessrung Eros*

So, what was the worldview that corrupted Phaedrus? What was the worldview that, during, and even beyond, his rebellious youth, Phaedrus had assumed? Did Phaedrus have a view of an ultimate whence that could lead him to a beneficial whither?

We know Phaedrus's worldview, or what appears to be his worldview, from his appearance in the *Symposium*. In the *Symposium*, Phaedrus's speech on *eros* referred to an ultimate whence. We have to be a little cautious here. Richard Hunter reminds us we should be wary of taking any of the speeches in the *Symposium* entirely at face value, for at least a couple of reasons: a) the speeches in the *Symposium* were allegedly recollected by Aristodemus, whose memory is not particularly stellar; and b) speeches given at banquets were expected to be playful or "seriocomic" (*spoudaiogelogon*).[27]

We would do well to take Hunter's counsel under advisement, *mutatis mutandis*. However, we might also note Phaedrus's inclination to demythologizing in *Phaedrus* (or co-opting myth in a way that justifies his mundane worldview) and his apparent preference for naturalism, as suggested by the reference to him in *Protagoras*.[28] So we may treat Phaedrus's speech from the *Symposium* very much as Rhodes does: at face value, at least relative to how Phaedrus in turn lived his life.

Phaedrus's speech in the *Symposium* offers a quirky account of human origins similar to the cosmology of Empedocles. Phaedrus's worldview operates on the premise that there are two imminent cosmic principles, love (*eros*) and strife. Yet, instead of Empedocles's moral dualism mixed with a pluralist ontology—that is, a principle of individuation based on a ratio of the four elements, Earth, Air, Fire, and Water—Phaedrus's speech on *eros* promotes a novel monism.

The (intentionally?) comical part of Phaedrus's *Symposium* speech is that Phaedrus's worldview singles out the dullest of the four elements, Earth, as its ontological ground (no pun intended). No other monistic worldview had ever adopted Earth as an ontological ground. Worse yet, in Phaedrus's *Symposium* speech, Earth is a derivative ground at that. Citing Hesiod, Phaedrus argues that Earth emerged from Chaos. Yet, Earth, the most inert of the elements, apparently resisted individuation and perfection. So, somehow, *eros*, *sui generis*, gave rise to itself to generate motion, individuation, beauty, etc.

Phaedrus's speech accordingly called *eros* the most honorable god. Both men and gods honor *eros*, because, *sans Eros*, nothing would move, desire, or think. *Eros*, resisting otherwise inert and undifferentiated Earth, not only aims at states of individuation but individuated perfection.

Eros is therefore heroic *de facto*. *Eros* strives; strives always to attain states of individuated perfection by struggling to counter Earth's inertia that would otherwise dissolve all beings into the one, undifferentiated, awful, prime origin, Chaos. As Rhodes notes summarily, *Symposium* Phaedrus deems *eros* "an epiphenomenal force of Earth that pulls its matter not

---

27. Hunter, *Plato's Symposium*, 23–24.
28. *Protagoras*, 315c.

only away from the fate that awaits it, but also toward a *telos* of honor with regard to the beautiful."[29] Rhodes writes otherwise:

> This account of *eros* begins to clarify Phaedrus's choices. His nebulous epiphenomenon of Earth exerts its pulls on each piece of matter that it instantiates as consciously appetitive and rational. . . . Each operation of the mysterious force strives first to ensure the foundation of the success of its own matter. . . . Hence, Phaedrus's crass selfishness and valetudinarianism now appear as symbols of a wish to become the most successful specimen of Earth by being the most perfectly erotic.[30]

Empedocles's cosmology was comical and problematic enough for Plato and Socrates, and later, Aristotle, especially due to the dubious morals and epistemology derived from it. Phaedrus's essentially naturalist, neo-Empedoclean worldview offered in the *Symposium* would be subject to criticisms similar, for example, to Socrates's reduction to the absurd of any naturalist explanation for Socrates's presence in prison in *Phaedo*. A naturalist explanation would suggest Socrates had been blown into prison by some wind rather than forced there by a deliberate, immoral injustice. While that Socratic point in *Phaedo* was directed more obviously at the limitations of the thought of Anaxagoras, that criticism could apply just as well to Empedocles's materialism or Phaedrus's monism.

Furthermore, for Phaedrus, only male homosexuals can best honor *eros* by becoming the healthiest, wealthiest, and most competitive individuals: "They would avoid all dishonor and compete with one another."[31] This position is the basis of Phaedrus's *apologia* for competitive, honor-love oriented male homosexuality in the *Symposium*, and in the position he held his entire adult life, even up to the alleged time of *Phaedrus*. Women may be able to exercise occasional courage borne of love, as in the case of Alcestis, but that is rare; and Phaedrus essentially denigrates women in the same context in the *Symposium* in which he momentarily praises Alcestis. Phaedrus notes that Orpheus was not really courageous and for that was consigned to an ignominious death "at the hands of women."[32] Nothing on that argumentative front, that male homosexuality is superior to all forms of *eros*, has changed when we see Phaedrus later in *Phaedrus*.

29. Rhodes, *Eros, Wisdom, and Silence*, 211.
30. Ibid., 211.
31. *Symposium*, 178e.
32. Ibid., 179d.

Who Is Phaedrus?

For Phaedrus, male homosexual, Typhonic love, is not just a lifestyle but a virtual religion. Typhonic love is vastly superior to all other forms of love. For Phaedrus and his Typhonic fellows, such as Alkibiades, the male homosexual cannot or should not suffer the deficiencies in physical and mental health that befall others, especially females. The duty of the Typhonic male is to emerge glowingly from the muck of humanity, much as *eros* allegedly emerged from otherwise inertia-prone Earth. As the creative non-fiction writing Plato more than implies, the famously handsome Phaedrus seems born to play the role of beaming Typhonic lover and champion of the cause: Phaedrus's very name suggests "glowing" or "shining."[33] Phaedrus had always stood out, at least physically, among the muck of humanity: thus Socrates's tailor-made myth in the *PL* in which it is revealed that, in the Essence Wheel, Beauty shines the truth of each Essence through each Essence. What better image to engage the beaming Phaedrus? The image, that actually defied reduction to an image, of shining Beauty was to reveal to Phaedrus that Phaedrus owed his beauty to a source outside himself.

Phaedrus's cosmology, however, was superficial by comparison with Socrates's philosophy. In Phaedrus's worldview, with love as the principle of the realization of individuated perfection, the male homoerotic honor-lover does not love his beloved unconditionally. Rather, he competes with his partner at every turn, on every level, to prod him to become the perfect human specimen. The other side of that honor-love is shame. The male homosexual should be ashamed, and should be made to feel ashamed, for falling short of being the wealthiest, healthiest, and most superbly sexual of human beings. Given this mutual prodding and shaming between the two men, one could term this kind of *eros Schadenverbesserung eros*, shame-improvement *eros*.

There are references to *Schadenverbesserung eros* in *Phaedrus* that render obvious this peculiar form of honor-love that Phaedrus treats as a kind of civic religion. Socrates refers to those who "live a life less noble and without philosophy . . . ruled by the love of honor . . ."[34] Further, it is not accidental that soon after Socrates finishes the *PL*, which Phaedrus finds remarkable, Phaedrus remarks that Lysias would be afraid to try to "compete" with it.[35] Phaedrus then refers to shame: how many men in the city are "ashamed" to write speeches and leave them behind for fear of being

---

33. Sallis, *Being and Logos*, 106.
34. *Phaedrus*, 256b
35. Ibid., 257c.

called sophists? Phaedrus's comments reflect his *Schadenverbesserung eros* ethic. The honor-lover, especially the Typhonic lover, should always strive to avoid shame.

Phaedrus was not born into his *Schadenverbesserung eros* ethic. It is something he learned, much as his Earth-oriented worldview in the *Symposium* was not his original worldview. Most likely, the ontology in Phaedrus's *Symposium* speech was the joking part of a speech written by Erixymachus, Phaedrus's lover at the time. If that is so, and it is entirely likely, then Phaedrus's *Symposium* speech emerges as a kind of cruel joke on the young Phaedrus; a joke of which the young Phaedrus was not even conscious.

Would Erixymachus stoop to such a cruel comic play?

The banter in the *Symposium* suggests that Erixymachus in particular was quite inclined to jocularity.[36] Further, Erixymachus was the ring-leader of the speeches in the *Symposium*. Ostensibly it is Phaedrus who spurs the speeches on love in the *Symposium*, according to no less than Erixymachus himself. Yet, Erixymachus really generates the plan.[37] And Erixymachus even recommends the order in which the speeches will be delivered.[38] Surely Erixymachus had put all of the words of Phaedrus's *Symposium* speech in Phaedrus's mouth over a period of time, as Erixymachus was, by all appearances, Phaedrus's *erastes*. Erixymachus, that is, was surely being disingenuous when he said: "I'd like to do him [Phaedrus] a favor and make my contribution."[39] Erixymachus was no mere contributor. He was the master of ceremonies. If the *Symposium* were a more typical Platonic dialogue and had a personal nomination like so many do, it could easily be called the *Erixymachus*.

It is thanks, really, to Erixymachus that Phaedrus's *Symposium* speech establishes a view of love that situates the operations of love within the context of the elements, the stock and trade of the physician, Erixymachus. So, by the time the speeches make their way to Erixymachus, it is that much easier for Erixymachus's discourse on love that treats of the relationship of the opposing functions of the elements to seem not just *a propos* but perfectly suited to the circumstance, certainly in comparison with the simplistic offering delivered by Phaedrus.

---

36. *Symposium*, 193e.
37. Ibid., 177c.
38. Ibid., 177d.
39. Ibid., 177c.

Who Is Phaedrus?

It is thanks to Erixymachus (thanking himself) that Phaedrus's speech was so bad and simplistic. This was all by Plato's poetic design, of course, but it reinforces what John Dillon says of the *Symposium*: the procedure of the successive speeches in the *Symposium* amounts to "a process of intellectual development which is likened to an ascent from which ever-broadening vistas are obtained."[40] From Phaedrus's superficial speech there was nowhere to go but up, and by Erixymachus's design.

The joke, sadly, was on Phaedrus; and a cruel joke it was because Phaedrus believed the ontology/cosmology he was delivering; and, worse, Phaedrus would proceed by living the speech to his detriment. Erixymachus, who knew the sarcastic elements of sympotic protocol, let Phaedrus embarrass himself. Indeed, it is likely Phaedrus was about to be abandoned by his *erastes* at the time, Erixymachus himself, because Phaedrus's cluelessness demonstrated Phaedrus would not be very worthy as a Typhonic lover over the course of time. Phaedrus was a handsome catch and, obviously, many of the Typhonic lovers in Athens wanted to bed him. To shift the imagery to more recent popular culture, many men would like to say that they made it to bed with Paris Hilton. Yet, no one who bedded that beauty would consider her an intellectual equal.

Socrates says to Phaedrus, after all, that Phaedrus is an ἀτεχνον/ ἀτεχνων wonder when it comes to speeches:[41] That is, Phaedrus is an "utter" wonder; and, by the play on words, Phaedrus is an "artless" wonder: a "naïve" wonder when it comes to speeches. *Symposium* Phaedrus was naïve to the point that he delivered a speech he did not fully understand, yet believed and lived. Phaedrus still believed the core and details of that *Schadenverbesserung eros* speech years later when we see him next in *Phaedrus*.

Indeed, when we look at Phaedrus's Platonic career, as it were, we see him as a dupe on both occasions; and a dupe, sadly, in the area of his favorite endeavor, speechifying. Phaedrus gives one speech about Typhonic shame in the *Symposium* in which he is actually being shamed in the very delivery of it. Later, he gleefully reads another speech in *Phaedrus* in praise of the non-lover, written by no less than his own "lover," Lysias, who is telling Phaedrus, through that very speech, that Lysias is really a non-lover. Not surprisingly, Socrates states that the person who falls for the non-lover

---

40. Dillon, "Comments on John Moore's Paper," 74.
41. Cf., "Phaedrus the Artless."

ends up in the role of "wanderer" and "fool"[42] Those words describe the mostly aimless and clueless Phaedrus.

More, Pheadrus's *Symposium* speech in praise of Typhonic love that calls for competition with the beloved to obtain homosexual perfection elides easily with the first glimpse we have of Phaedrus in *Phaedrus*. In *Phaedrus*, when Phaedrus comes on the scene, we see a superficial hypochondriac concerned with his physical perfection and appearance. Phaedrus is embarking on a therapeutic walk on the softer roads on the advice of his new physician, Acumenus, father of his former lover, Erixymachus, who had almost certainly abandoned Phaedrus for not being able to compete Typhonically.

Phaedrus Phaedrus, fighting aging, was trying to maintain his legendary good looks as long as possible in keeping with his *Schadenverbesserung eros* ethic. The only thing that has changed in Phaedrus's world from the time of the *Symposium* to the time of *Phaedrus* (aside from the intervening years in exile) is Phaedrus's lover: once the physician, Erixymachus; now the rhetorician, Lysias.

Much poorer but still concerned with his, albeit waning, good looks, Phaedrus was still keen to compete as much as he could with his new rhetorician-lover, Lysias: hence Phaedrus's lingering preoccupation with speech and speeches; and his rather pathetic embrace of all things democrat due to the man who was now his new *erastes* of a sort despite their near equality in age.

Socrates sees the situation. Other than lovers, little had changed with Phaedrus from the time of *Symposium* to the time of *Phaedrus*. If anything had changed, it was simply exacerbation. The Phaedrus of *Phaedrus* might have become even more preoccupied with speeches than ever, if that was possible. This is not surprising, as Phaedrus's lover had changed from Erixymachus, the physician, to Lysias, the rhetorician. Yet, Phaedrus's intense concern with speeches was now rather pathological. Thus Socrates's diagnosis of Phaedrus's situation that synthesizes, appropriately, the arts employed by Phaedrus's two prominent boyfriends: medicine and rhetoric. Phaedrus's fervor for speeches seems like a disease.[43] Socrates, the true lover, was the only man who could replace, nobly, the harmful dyad of Phaedrus's non-lovers.

---

42. *Phaedrus*, 257a.
43. Ibid., 228c.

Who Is Phaedrus?

Phaedrus in *Phaedrus*, as Typhonic, *Schadenverbesserung eros* lover, thinks he must learn to compete with his new lover, Lysias: thus Phaedrus's even greater preoccupation with rhetoric. According to his *Schadenverbesserung eros* ethic, if Phaedrus could not compete with Lysias in rhetoric, Phaedrus might find himself jilted; shamed out of the relationship. Phaedrus thought he had to learn to be more competitive in speech-making or, at the very least, speech appreciation.

Socrates therefore saw competition-based, *Schadenverbesserung eros* as a dubious form of honor-love, not because it was homosexual but because it was not built on the love of wisdom. In love guided by the love of wisdom, the lovers are willing to suffer for one another in the attempt to gain divine understanding, even if they do not always meet the standards of human perfection.

Again, the love bestowed by the lover of wisdom, Socrates says, is greater than that conferred by "divine inspiration."[44] This is the direct counter to Phaedrus's view of pederasty in the *Symposium*, where Phaedrus refers to the *erastes* as "divinely inspired."[45] Socrates's cure for Phaedrus's perverted sense of honor-love comes indispensably in philosophy, the love of wisdom, the highest calling of the soul. In the terms and images of *Phaedrus*, the love of wisdom is perfected in the contemplation of the Essence Wheel presented in the *PL*. That myth is, in effect, the poetic presentation of the ultimate effect of dialectic, the necessary means by which the soul is capable of conceiving of perfection in the first place.

We see Socrates, therefore, playing the role of sublime rhetorician to show he loves Phaedrus more than Lysias does. Also, Socrates plays the role of sublime physician to show he loves Phaedrus more than did Phaedrus's former lover, Erixymachus, the whimsical physician. Here John Anton's words ring true: "Plato's Socrates is committed from the time of the *Gorgias* to a belief that reversing the state of diseases of the soul intimately depends upon the practice of a set of arts, chiefly among them the art of dialectic."[46]

In the greater context of *Phaedrus*, Socrates's philosophy offered more of a cure for the soul than any of the mystery religions of the city, or any other account of an ultimate whence. On the level of the ethical, Plato's presentation of the function of Beauty in the Essence Wheel augments what Charles Taylor claims the appreciation of the Good does in the *Republic*.

---

44. Ibid., 256b.
45. *Symposium*, 180b.
46. Anton, "Dialectic and Health in Plato's *Gorgias*," 50.

Phaedrus's Ultimate Whence

The *Republic* reassesses the alleged priority of the form of honor-love that is most obvious in the city, the soldier ethic.[47] In *Phaedrus*, Plato reassesses another form of honor-love prominent in Athens: male homosexual *Schadenverbesserung eros* Socrates deems problematic and manifestly inferior to a Zeus-inspired love of wisdom.

Phaedrus's *Symposium* speech had, in fact, tried to conflate the civilian and military versions of honor-love. In the *Symposium*, Phaedrus argued that *eros* could generate artificial courage in persons who were not "naturally courageous."[48] At the time, Phaedrus did not realize he was actually maintaining a Socratic view of virtue and lodging a self-criticism at the same time. For Socrates, courage is "natural" to all persons as a function of the soul, lest they become corrupted. A person's need for artificial courage would be evidence of their corruption; and, moreover, Socrates would surely argue that the "naturally courageous" person is actually the person motivated by genuine love, the love of wisdom, as the soldier would fight to realize human laws that would reflect the divine law recognized by Socratic philosophy. The honor-loving Typhonic warrior would actually be fighting from the opposite of courage—fear; fear of losing his beloved whom he deems as little more than a commodity with whom he is to compete on a regular basis.

Socrates has to save Phaedrus from Phaedrus's own worldview that brings with it not only a risible ontology, but that also operates with an ethic steeped in a skewed sense of shame. Socrates therefore has to impart to Phaedrus a proper sense of shame, one oriented relative to a divine, constant standard conceived in the recollection of the unchanging Essence Wheel, not a democrat-oriented shame that shifts with the winds of popular opinion or is determined pell-mell by the likes of Lysias and Epicrates.

Socrates's mystery philosophy would show Phaedrus Truth and its fundamental relationship with Beauty. This is crucial because in every phase of Phaedrus's worldview, Phaedrus betrays he is motivated by a preoccupation with beauty, if mainly his own. Phaedrus's worldview, however, does not pose Beauty as an hypothesis in the Socratic sense of *hypo-thesis* as presented in the discussion of *dianoia* in the *Republic*. Phaedrus's worldview does not pose an ontological difference between Beauty, the Essence *par excellence*, and the beautiful thing or individual. Without any serious awareness of that ontological difference, Phaedrus will never be able to

---

47. Taylor, *Sources of the Self*, 117.
48. *Symposium*, 179a.

Who Is Phaedrus?

abandon his superficial and confused worldview that leads him to think that a life-justifying beauty somehow originates in the fortuitous coagulation of the elements, or, more precisely, one element, Earth.

Phaedrus did not have to look far to find a counter to his worldview's simplistic understanding of beauty. Phaedrus had always been famously handsome, and his good looks, which came naturally, made for a relatively easy life in his long enterprise of social climbing. Yet, the Phaedrus we see in *Phaedrus* was losing those natural goods. Phaedrus's very waning health was the counter to Phaedrus's own bizarre Earth-ontology and his *Schadenverbesserung eros* ethic. Soon, almost certainly, the aging Phaedrus would be summarily dismissed by his new "lover," Lysias, for not living up to financial, physical, and sexual perfection.

If and when Phaedrus found himself rejected by Lysias for becoming unattractive, somewhat as Phaedrus had likely been rejected by Erixymachus for being relatively stupid, Phaedrus would have nothing to blame but the *Schadenverbesserung eros* ethic he had praised for many years. At some point, Phaedrus would not be able to compete; and Socrates's mystery philosophy, with its proper whence and whither, would be the only system left, not only for Phaedrus's consolation, but as the means, the only means, for Phaedrus's recovery and conversion.

5

Phaedrus's Middle Whence
Was Phaedrus Bi-rebellious?

α) Why Mutilate the Herms?

"WHENCE AND WHITHER?" THIS is Socrates's opening question. Every human being has an ultimate, middle, and immediate whence (at least). So, what about Phaedrus?

Socrates addressed the issue of Phaedrus's ultimate whence *per* the *PL*; at least Phaedrus's intellectual origin as a rational human. Souls, inherently immortal, find their true origin in the contemplation of Essences in the Essence Wheel. (In the next section we address Phaedrus's immediate whence, Phaedrus's meeting with Lysias at the house of Epicrates.) But what about Phaedrus's middle whence?

Phaedrus's middle whence pertains to the turbulent times that led to his prosecution and banishment from Athens for several years.

In *Phaedrus*, Socrates apparently encounters Phaedrus for the first time since Phaedrus's return from exile. In this rather complicated context, at least one simple point should be at the fore. Athens itself was both a whence and whither for the exiled and returned Phaedrus. So, given Socrates's peculiar status as the god's gift to Athens, Phaedrus's relationship with Athens is the focal point for all of Socrates's service on Phaedrus's behalf.

Why was Phaedrus banished? Further, given that Phaedrus had returned to Athens from exile, had he made a good return? What would constitute a good return in Socrates's view?

Who Is Phaedrus?

In *Phaedrus*, Socrates does not refer explicitly to the turbulent events of Phaedrus's middle whence, the controversies over the *MH* and the *PEM*. Socrates does manage to insert a telling rhetorical question, however, saying to Phaedrus: "But is it not better to be ridiculous than to be clever and an enemy?"[1] Socrates is ridiculous; Lysias is clever; (he and others like him are called so on more than one occasion); and Phaedrus was once regarded an enemy of the state.[2]

While there is not much mention of the controversies to which Phaedrus had been party, some familiarity with that pretext is important for appreciating *Phaedrus* fully. This is similar to how awareness of the post-text of *Charmides* is crucial for understanding the internals of *Charmides*: "When reading *Charmides*, we are no doubt supposed to have in mind the subsequent careers of Charmides and Critias; part of the drama of that dialogue consists in Socrates talking about *sophrosyne* with several characters who later ('later' in the sense of 'after the dramatic date of the dialogue') showed a marked lack of that virtue. Part of Plato's meaning—conveyed over the heads of the *dramatis personae*—is that we are to see this."[3] As awareness of the post-text of *Charmides* is crucial for appreciation of the drama itself, the turbulent events of Phaedrus's middle whence, the pretext, are keys to grasping the internals of *Phaedrus*.

The turbulent times of Phaedrus's middle whence concern his involvement, or apparent involvement, in both of the two most infamous Athenian political-religious controversies, the *MH* and the *PEM*. Apparently Phaedrus was officially found guilty in the *PEM* only. However, with many others, including Rhodes and Nussbaum, I conclude Phaedrus was very likely involved in the *MH* also.[4] Yet, unlike Nussbaum, Rhodes, and others, I maintain that Plato himself is the best source for suggestions, or something like evidence, that Phaedrus was involved in both scandals.

---

1. *Phaedrus*, 260c.
2. Ibid., 227c, 228c, 229d.
3. Griswold, "Comments on Kahn," 134.
4 A Herm was a sculpture with a head above a plain lower section, usually squared off, on which male genitals were carved. Debra Hamel describes Herms as "like big Pez dispensers with penises" (Hamel, *The Mutilation of the Herms*, 1). Herms were thought to ward off evil and were placed at key locations—near boundaries, tombs, temples, crossings, the gymnasia, in streets, outside houses, etc.—for protection and good luck. Hamel sums up the mutilation of the Herms as follows: "in addition to smashing or somehow scratching the herms' faces, the *hermokopidia* [herm-smashers] also lopped off their penises whenever they could."

Plato assumes his contemporary audience, at least, would be aware of the controversies to which Phaedrus had been party. And, there is a subtle allusion to Phaedrus's exile from, and return to, Athens in the opening dramatic setting. When Phaedrus is explaining the course of his morning constitutional, he refers to his new physician, Acumenus. The mention of Acumenus is likely more than a reminder that Phaedrus had known Acumenus, father of Erixymachus, a long time. Acumenus and Phaedrus had something more particular in common. Like Phaedrus, Acumenus had also been tried, after testimony given by the slave, Lydus, for participation in the *PEM*.[5] Apparently Acumenus, like Phaedrus, had also returned to Athens from exile.

Overall, the key to the appreciation of the historical elements of the pretext of *Phaedrus* lies with the not so subtle reference to Phaedrus's character flaw. Socrates summarily describes Phaedrus as *epamphoterious*; torn between two ways.[6] Granted, Socrates could intend this negative attribute in numerous ways; and, indeed, in almost every facet of his life, Phaedrus seems to have been *epamphoterious*. For all of his promotion of male homosexuality as a virtual religion, Phaedrus was bisexual when he needed to be: he had married his female cousin, most likely for a dowry.[7] Yet, for the purposes of *Phaedrus*, when Socrates refers to Phaedrus's *epamphoterious* inclination, Phaedrus's dyadic flaw, Plato is also hinting that Phaedrus was involved in both the *MH* and the *PEM*.

Throughout *Phaedrus*, Phaedrus is even assumed to be *epamphoterious*, torn between two ways: follow Lysias or follow Socrates? In that sense, to a degree, Socrates will have to play upon Phaedrus's flaw. At the beginning, Phaedrus clearly favors Lysias. So, Socrates will have to seduce Phaedrus in *logos*; not for sex but to lure Phaedrus away from Lysias's rhetoric and the democrat sentiments associated with Lysias's rhetoric.

James Nichols has summed up the matter very concisely, and relates the issues involved in *Phaedrus* to issues in our own time:

> This problem of rhetoric's elitism, like the issue of deception, has been around from the start. Plato deals with it as we shall see in the *Gorgias* and delicately touches on it in the *Protagoras*, where Socrates compels that famous Sophist to come to terms with the

---

5. Nails, *The People of Plato*, 2.
6. *Phaedrus*, 257b. For linguistic economy, I render the third person ἐπαμφοτερίζηι adjectival.
7. Nails, *The People of Plato*, 232.

> problematic relation of sophistry to democracy. The problem perseveres in modern democracy, reinforced by a relativism about good and bad, noble and base things, which Plato himself had already diagnosed as an endemic tendency of democratic thinking and character. The democrat man, Socrates argues, "doesn't admit true speech . . . , if someone says that there are some pleasures belonging to fine and good desires and some belonging to bad desires, and the ones must be practiced and honored and the others checked and enslaved. Rather, he shakes his head at all this and says that all are alike and must be honored on an equal basis."[8]

Thus Phaedrus's dilemma after his return from exile: Follow the ugly, ridiculous, and indigent aristocrat Socrates, or follow the attractive, clever, and wealthy democrat Lysias? Why should Phaedrus follow the poor aristocrat, Socrates, when democrats like Lysias were the powers of the time? That dilemma reflects a similar dilemma *epamphoterious* Phaedrus confronted back in his middle whence. Back in those turbulent years, Phaedrus faced the choice of following either Socrates or his opposite, Alkibiades, Socrates's one-time favorite. Back then, Phaedrus chose Alkibiades, and that decision is almost certainly what led to Phaedrus's banishment from Athens.

In those years of Phaedrus's middle whence, when Phaedrus chose Alkibiades, *epamphoterious* Phaedrus was trying to have it both ways. Phaedrus understandably associated Alkibiades with Socrates, knowing, no doubt, that Alkibiades had once been Socrates's favorite. Yet, Phaedrus was so superficial he appears not to have realized that Socrates had disowned Alkibiades.

Alkibiades, himself *epamphoterious*, yet clever enough to be successfully duplicitous, became so different from Socrates that Alkibiades and Socrates were virtual opposites. Phaedrus had no excuse for not noting a significant difference between Socrates and Alkibiades as time went by. Yet, it is understandable, given Alkibiades's somewhat begrudging, half-drunken encomium to Socrates at the end of the *Symposium*, that Phaedrus might be somewhat confused as to the actual distance between Socrates and Alkibiades. Phaedrus would have been further confused had he stayed long enough to hear Alkibiades's drunken praise of Socrates for Socrates being a different kind of *erastes*: one who did not engage in sexual relations with his charges but merely tended to their souls. Phaedrus, however, did not hear that speech because, in the name of moderation, Phaedrus left the

---

8. Nichols, *Plato, Phaedrus*, 9.

banquet early with his *erastes* at the time, Erixymachus, at Erixymachus's allegedly medically informed recommendation.

Whatever identity might have existed between Alkibiades and Socrates was to be dissolved in *Phaedrus*, once and for all. *Phaedrus* serves, in part, as Plato's disavowal of Alkibiades on Socrates's behalf, as much of the focus of *Phaedrus* has everything to do with an Athens in decay due to harmful influences from scoundrels like Alkibiades and frauds like Lysias. (In turn, however, Lysias himself despised Alkibiades and Alkibiades's whole family.[9])

When Wohl writes about the young Alkibiades relative to Socrates, if for reasons not limited to the subject of *Phaedrus*, she could be addressing *Phaedrus* and its underappreciated pretext: "The contest between philosophy and democracy over Alcibiades is above all a contest over his eros and, through him, the eros of Athens."[10] Socrates had lost Alkibiades; and, most likely, it was Alkibiades who had corrupted Phaedrus. Phaedrus would never develop Alkibiades's kind of influence. But Socrates's de-corruption of even the (aging) youth of Athens, personified by Phaedrus, had to start somewhere.

Epamphoterious Phaedrus embraced the speeches of democrats like Lysias who also liked to have everything both ways. Lysias, *qua* democrat, pretended to be a man of the "people." Yet, Lysias lived a lavish life; a life more legendarily associated with aristocrats. Lysias certainly lived more lavishly than the supreme aristocrat of the soul, Socrates.

Another element of the *epamphoterious* character of Phaedrus can be seen in the fact that Phaedrus, an Athenian, could enjoy all the rights of being a citizen of Athens while appearing to be unprovincial. For many years over the course of his career, Lysias was a metic, a non-Athenian. By embracing Lysias, Phaedrus wanted things both ways again: he could be both an Athenian and a cosmopolitan super-Athenian at the same time, as a simpatico with the prosecutor from Pireus. By contrast, Socrates seemed ridiculous and hyper-provincial. For Socrates, for reasons still mysterious to us, Athens might as well have been the center of the cosmos, even though Socrates's philosophy was as universal as any.

Epamphoterious Phaedrus always wanted things both ways without having to commit. So, over the course of *Phaedrus*, Socrates would try to move Phaedrus from *epamphoterious*, dyadically confused, to "simple."

---

9. Furley, *Andokides and the Herms*, 44. Cf, "Plato's Rehabilitation of Zeus."
10. Wohl, *Love Among the Ruins*, 160.

Who Is Phaedrus?

Phaedrus was to learn how to choose to be "all in" in one way.[11] Phaedrus was supposed to choose Socrates over Lysias; or, more particularly, Socrates's dialectic, and everything associated with it, over Lysias's rhetoric and everything associated with it.

How does all of this bear on Phaedrus's relation to Athens, his possible involvement in both the *MH* and the *PEM*, and his de-corruption via Socrates?

On the whole, we have to resign ourselves to considerable speculation about scandals as complex as the *MH* or the *PEM*. Yet, on the dyadic front, a key to understanding Phaedrus, the man, and *Phaedrus*, the dialogue, is that the *MH* was considered especially offensive to the democrat, while the *PEM* offended more the aristocrat. W. D. Furley has persuasively argued that this was a peculiar dyadic dynamic relative to the *MH* and the *PEM*. The Herms were considered "popular monuments of the democracy . . . despite their proliferation under the Peisistratid tyranny."[12]

Furley concedes that there were surely many motivations behind the *MH* that will always be a mystery, for at least a couple of reasons: 1) there were probably many different parties, factions, or social clubs who wanted to offend the democrats for different social, political, and religious reasons; and 2) the *MH* was really more than just a one-time event.

Desultory mutilations of Herms had occurred in Athens over the course of many years. Yet, we have come to identify the *MH* scandal with the city-wide, especially aggravated *MH* on the eve of the expedition to Sicily. Out of literally hundreds of Herms scattered throughout Athens, and on the borders, there was hardly a Herm that was not mutilated on the eve of the expedition to Sicily. The expedition eve *MH* was so pervasive and severe it stayed in the minds of Athenians for generations; much as *Kristalnacht* does for the Jew, despite previous and regular persecution otherwise; and the way 9/11 does for the American, despite repeated attacks on American installations and forces over many years prior to 9/11 itself.

While the *MH* offended more the democrat faction, the *PEM* contrarily offended more the aristocrat, as aristocrats originated and maintained the Eleusinian mysteries. The *PEM* was considered more an attack on noble families, noble intentions, and noble traditions, while Hermes, hence the Herms, was the more "popular" god of the democrats.

11. Cf., "Phaedrus's Whither."
12. Furley, *Andokides and the Herms*, 20.

How much detailed justification of this dichotomy can be made will be debated forever. Yet, on the more plainly political level, the democrat faction feared the effects of both scandals, as both scandals occurred when the democrat faction held most of the power in Athens.

Aside from the *MH* appearing to be a frontal assault on religious elements associated with democrats, the democrats clearly feared they would suffer the more simply by being associated with such a negative and unprecedented event. More, something similar could be said about the rise in instances of the *PEM* under democrat rule. Even if, on the level of the strictly religious, the *PEM* offended aristocrats more than it did democrats, the democrat faction could not afford to be seen as losing so much social control that nothing seemed sacred: neither democrat-inclined Herm-respect, nor the aristocrat-established Eleusinian mysteries. A city as instinctively religious as Athens was could not abide nihilism.

Aside from the supposition, well-supported by Furley, that the *MH* offended more the democrat and the *PEM* more the aristocrat, there were other differences between the two scandals. The *MH* was noticeably public, even if few witnessed the actual action since it occurred in the darkness of night. The *PEM* was much more private, occurring mainly in private homes and at private parties. So, even when we come to understand some of the more obvious parameters of the two scandals, the primary being that the *MH* seemed to offend democrats and the *PEM* aristocrats, a foundational perplexity remains. Why would anyone be motivated to participate in *both* stems of this *CO* of scandals? Why would Phaedrus participate in *both* (if, in fact, he did)? Was Phaedrus in fact bi-rebellious?

From the evidence we have, it is difficult to conclude anything definitive about the nature and scope of Phaedrus's guilt relative to both the *MH* and the *PEM*. Some commentators accept with little hesitation that Phaedrus was involved in both scandals. Nails, contrarily, reminds us that Phaedrus was officially charged in the *PEM* only. Nails claims that in the trial of Andokides, who was also alleged to have participated in both scandals, Andokides did not interpolate Phaedrus's name when Andokides asked for a rereading of the names of those implicated in the *MH*, a list that might have included Phaedrus's name.[13] From this non-interpolation of Phaedrus's name by Andokides it seems Phaedrus was spared prosecution for participation in the *MH*.

---

13. Nails, *The People of Plato*, 233–34.

Who Is Phaedrus?

Yet, the full historical verdict is still out. It could well be that Phaedrus actually participated in both the *MH* and the *PEM*, even though he was formally charged and prosecuted only for the latter.

While we should not accuse Phaedrus hastily, the court records that led to Phaedrus's dismissal were probably unreliable in the first place, as Furley reminds us. When Andokides was tried for involvement in both the *MH* and the *PEM*, the most revealing trial of all relative to the two scandals, some of the "evidence" in his particular case did not emerge until some fourteen years after the events.[14] In the political aftermath of the *MH*, and with the bothersome phenomenon of ongoing *PEM* lurking in the background, the democrats started proceedings to accuse many for participation in both scandals.

Regarding Andokides's confession of guilt for participation in the *MH* rather soon after the *MH*, Furley says: "It is worth noting how limited is the overlap between those named in connection with the mutilation and those named in connection with the profanation."[15]

Yet, not to accuse hastily, if Phaedrus's name was not prominently impressed on the actual writ relative to the *MH*, and if Andokides was incapable of implicating Phaedrus for involvement in the *MH*, it may have been that Phaedrus was such a marginal figure among the scores of perpetrators of the pervasive *MH*, that Andokides saw no need, or ability, to interpolate Phaedrus's name on the formal writ.

Even if Nails is right, and Phaedrus was never officially associated with the *MH*, the Phaedrus of *Phaedrus* was still likely proceeding about Athens under a cloud of suspicion of having been involved in both scandals, even after his return from exile.

It seems, however, that none other than Plato himself is telling us that Phaedrus was involved in both the *MH* and the *PEM*. In *Phaedrus*, Plato's very choice of terms to describe Phaedrus himself suggests that Phaedrus was involved in both the *MH* and the *PEM*.

There was a linguistic curiosity to the term used to promulgate the guilt of those involved in both the *MH* and the *PEM*. Relative to Andokides's testimony soon after the *MH*, only one man actually, Pherekles, was publicly declared guilty in both scandals. This is not to say that others were not guilty in both scandals, but only one man was found guilty in both

---

14. Furley, *Andokides and the Herms*, 68.
15. Ibid., 48n.

given Andokides's testimony in particular, and that publication of Pherakles's guilt seems to have implications for *Phaedrus*.

The publication of Pherekles's guilt was rendered by the carving of Pherekles's name in *Stelai*. That publication read as follows: περι αμφοτερα, "involved in both."[16] Pherekles alone was called, by the city, *amphoterious*; guilty in both the *MH* and the *PEM*. Here Socrates's claim regarding Phaedrus's character flaw as *epamphoterious*, torn between two ways, is likely more significant than just a summary assessment of Phaedrus's key flaw. Even if [*ep(i)*]-*amphoterious* suggests being on the periphery of the *amphoterious*, the epicenter is still connected to the center.

Again, not to accuse Phaedrus hastily, but Plato and Socrates knew Alkibiades and Phaedrus better than most; and they probably knew, or legitimately inferred, that where Alkibiades went, there went Phaedrus, short of the battlefield; and they probably knew Alkibiades was involved in both the *MH* and the *PEM*. So, it is very likely Phaedrus had been bi-rebellious, *amphoterious*, like Pherekles, "involved in both," precisely because Phaedrus was *epamphoterious*, always wanting things both ways. Plato, using a variant but virtual synonym of the legal term for "involved in both," is telling us he knew, or reasonably inferred, that Phaedrus was indeed involved in both the *MH* and the *PEM*, even if prosecuted only for the latter only.

β) Why Profane the Mysteries?

Even if Phaedrus was involved in only the *PEM*, Furley has shown that anyone involved in only the *PEM* could still be considered bi-criminal on that charge alone. Those accused of involvement in the *PEM* alone were still under a dual charge: "we note that the offence of profaners against Eleusis is expressed by two different phrases: *peri toi theooteri* and *peri ta musteria*. These might appear to be two different ways of putting the same thing, but it is odd that different expressions are used: is it conceivable that some men offended against the Mysteries directly, whilst others insulted Demeter and Kore more personally?"[17]

What Furley reveals, curiously, is that in the famous dyad of scandals, the *MH* and the *PEM*, we actually have a scandal *triad*. In brief, Plato was likely aware that the juvenile joiner, Phaedrus, while only officially charged with participation in the *PEM*, had actually participated in both the *MH*

16. Ibid, 47.
17. Furley, *Andokides and the Herms*, 48.

and the *PEM*, and was, in effect, not just bi-rebellious but *tri*-rebellious. More, while Alkibiades always repudiated the suggestion that he, Alkibiades, participated in both scandals, he almost certainly did, with Phaedrus and others in tow.

Phaedrus was certainly not alone in being caught up in the crazy wake of Alkibiades's frenetic political actions. Short of combat, it would have been difficult for Phaedrus not to participate in something pursued by the charismatic, Typhonic Alkibiades. Rhodes even surmises that Phaedrus was involved homosexually with Alkibiades. Even if that were true, it is unlikely Phaedrus, by all appearances a rather soft hypochondriac, could sustain a long-term Typhonic, *Schadenverbesserung eros* relationship with the highly competitive and ambitious Alkibiades. Surely the aggressive, rough-and-tumble Alkibiades would have found the effeminate Phaedrus little or no serious *Schadenverbesserung* competition. Yet, both Phaedrus and Alkibiades were legendarily handsome and ran in the same circles: witness the *Symposium*. So it is entirely possible, back in Phaedrus's middle whence, that Phaedrus had become at least a devoted follower of Alkibiades, if not also a lover.

In this regard, while Alkibiades's name never appears in *Phaedrus*, Alkibiades looms rather large in the pretext: thus a profound connection between *Phaedrus* and the *Symposium*. What Mark Moes argues regarding the *Symposium* applies, if obliquely, to *Phaedrus*: there is a basic moral about Alkibiades to be gleaned from the *Symposium*, especially given that Plato set the *Symposium* in about 404: "the text forces readers to consider the events of the banquet in the retrospective light of the tremendous personal and public losses which resulted from Socrates's failure to cure Alcibiades from his character defects."[18]

Indeed, the *Symposium* provides a series of lessons in negative imitation: "It [*Symposium*] motivates [readers] to do everything in their power to avoid becoming like Alcibiades, prompts them to see certain character disorders or flaws in the proud and self-sufficient attitudes of the speakers at the banquet who idolized him . . ."[19] One of those speakers, of course, was Phaedrus. So, it is quite likely that Phaedrus had become involved in both the *MH* and *PEM* because of his attachment to Alkibiades.

It is also likely that Phaedrus's return to Athens was due to that attachment. Rhodes notes how triumphantly Alkibiades returned to the fickle

---

18. Moes, *Plato's Dialogue Form and the Cure of the Soul*, 63.
19. Ibid., 63.

democrat Athens that had essentially banished him. It is entirely likely that Phaedrus, following along in all things Alkibiades, had returned to Athens in that wake. This attached-to-Alkibiades return might explain further Phaedrus's embrace of Lysias and democracy. Phaedrus's embrace of democracy after his return did not necessarily mean that Phaedrus had not offended the democrats by not participating in the *MH* years before. It simply meant, once again, that Phaedrus, a man with little core, wanted to curry favor with the current power.

Phaedrus, relative to both the *MH* and the *PEM*, might have to answer more charges at some point, even after his return. He might have to claim he had not actually participated in both scandals, and why. Later, that is, Phaedrus might need a Palamedes-like defense; a dyadic defense.[20] That, however, concerns Phaedrus's future, his whither. Here we are still concerned with Phaedrus's past, and his middle whence in particular.

So, why might Phaedrus have participated in both the *MH* and *PEM*?

We have more than hinted at the answer: Phaedrus was a rather blind follower of Alkibiades. What emerges therefore, all the more, is that *Phaedrus* is a study of how a corrupted youth appears as an adult. So, *Phaedrus* is also a peculiar kind of apology. Despite what the "men of Athens" said or implied when they accused Socrates of corrupting the youth, it was not Socrates's fault that Socrates's most famous charge, Alkibiades, became a duplicitous scoundrel. Alkibiades simply went his own way and corrupted others, including Phaedrus.

There is a strange mix of personalities here. If Diogenes is correct, Phaedrus, for some reason and at some point, became one of Plato's favorites; surely not on the level on which Alkibiades was once Socrates's favorite; but a favorite nonetheless.[21] The following analogy, therefore, albeit loosely, is operative between the lines of *Phaedrus*: Alkibiades : Socrates :: Phaedrus : Plato.

In *Phaedrus* there is, however, a peculiar skewing of this analogy. Phaedrus's middle whence suggests that Phaedrus had been corrupted by none other than Alkibiades himself, whose corruption, long before, Socrates could not prevent. So in *Phaedrus* we see the Socratic remedy of Phaedrus's corruption by Alkibiades; another apology for Socrates. This reading, based on Diogenes's reference to Plato's and Socrates's favorites, is at least as plausible as Nussbaum's suggestion that Phaedrus is significant only as the

---

20. Cf. "The Palamedes Triad."
21. Nails, *The People of Plato*, 234.

historical-dramatic substitute for Plato's more legendary favorite, Dion.[22] Of course, given the richness of Plato's thought, not to mention the complexities of Phaedrus's circumstance relative to both Athens and Alkibiades, my thesis about favorites and Nussbaum's thesis about favorites are both plausible at the same time.

Yet, I see no need to liken Phaedrus to someone otherwise famous, such as Dion. If Phaedrus was one of Plato's favorites, it is not because Phaedrus had anything remarkable to commend him, except, perhaps, his inability to resist the power and company of Socrates, even if Phaedrus was not bright enough to follow Socrates well or heed Socrates's help. Plato seems to have favored Phaedrus less out of respect, and more out of a sense of sympathy, like a parent might have for a child whose physical presence and charm are irresistible but who is, sadly, almost always easy to outwit. As Michael Stoeber says, Phaedrus always comes across as "sincere and naïve."[23]

The greater question is this: is it possible in the end, or in the post-text, that Phaedrus finally embraced Socrates's philosophy, became uncorrupted, and disowned Lysias, or, better yet, set to the task of converting Lysias to "true opinion?"

If it seems odd that we see Socrates trying to de-corrupt a grown man, there are many suggestions, and not just in *Phaedrus*, that Phaedrus was always a kind of man-child, or man-boy. Lysias clearly has serious sway over Phaedrus, even though Lysias may be younger or roughly equal in age to Phaedrus at the alleged time of *Phaedrus*. Phaedrus certainly comports himself toward Lysias, though absent, like the fawning boy in a pederasty relationship.

Moreover, aside from that already odd situation, Phaedrus would be old enough (if Rhodes's dating is correct) to assume the role of *erastes* himself. Were Phaedrus able to amass a minor fortune and find a boy to influence, he could corrupt the next generation of Athens as easily as Alkibiades and Erixymachus had corrupted him.

So, if Socrates indirectly corrupted Phaedrus by not being able to tame Alkibiades, Socrates might make amends by de-corrupting Phaedrus. That remedy would be more than a merely personal favor to Phaedrus; it would be a favor to Athens. Socrates would de-corrupt Phaedrus lest Phaedrus return to Athens, adopt a boy, and shape the boy, and therefore the city, in

22. Nussbaum, *The Fragility of Goodness*, 229–30.
23. Stoeber, "Phaedrus of the *Phaedrus*," 273.

Phaedrus's corrupted image. Once again, Socrates was trying to halt the onslaught of democrat decadence.

γ) Alkibiades: Apotheosis by Other Means

Phaedrus likely participated in both the *MH* and the *PEM*, scandals that required opposed motives, simply because Alkibiades did. The question then becomes this: why would Alkibiades participate in both scandals? Indeed, why might Alkibiades have taken the lead in both?

Even though participation in both the *MH* and the *PEM* ostensibly required opposed motives, there was a common denominator in them, the political-religious. If Alkibiades learned nothing otherwise from Socrates, even if he did not comprehend Socrates's aims, Alkibiades inferred that persons and entire states are, or can be, deeply motivated by religion, pro- or con-.

Alkibiades clearly saw what we can see now, especially *per* Thucydides, Plato, Aristophanes, and so many others who relate numerous debates about piety (and impiety). In Athens, Alkibiades could see religious motivation in whole factions. Thucydides and Furley remind us how different the motivations behind the *MH* and the *PEM* might have been, yet also how quickly and easily the conflation of the *PEM* and the *MH*, as scandals, came about in the minds of many in democrat-dominated Athens. It would not be surprising if Alkibiades, who spent a career dividing aristocrats from democrats to conquer both, was deeply involved in the anti-aristocrat *PEM* and the anti-democrat *MH* as well. If Alkibiades did not always divide and conquer, he was pleased as much to confuse and conquer.

Alkibiades, it seems, might have his defenders against the charge that he was involved in both the *MH* and the *PEM*. Furley, following the lead of Thucydides, suggests that Alkibiades may not have participated in both scandals but that, given Alkibiades's infamous character, it was easy to conflate the *MH* and the *PEM* relative to Alkibiades and accuse him in both, if only in the court of public opinion.

Yet, as part of the complicated pretext of *Phaedrus*, it was no less than Lysias who used rhetoric to keep the dual accusation of Alkibiades alive in Athenians's thoughts:

> In fourth-century Attic oratory ... Alkibiades' name becomes inseparably linked with both mutilation and profanation. At Lysias 14.41–42, for example, the speaker castigates "men like Alkibiades"

Who Is Phaedrus?

who do such things as profane the Mysteries and mutilate Herms; Demosthenes 21.147, in the mid-fourth century says flatly that Alkibiades mutilated the Herms. The tendency to attribute both impieties to Alkibiades recurs in later writers such as Diodorus Siculus (13.2.3; 5.1) or Pausanias Atticistas.[24]

As wrong as Lysias was about many things, he may have been right about Alkibiades having a hand in both the *MH* and the *PEM*. Lysias was hardly alone in reminding his audience of Alkibiades's knack for duplicity. James Arieti summarily describes Alkibiades's infamous career that was marked by so much wrangling, shenanigans, and duplicity:

> Implicated in the profanation of the Herms on the eve of the Sicilian Expedition and reputed to have mocked the mysteries at private parties, Alkibiades fled to Sparta rather than stand trial in Athens. There he gave Sparta the advice that enabled it to defeat Athens in Sicily and by the fortification of Decelea, to ravage Attica, a maneuver that—as Thucydides says—was the ruin of Athens. Later estranged from Sparta, he was able to get Persian help for Athens, which welcomed him back. Defeated at the battle of Notium, he fled to the Propontis and was later executed by the Persians.[25]

The inference that Alkibiades was involved in both the *MH* and the *PEM* is fairly easy to adopt; and I surmise that Alkibiades proceeded with an especially ingenious motive in the *MH* in particular.

In the case of the *MH*, timing was everything. It was Alkibiades himself who urged the Athenians to undertake the expedition to Sicily, with him leading the charge. Given his imminent crossing to Sicily, and as the Herms were signs of hope for good crossings, the citywide *MH* on the virtual eve of the expedition to Sicily might have stirred mass sympathy for Alkibiades. This assumes, of course, that the citizens would not suspect Alkibiades of participating in the *MH*, much less heading it.

Who would suspect Alkibiades of even being involved in the *MH*, to say nothing of taking the lead in the scandal? The *MH* might generate a horrible jinx in the minds of Athenians, especially democrats. Alkibiades surely would not be involved in the *MH*, so the citizen would think: otherwise Alkibiades would be putting his life in certain peril were he to try to

---

24. Furley, *Andokides and the Herms*, 44.
25. Arieti, *Interpreting Plato*, 109–10.

cross to Sicily the very day after the offense to the god who guaranteed good crossings, so the citizen would think.

Yet, for Alkibiades the Typhonic atheist, Hermes meant nothing; the Herms meant nothing; the *MH* meant nothing. A jinx? For Alkibiades a jinx was a joke. The *MH* on the eve of Alkibiades's crossing to Sicily emerges as an exceptionally clever political ploy, if not instigated by Alkibiades, then perhaps instigated by others on his behalf.

The *MH* gave Alkibiades complete cover in his Sicilian endeavor. Should he fail, he would seem destined to do so, jinxed by the *MH*. Were he to succeed, despite the lingering jinx from the *MH*, he might emerge as more than just a general. He might emerge as a god.

This latter point was of utmost importance to Alkibiades. The young Alkibiades had been raised in the household of a virtual political god, Pericles. More, Alkibiades had been mentored for a time in Socrates's "divine philosophy"; so he was, it seems, always taught to aim at some kind of apotheosis. Yet, Alkibiades would go his own way. He would not seek what he regarded pseudo-apotheosis by a mystery found in the city or by Socrates's philosophy. Alkibiades sought apotheosis by other means. He sought apotheosis by the accumulation of military might by political cleverness. If apotheosis by other means meant resorting to bad behavior, so be it.

Regarding the charges surrounding the *MH* in particular, Alkibiades's political enemies waited to bring charges against him *in absentia* during his expedition to Sicily. This much informs us of the obvious: some parties suspected Alkibiades's involvement in the *MH* almost immediately. By delaying charges against Alkibiades for participation in the *MH*, and by allowing him to leave to pursue the expedition to Sicily, those in the city suspicious of him would prevent the charismatic Alkibiades from mustering sympathy from Athenians who supported the expedition. The timing of the accusations aside, it did not dawn on most democrats what Alkibiades's motivation in the *MH* might have been. The *MH* gave Alkibiades political cover no matter the outcome of the expedition to Sicily. If he failed in Sicily, something else, the *MH*, could be blamed. If all went well despite the jinx after the *MH*, Alkibiades's apotheosis would be final. He would prove himself greater than Hermes.

As a promoter of Typhonic, *Schadenverbesserung eros*, Alkibiades was opposed to everything Zeus. So, the sexual element in the *MH* would also be in Alkibiades's purview. As Wohl writes: "A man of almost irresistible charm, Alcibiades is one of the most explicitly sexualized figures

Who Is Phaedrus?

in fifth-century politics. Plutarch (Alc. 16.1–2) tells us he carried a shield emblazoned with a thunder-bearing Eros, and that is something of the role he played in Athens: eros and power are never far apart with him."[26] Alkibiades wanted to dominate every scene. The *MH* provided occasion for Alkibiades to humble Hermes, Zeus's son, at least.

Alkibiades thought politics was the only means for apotheosis; but not just any politics, war politics. Alkibiades had decided that philosophy and religion, especially the Eleusinian mysteries, were for sissies. The Eleusinian mysteries were peculiar, as they entailed elements not only pertinent to military logistics but also to appeals for political peace. Here Furley's analysis of the role of the Eleusinian mysteries is very helpful: "the Delphic oracle had confirmed Eleusis' claim to have been the first land to receive grain from Demeter and to pass on the gift to other Greeks, and had sanctioned the annual payment by all Greek states of first-fruit offerings of grain payable to Eleusis prior to the festival of Proerosia."[27]

Eleusis became more than religiously significant. With all of the influx of grain to Eleusis from other Greek cities, and given Eleusis's peculiar geographical place, Eleusis became strategically important. Also, Eleusis came to be identified with peace:

> Sometime during the period of unstable peace between 423–415 (probably), an edict was passed in Athens calling on all the Greek states to remember their duty to send first-fruit offerings of grain to Demeter at Eleusis, . . . the Eleusinian Aparchai Decree. . . . [T]he conditions it envisages in all the Greek states sending grain to Eleusis seem to presuppose peace; otherwise the foreign city-states would hardly have been forthcoming with their tithe for Eleusis.[28]

Peace Alkibiades could not abide; peace agreements were antithetical to his ambitions. They were worse when reinforced by a religion sanctioned by the state. The military man in Alkibiades called for strife now and then; preferably now. In Alkibiades's thinking, the citizens of whatever faction needed to be reminded, often, that they needed, or might need, the mercenary services of Alkibiades. The peace-fostering Eleusinian mysteries needed profaning. One can easily imagine the drunken Alkibiades, like the one we see in the *Symposium*, amuse himself and others by the *PEM* at

---

26. Wohl, "The Eros of Alcibiades," 352.
27. Furley, *Andokides and the Herms*, 35.
28. Ibid., 36.

private parties. Perhaps a modern parallel would be Alkibiades assuming the role of pseudo-priest at a mock Mass. We can imagine a crazed Alkibiades, with all manner of cant and incantation, trying to transubstantiate pita and mavrodaphne.

Aside from the drunken fun to be had in mocking the piety of aristocrats, in Alkibiades's mind the mocking of the *PEM* was just part of doing business as a duplicitous mercenary. For Alkibiades, the charm or appeal of the peace-affirming mysteries had to be dissolved, or at least damaged. The Eleusinian mysteries, after all, mitigated tensions between the different classes within Athens, and different cities without. Alkibiades needed tension. He needed to be needed, so he needed crisis, within the city and without.

Given Alkibiades's charisma, and the likelihood that Alkibiades was indeed involved in both the *MH* and the *PEM*, if Phaedrus was in fact involved in both, surely no particularly profound motive need be attributed to Phaedrus other than desire to be a part of everything Alkibiades. Phaedrus and Alkibiades had this much in common: they were always ready to demythologize the religions of the city; and they were both devoted to their own virtual religion, the alleged superiority of male homosexual, Typhonic, *Schadenverbesserung eros.*

δ) Phaedrus the Nihilist and the *Heteratai*

Phaedrus emerges in part as a study in nihilism. In the wake of Alkibiades's duplicities, Phaedrus, who seemed to believe in nothing other than personal expediency, saw in the *MH* and the *PEM* the means to exercise his nihilistic bent. It did not take Socrates long to diagnose the problem.

Socrates surely knew that the juvenile, bi-rebellious tendencies in Phaedrus were what landed Phaedrus in trouble with Athens. Phaedrus's actions could be regarded as simply vacuous compared with the same act of rebellion performed by others, for example, the so-called *heteratai*.

The *heteratai* were oligarchy-loving, anti-democrat, private club members who carried out the *MH* for a cause, to undermine the democrats. The city-wide *MH* on the eve of the expedition to Sicily was just the most momentous mutilation event. There had been others. The *heteratai* did not engage in the *MH* merely for some fraternity prank. Here J. McGlew's reading, that the *heteratai* who carried out the *MH* were already a

Who Is Phaedrus?

virtual political organization, is compelling.[29] If the *heteratai* were as well-organized as McGlew surmises they were, that would suggest it would have been relatively easy for Alkibiades to recruit them for the momentous *MH*, or to join them in the deed for his own reasons.

The *heteratai* were *sophrosune*-obsessed oligarchs of a Protagorean stripe. They were moderation-mongers, as it were; so fond of moderation that, oddly, they resorted to immoderate means in the *MH* to undermine the confidence and rule of the democrats, whom the *heteratai* viewed as undisciplined decadents.

In the obviously immoderate action of the *MH*, the *heteratai* thought they had to fight fire with fire, immoderation with immoderation. Their basic complaint was that democrats were too lax in their laws and needed some civic sobering. In the view of the *heteratai*, Athens was an otherwise strong dog being wagged by an idiotic tail, the democrat faction.

Yet, the *MH* was not rank nihilism on the part of the *heteratai*. The *heteratai* thought they could bring more discipline to Athens than the democrats could, or would. In particular, following Protagoras's pedagogical argument, the *heteratai* thought virtue could be taught. They thought moderation in particular could be taught on the personal level, but only to the few: others would have to be made moderate via the laws. Thus the fundamental social problem *per* democracy, as the *heteratai* saw it: since the majority of persons were not really teachable, the people needed guidance and instruction via the laws; but the lax laws of the democrats did not bring sufficient discipline.

Democracy, especially democracy that appointed leaders by lottery, so argued the *heteratai*, was doomed to fail because of this intractable pedagogical problem. The city should be run by the few who could individually learn and exercise moderation, and make laws that would indirectly, at least, impress moderation on the majority incapable of learning moderation individually. As a sure sign of decadence, the democrat practice of picking leaders by lottery would insure that Athens's rulers, as a matter of ineluctable probability, would be as undisciplined as the pleasure-loving masses. Of course, Socrates would eventually live, and die, this political pox in his own right. His lottery pebble was once drawn, so Socrates served on Athens's council, a position that only brought him more antipathy from democrats.

---

29. McGlew, "Politics on the Margins," 1–22.

Socrates was manifestly suspicious of almost all things democrat, but he was surely also suspicious of groups like the *heteratai* and their over-reliance on Protagoras. The *heteratai*, Protagorean oligarchs, were not as misguided as the democrats, many of whom apparently used Protagoras's epistemology, or something like it, as the basis of their moral relativism. Yet, the *heteratai* were still misguided regarding the basics of virtue and pedagogy. There is an indirect, albeit subtle, reference in *Phaedrus* to such Protagorean fervor, to which Socrates's thought offered an alternative. In *P'/S'*, when Socrates was rhetorically improving *L'/P'*, Socrates referred to two alleged principles of the passions: an innate desire for pleasure; and an acquired conviction for virtue. Socrates referred to the latter as "moderation."[30]

Yet, in *P'/S'*, Socrates was not speaking as himself. In *P'/S'*, Socrates was speaking *a la L'/P'*, as Lysias. For Socrates, virtue, and moderation in particular as one of the pillars of virtue, is innate in the soul, not really teachable. But virtue is teachable according to Protagoras. For this reason Socrates, to counter the likes of Lysias, refers to rhetoric as an exercise in "soul-leading." Rhetoric should lead the soul on its naturally virtuous course, where the supposition is that the soul is inherently virtuous but might become corrupted. That is why Socrates says that what he reveals in the *PL* is superior to "human wisdom" or, more precisely, "human *sophrosune*," "human moderation." By "human moderation" Socrates surely means a two-fold pretense: 1) the democrat conceit that pleasure is the end of human existence, such that some pleasures must be abandoned for the sake of pursuing others, which, for Socrates, is *faux* moderation; and 2) the Protagorean principle that virtue can be taught.[31]

So, relative to the *MH*, even assuming the fairly sophisticated motivation of the *heteratai* and the kernel of truth in the premise that democrat inclinations and institutions must be undone because they are not inherently virtuous, Socrates could not wholeheartedly embrace the *heteratai*. Socrates would agree that most persons are corrupted. He reminds Phaedrus that only a "few" bother with dialectic. More, Socrates certainly maintained that democrat inclinations and institutions were problematic to the point of being very dangerous. Socrates saw Phaedrus embracing superficially the same undisciplined democrats, the "men of Athens," who would put Socrates himself to death. At least the *heteratai* had a position

---

30. Cf., "Triads and Dyads of Speeches."
31. *Phaedrus*, 256b.

Who Is Phaedrus?

from which to replace the decadent democrats. Phaedrus, by comparison, was a nihilist.

The nihilist in Phaedrus, moreover, was not easily suppressed. Phaedrus was fascinated with the unconventional for its own sake. In Phaedrus's praise of *L'/P'*, we see more than a hint of the nihilist in Phaedrus. Phaedrus saw in *L'/P'* a rethinking of the unconventional by the unconventional.

The marginally conventional phenomenon understood in *L'/P'* was the pederasty relationship, a "love" relation in which an older, socially and financially advantaged man, the *erastes*, mentors a boy on the verge of manhood so as to shape the boy in the image of the man. As there were no obvious schools in Athens, the pederasty relationship was accepted in parts of Athenian society as a way in which the *erastes* might fashion a boy, and therefore a future Athens, in the man's social image.

There were certainly unconventional elements in the pederasty relationship. In that relationship, the boy would be obligated, at the *erastes*'s whim, to offer the man unconventional sexual relations. In a kind of shaming rite of passage, the boy would be forced to dress up as a girl, and then, sometimes, provide the man intercrural sex. The man would come to climax by rubbing his member between the boy's thighs. In return for this unconventional activity, the boy/girl would reap his rewards: money, attire, and introduction into broader social circles.

There is an ingenious play on words in *Phaedrus* by which Plato satirizes this exercise. When Phaedrus and Socrates settle on the grove as the place for their conversation, conversation that at times becomes banter with sexual overtones, Phaedrus says the place is perfect "for girls to play": κόραις παίζειν.³² As *pazein* provides a play on words between "education" (*paideia*) and "boy," (*pais*), what Phaedrus is unwittingly saying is that the grove is a good place for the posing of boy/girls in keeping with the unusual practice of pederasty. By this play on words, Plato informs us that the dynamics of pederasty underlie the drama from the beginning. The suggestion of pederasty becomes obvious with Phaedrus's reading of *L'/P'*, a speech that argues a new, unconventional operating premise for pederasty: any pretense to affection between *erastes* and *pais* should be dropped. The suggestion of pederasty continues when, in *P'/S'*, Socrates play-acts the *erastes* in his delivery of *P'/S'* by dawning a hood on his head, perhaps the protocol when the *erastes* engages the boy in a sexual encounter.

---

32. Ibid., 229b.

Moreover, there is another play on words in Plato's economical use of *korais paizein*, as *korais* is the dative plural of *kore*, "girl," which also happens to be the proper name of Kore.[33] Kore is the daughter from the incestuous relationship between Demeter, the honoree of the Eleusinian mysteries, and Zeus. By extension of the play, Phaedrus is unwittingly suggesting that, in the setting at least, he and Socrates are the spawn of Zeus. Socrates is trying to persuade Phaedrus that Phaedrus should consciously conceive of himself as a child of Zeus; yet hardly the Zeus depicted badly in the myths of the city. Phaedrus should consider himself a child of Zeus when Zeus is properly rehabilitated as the god of the love of wisdom. From that perspective, the superficial Phaedrus might seriously re-think his preoccupation with mere novelty and cleverness; that is, Phaedrus should become aware of his own inclination toward nihilism, lest he find himself lost for the rest of his days.

---

33. Zeruneith, *The Wooden Horse*, 95.

6

Phaedrus's Immediate Whence
Athens's and Phaedrus's Decline

α) The Morychus-Epicrates-Lysias Triad

SOCRATES ENCOUNTERS PHAEDRUS SOON after Phaedrus had met with Lysias at Epicrates's house. Epicrates's house is Morychus's former house. That house is in the vicinity of the Olympieum, the temple of Zeus. Plato is telling us much by this dramatic shorthand.

Chief among the dramatic elements is the reference to the Olympieum, the temple of Zeus. Given the many and crucial references to Zeus throughout *Phaedrus*, one cannot overestimate the importance of recalling that, while Phaedrus and Socrates move outside the city limits, the action of *Phaedrus* occurs in the virtual, if not actual, shadow of the temple of Zeus.

Moreover, Plato bothers to mention three persons relative to the action on the whole: Morychus, Epicrates, and Lysias. Those three men, in Plato's thought-experiment extension of dianoetic reckoning as treated in the *Republic*, function like the three fingers in *Republic*. They constitute a triad that reduces to compare-and-contrast dyads. By a dianoetic triad-dyad reduction, one can better discern the nature of Phaedrus's relationship with Lysias, given Lysias's relation to the other persons in this opening triad.

So: Phaedrus's immediate whence? Phaedrus had just met Lysias, rhetorician and champion of democracy, at the house of Epicrates, another champion of democracy. Plato bothers to note that Epicrates's house had previously belonged to Morychus, a tragedian.

Phaedrus's Immediate Whence

Little is known of Morychus or his work. But Morychus garnered enough fame, or infamy, in his lifetime to be labeled, repeatedly, a sybarite. In various forms of literature there are desultory allusions to Morychus's wealth and his "indulgence of the appetite."[1] De Vries rightly notes that the name Morychus came to be associated automatically with a certain "irrisio," whether "festiva" or not.[2] What De Vries fails to note is that the "irrisio" might depend on the position of the person: what democrats find risible, aristocrats might not, and *vice versa*.

Long before De Vries, W. H. Thompson recognized not only that Morychus's name was associated with a habit of indulgence, but that, regarding the house in question: "The character of the entertainments had changed with the change of possessors."[3] Thompson does not inform us at any length of the nature of that change in character of entertainments when the house of Morychus became the house of Epicrates. Yet, Thompson does claim that the change was not just from aristocrat to democrat, but from aristocrat to demagogue.[4]

The few references to Morychus we have are scarce indeed, but there seems to be a constancy regarding Morychus's reputation for a considerable indulgence of the appetite. Mary Lefkowitz correctly writes that Aristophanes and Teleclides more than suggest that Morychus was a sybarite; and she is certainly correct to say that "it appears to take only a generation for comic jokes to be transmuted into historical data."[5] Virtually every reference to Morychus we have comes with a hint of derision. Yet, we should hesitate to call so many indirect references exact "history." It is likely that the portrayals of Morychus as a sybarite survived as juvenile jabs of democrats who resented Morychus's wealth and sense of aristocracy. One thinks of democrat jokes in contemporary U.S. politics that convey the same sentiment: for example, the one about the size of a certain hot tub that could hold six Democrats or four Republicans. Yet, of course, there are just as many sybaritic Democrats as there are Republicans, if not more.

We know, too, that while Morychus was portrayed as a sybarite in Aristophanes's comedies, we also know that Aristophanes's comedies are not exactly sources for precision history. The case of Socrates in

1. Crosby, "An Unappreciated Joke in Aristophanes," 329.
2. De Vries, *A Commentary on the Phaedrus of Plato*, 35.
3. W. H. Thompson, *The Phaedrus of Plato*, 4n.
4. Ibid., 2n.
5. Lefkowitz, "Aristophanes and Other Historians of the Fifth Century Theater," 146.

Who Is Phaedrus?

Aristophanes's *Clouds* is the most obvious. Further, while Lefkowitz rightly notes that Morychus has been handed down to us as a sybarite, she is incorrect on another point. She says further that Morychus would be the kind of decadent host, "at least in Plato's characterization," that would appropriately entertain another decadent such as Lysias.[6] Yet, the "characterization" of Morychus as a sybarite is not Plato's characterization. We have no Platonic characterization of Morychus. In *Phaedrus*, Epicrates is the host of Lysias, not Morychus.

It is entirely possible that Plato had a favorable view of Morychus. Without reading too much of Nietzsche's *The Birth of Tragedy* into Plato's *Phaedrus* (although it would not be the first time Plato had the anticipatory better of Nietzsche), I maintain that Plato mentions Morychus as a kind of shorthand reference to someone who, as aristocrat and tragedian, at least took the divine seriously. Plato probably did not have any inordinate respect for Morychus; but perhaps Plato had some regard for Morychus as someone maintaining some recognition of the divine *qua* traditional tragedian.

Further, the implication in Plato's mention of Morychus is that the house of Morychus, now occupied by Epicrates, was close to the temple of Zeus, the Olympieum, for a reason, perhaps by design in the case of Morychus.[7] While it is difficult to determine Plato's precise estimation of Morychus, Plato apparently saw in Morychus, *qua* tragedian, someone who at least recognized the activities of mortals in light of the activities of the divine, and *vice versa*. Morychus, like Plato, if not nearly as competently, meant to keep the spirit of divinity and aristocracy central in all things Athenian. This is why Plato's pointed reference to the temple of Zeus early in the dialogue serves to intimate one of the key reasons for the publication of *Phaedrus*: to rehabilitate the reputation of Zeus.[8] Every reference to Zeus in *Phaedrus* recommends a god who is noble and constant, in contrast with the common and deceitful Zeus depicted in the pedestrian theology of the city.

What, then, of the Lysias-Epicrates-Morychus triad?

Morychus and Epicrates constitute a dyad within the Lysias-Epicrates-Morychus triad. Morychus and Epicrates are identical insofar as they owned or own the same house, and were both wealthy. But they are different as

---

6. Lefkowitz, "Aristophanes and Other Historians of the Fifth Century Theater," 146.
7. *Phaedrus*, 227b.
8. Cf., chapter 7, "Plato's Rehabilitation of Zeus."

Morychus may be associated with aristocratic Athens, while Epicrates is an elitist champion of democracy. In Plato's dramatic shorthand, it is a sign of cultural decline that the house of Morychus should become the house of the decadent democrat, Epicrates, friend of Lysias. More, even though Epicrates and Lysias would eventually part ways, for Plato's purposes in *Phaedrus* they were basically the same person. The decline from Morychus to Epicrates signals the decline of Athens.

Accordingly, as Phaedrus and Socrates decline their way outside the city, the metaphorical point is that while Socrates assumes this decline, he tries to provide an ascent for Phaedrus back to the heights of Athens, symbolized especially by the Olympieum, the temple of Zeus. While Socrates would otherwise never leave Athens, except to defend the city in war, he saw fit to leave on this occasion with Phaedrus to give Phaedrus some distance from the city. The formerly exiled Phaedrus, who had now returned to Athens, needed some perspective on his precipitous embrace of the new democrat-dominated Athens to which he had returned. Phaedrus could use some distance from the elitist and demagogic lords of the city like Lysias and Epicrates. The former, as Socrates saw it, the most influential person in Phaedrus's life at the time of *Phaedrus*, was especially insidious.

Moreover, it is telling that Socrates encounters Phaedrus as Phaedrus is on the verge of crossing the border of the city. The god of crossings was Hermes, in whose honor the Herms, statues marking borders or crossings of all kinds, were erected in so many places in and around Athens. If there was no hard evidence that Phaedrus had been involved in the *MH*, as he was prosecuted for participation in the *PEM* only, Plato is suggesting that Phaedrus, blithely passing the city's border, was still indifferent regarding crossings, the peculiar bailiwicks of Hermes. Socrates therefore agrees to go into a kind of second exile with Phaedrus to convert Phaedrus to true philosophy, the necessary condition for Phaedrus to make a good return to Athens, once and for all.

β) The Morychus-*Epicrates Dyad/Triad

So, further, who is Epicrates as part of the Morychus-Epicrates dyad within the Morychus-Epicrates-Lysias triad?

Here we have to consider just how ingenious the creative non-fiction writer Plato was. We know Plato played with disguises. Later in *Phaedrus* the issue of disguises is raised explicitly; but here Plato could even be referring to a second Epicrates along with the bald reference to the Epicrates who had purchased the house of Morychus. As a composer of creative non-fiction, Plato was seizing advantage of a quirky coincidence: he had two cultural enemies in his vicinity at the same time and with the same name: Epicrates of Athens, rich democrat businessman and would-be rhetorician; and Epicrates of Ambracia, comic playwright and champion of democracy. Why not counter the two at once, especially in a dialogue in which the dyadic is thematic?

These homonymous enemies of Plato are disguises for one another and, according to Plato, equally harmful to the city, if in different ways. Politically regarded, Epicrates of Athens, the democrat activist, is in effect the same person as Epicrates of Ambracia. They had different arts but their demagogic cause was the same. So, within the Morychus-Epicrates-Lysias triad there is actually an exceedingly clever dyad within the name "Epicrates" alone. We have essentially a dyad of Epicrateses conflated into one name and one purpose: to champion democracy. Epicrates of Athens champions atheistic democracy, like Lysias, by amassing enormous wealth and wielding great political influence. Epicrates of Ambracia champions atheistic democracy, like Lysias, by being clever: the former writing comedy, the latter writing (in Plato's view) risible speeches for courts, assemblies, and private citizens. For Plato's purposes, we could effectively refer to Epicrates of Athens and Epicrates of Ambracia as one: Epicrates with an asterisk; or *Epicrates who was/were, in effect, the same as Lysias.

Epicrates of Ambracia wrote comedies critical of aristocrats at large and Plato in particular. One of Epicrates's comedies lodged an especially biting attack on Plato's thought, and apparently Plato's Academy. The following is part of a satire by Epicrates that mocks the procedures at Plato's Academy or Socrates's notion of dialectic, or both:

> What about Plato, Speusippus, and Menedemus? What subjects are they dealing with now? What thought, what argument are they investigating? If you've come knowing anything please tell these things to me with discretion.
>
> I can talk about these things clearly. At the Panathenaic festival I saw a band of gay youths in the gymnasium of the Academy and heard them say unutterably weird things. They were making distinctions concerning nature, the life of animals, the nature of trees, and the genera of vegetables. Among other things they were studying the genus of the pumpkin.

> How did they define it? What is the genus of the plant? Reveal this to me if you know.
>
> Well, first they all stood silently, bent over, and they thought for a considerable time. Suddenly, while the young men were still bending over and reflecting, one of them pronounced it a round vegetable, another a grass, a third a tree. A Sicilian doctor who heard these things blew a fart at the fools.
>
> That must have made the students very angry. I suppose they shouted out against the man's derision. For it is out of place to do such things during a discussion.
>
> It didn't bother them. Plato was there, and he enjoined them, very gently and without agitation, to try again from the beginning to distinguish the genus of the pumpkin. They proceeded to do so.[9]

Plato surely had no fondness for Epicrates of Ambracia. Plato probably deemed Epicrates of Ambracia "clever," a word used often by Socrates, insultingly, with regard to Lysias. Epicrates of Ambracia was not particularly funny; not to Plato at least.

γ) The *Epicrates-Lysias Dyad/Triad

What, then, of the *Epicrates-Lysias triad/dyad?

*Epicrates and Lysias are ostensibly different: the former is/are a comic playwright/businessman-rhetorician, the latter a businessman-rhetorician. Yet, Plato invites us to consider the sense in which the comic playwright Epicrates is identical to, or at least similar to, the rhetorician Lysias.

The conflation of the comedian, Epicrates, with Lysias, the rhetorician, accords with Plato's complaints about the confusion of poetry and rhetoric otherwise. For example, Socrates complains in *Gorgias*: "And so wouldn't rhetoric be a public speaking? Or don't the poets seem to you to be making rhetoric in the theatre?"[10]

*Epicrates and Lysias are identical yet different. One Epicrates writes for the stage, the other Epicrates for assemblies, and Lysias for the courts and public assemblies. The functions of these writers would easily intersect. Both courts and assemblies, in democracies, tend toward the superficially theatrical. Socrates knew very well that the confounding language of the

---

9. Nicholson on Epicrates from *Comicorum atticorum fragmenta*. See Nicholson, *Plato's Phaedrus*, 69.

10. *Gorgias*, 502d.

Who Is Phaedrus?

courts often, and almost always for the worse, could be assumed by the masses without actual understanding, much as audiences in the theatre can be swayed by superficial discourse or sentimental song.

Thus Athens's cultural decline, according to Plato: Plato anticipates Nietzsche's career-long critique of democrats that begins with *The Birth of Tragedy*'s revaluation of theatre and the democrat-rhetorical ruination of the same *via* Euripides. *Phaedrus*, in effect, echoes Plato's complaint in *Gorgias* that there is too much democrat rhetoric in the theatre. The democrat turns politics into theatre, and theatre into politics, to the detriment of both.

Indeed, in *Phaedrus* Socrates complains openly and very particularly about the domination of democrat-inclined rhetoric at the expense of the divine. Socrates says provocatively of the god-imbued grove in which he and Phaedrus are talking: "Oh, how much more versed the nymphs, daughters of Achelous, and Pan, son of Hermes, are in the art of speech than Lysias, son of Cephalus!"[11]

As for Plato's almost certain antipathy for Epicrates of Ambracia, Plato was hardly opposed to humor. Plato's dialogues offer great comedy; and legend has it Plato deeply admired Aristophanes, so much so that Plato allegedly slept with Aristophanes's comedies under his pillow. Indeed, some commentators have noted how the ending of *Phaedrus* is framed with an allusion (homage?) to Aristophanes.[12]

For Plato, Aristophanes, for all of his unfair mockery of Socrates, was a great comedian in comparison with Epicrates; not just because Epicrates mocked Plato. Behind the comedy, Aristophanes had the ability to write with sophistication, at least. The same could not be said of *Epicrates and Lysias, who, like the sophists, simply wanted to demythologize religion to such an extent that the consequences would be cultural banality steeped in opinion: the stock and trade of the sophist. For all practical purposes, Phaedrus had become Lysias, or wanted to become Lysias. We see Phaedrus's Lysian denigration of myth and religion on open display in *Phaedrus*, and the pretext of the dialogue assumes Phaedrus's distaste for religion as evidenced in his participation in the *PEM*.

Via the Morychus-*Epicrates-Lysias decline, Plato was pointing to the dangers in the rise of irrational democracy. Superficial democracy, a redundancy for Socrates, held out far more dangers for Athens than anything the

11. *Phaedrus*, 263d.
12. Scully, *Plato's Phaedrus*, 70, n159.

old religions bore. The especially dangerous element in the rise of democracy is that democrats are dominated and motivated by sentiment, especially resentment. In another dialogue, even the remarkably ignorant Euthyphro realized how strongly and dangerously the Athenian democrats were ruled by their emotions: "I don't much desire to test their sentiments . . ."[13]

Of course, part of Euthyphro's ignorance lay in the fact that Euthyphro was also referring to himself when he spoke of the dangerous emotions to which democrat or polytheist Athenians were prone. Democrats resented aristocrats like Morychus, Plato, and, yes, dirt-poor Socrates, aristocrat of the soul.

Democrat envy and resentment would eventually be revealed in many ways, the most despicable being, of course, the democrats' prosecution of Socrates due to what Micheline Sauvage calls "the hardening of the public conscience."[14]

δ) The Lysias-Phaedrus Dyad

In *Phaedrus*, Phaedrus is oblivious to the cultural decline to which he has become party, now that he has embraced Lysias, the democrat's democrat. But how does Phaedrus relate to the parties representative of that decline?

How would the *Epicrates-Lysias-Phaedrus "triad" reduce to telling dyads?

If these triad-to-dyad reductions seem odd, it is worth recalling their dianoetic function in the *Republic*. They are immediately derivative functions of dialectic, *dianoia* in particular.

Granted, in the *Republic* the triad-dyad reduction issue was raised as a means for justifying the positing of Essences (as hypotheses). Here the triad-dyad reductions have a similar if extended function by which to note so many modes of similarity and dissimilarity, and of identity and difference, between and among various phenomena.

Christopher Gill is correct when he writes: "there may be stress on the idea that the individual dialogue constitutes a dialectical and dramatic unit, and that philosophical interpretation needs to register this fact";[15] and: "The dramatization of dialectic . . . [involves] attention to character,

---

13. *Euthyphro*, 3d.
14. Sauvage, *Socrates and the Human Conscience*, 13.
15. Gill, "Dialectic and the Dialogue Form," 146.

narrative frame, and other formal features."[16] One especially formal feature of *Phaedrus* is the presence of so many and various triads that demand dyadic reduction.

How are Epicrates, Lysias, and Phaedrus identical yet different? This dianoetic conundrum should not be overly difficult to resolve because, as Socrates says, oddly enough, Lysias, though absent, "is present."[17]

Regarding the especially important relation of Phaedrus to Lysias, other commentators, even if not making dyadic comparison thematic, have offered what they deem necessary comparisons pertaining to Phaedrus and Lysias. Note, for example, Ferrari's rather intense compare and contrast exercise regarding Phaedrus and Lysias. Ferrari argues that we can only really infer claims about Lysias's concealed character by studying that which is manifestly problematic about the character of Phaedrus.[18] Actually, the basis of inference should be reversed in this case. Historically, and by his own pen, we know much more about Lysias than we do about Phaedrus.

We know one very important point: Lysias was a metic, a non-Athenian. As a metic, were Lysias charged with anything, Lysias could not appear in court or other civic institutions without "a native patron, a *prostates*, who would represent him before the citizenry."[19] When Socrates said Lysias is "present" in *Phaedrus*, though Lysias never appears, Socrates could have been referring to Phaedrus as Lysias's native patron, or *prostates*, aside from the point that Socrates considers Lysias "present" because Lysias's text is present. In that sense, Phaedrus is Lysias, with Socrates as judge.

As Phaedrus is, in a sense, Lysias, the question then becomes whether or not Phaedrus can shift his identity from Lysian to Socratic. That is why so much by-play about the identity and difference between Phaedrus and Lysias is all but intertwined with playful references to the identity and difference between Phaedrus and Socrates. Hence Socrates's line: "If I don't know Phaedrus I have forgotten myself!"[20] Hence, too, Phaedrus's line that is, as it were, an echo: "O, Socrates, if I don't know Socrates, I have forgotten myself."[21] Phaedrus does not realize what he is saying in this moment. He is idly imitating Socrates. Yet, Socrates wishes Phaedrus really would

16. Ibid., 147.
17. *Phaedrus*, 228e.
18. Ferrari, *Listening to the Cicadas*, 228–30.
19. Ibid., 228.
20. *Phaedrus*, 228a.
21. Ibid., 236c.

identify more with Socrates than with Lysias. That is why occasions in *Phaedrus* have Socrates play the role of Lysias, as during the delivery of *P'/S'*, to challenge Phaedrus to note so many actual differences between Lysias and Socrates.

Socrates fears Phaedrus has become too much like Lysias and democrat-dominated Athens itself. Indeed, Athens had become so lax that a non-Athenian like Lysias could hold extraordinary sway in Athens's internal affairs. As John Bateman writes: "the peculiarities of Athenian legal procedure allowed the non-citizen, Lysias, to introduce into his speeches his own ideas and judgments on the political and social problems underlying many of his cases."[22] Lysias is an officious foreigner, and the abuse he is perpetrating on Phaedrus is representative of the harm he does Athens on the whole.

From the situation outside the city, Socrates could better cast suspicion on Lysias's democrat motives. Socrates had to reveal to Phaedrus, if only between the lines, that Lysias was a fraud. Very specifically, Socrates saw Lysias bastardizing the terms *aner apragmon*, a favorite term amongst aristocrats suggesting "a man who minds his own business." When Lysias publicly defended himself relative to one of his favorite endeavors, serving as a prosecutor of Athenians he did not like, especially oligarchs and aristocrats, he would describe himself, cleverly, as a non-meddler, which, in a sense, he was because he was not an actual Athenian.[23]

The wealthy aristocrat, the better *aner apragmon*, did not concern himself with political office, and, having sufficient wealth, was mostly free from the error of confusing money and honor. The better *aner apragmon* created for himself enough of a life of leisure to devote more time to the various forms of the love of wisdom. The best *aner apragmon*, Socrates, was the true aristocrat, an aristocrat of the soul, as Socrates had no real desire for money, so he never confused honor-love and money-love. Moreover, Socrates had no desire for political office, even though he served when his name was drawn in the political lottery. Socrates knew well, and always, that his love of honor, which he did indeed exercise, had to be grounded in his overarching love of wisdom.

So, Phaedrus had become too much like Lysias who had bastardized the title *aner apragmon* by eliminating the most important love to maintain, the love of wisdom. Lysias, by simply disowning all things divine and

---

22. Bateman, "Lysias and the Law," 276.
23. Lateiner, "'The Man Who Does Not Meddle in Politics,'" 3.

eternal, could reduce any so-called love of wisdom to the love of honor. In Lysias's insipid democrat ethic that Phaedrus had embraced, the love of honor would not be grounded in the love of wisdom. Rather, the Lysian, democrat version of honor-love was tied to cleverness, social status, and money-love.

Lysias was buying political power in Athens from outside Athens without having to live with the deleterious consequences of his influence in the city itself. That is why Socrates's moniker for his enemies in the *Apology*, "men of Athens," is such a telling and caustic criticism. Some of those actually bringing charges against Socrates for corrupting the youth of Athens were neither honorable men, nor citizens of Athens.

Phaedrus, outside the city with Socrates, is to gain some aristocratic distance from the insipid rhetoric of democrat-dominated Athens. Phaedrus is supposed to realize he needs distance from Lysias. Hence, again, Socrates's simple line about the very grove in which he and Phaedrus found refuge: even the minor divinities in the grove were far more worthy speakers than Lysias.

Worst of all, Lysias had not been willing to suffer for his (alleged) beloved, Phaedrus, and lead Phaedrus to the temple of Zeus to consecrate the pair's relationship. So, Socrates had to bring the spirit of Zeus's temple to Phaedrus. After Plato's rehabilitation of Zeus, entry into Zeus's temple, in some form, was the necessary condition for Phaedrus's de-corruption and good return to Athens.

7

Plato's Rehabilitation of Zeus

a) Socrates and Teisamenos

SOME MAY CALL IT "contrariety."[1] Yet, contrariety, or the more than occasional and hardly accidental CO, is an essential element in Plato's philosophy. The tension between opposites is a basic dynamic in reality itself for Plato.

We witness in *Phaedrus* a panoplies of opposites; one CO, express or implied, after another. Consider the two interlocutors themselves: Phaedrus is young (at least relative to Socrates), handsome, and superficial. Socrates is old, ugly, and wise. Phaedrus is an indecisive joiner, democrat, and virtual atheist. Socrates is independent, pious, and an aristocrat; certainly an aristocrat of the soul.

More, Phaedrus was an exile. Socrates, as the divine gift to Athens, would never go into exile. So, on this occasion with and for Phaedrus, Socrates assumes the role of his own opposite. Socrates agrees to leave the city, allegedly one of only two times he ever did so. The other time was to go to war.[2] One may assume Socrates's movement outside the city in *Phaedrus* had the same motivation as when he left Athens the other time. He left the city to save it. In this case Socrates would defend Athens from the likes of Phaedrus himself. Moreover, not incidentally, Socrates would help Phaedrus, the veritable personification of decadent Athens; defend Phaedrus from Phaedrus himself.

---

1. Chardin, "Les Contrariétés Merveilleuses de *Coriolan*," 27.
2. *Crito*, 52b.

Who Is Phaedrus?

Socrates's saving work for Phaedrus is to be viewed in light of *Phaedrus*'s particular theological backdrop: the presence of Zeus, nobly understood. The action of the dialogue has Socrates and Phaedrus descend away from an area near the Olympieum, the temple of Zeus. Despite that descent, Socrates is the Zeus-like leader in Phaedrus's life. In his dialectically charged effort, Socrates descends with Phaedrus away from the temple of Zeus in order to do something opposite: to lead Phaedrus back, in ascending *logos* that culminates in the *PL*, to a height associated with the temple.

The course of the descent of Socrates and Phaedrus has always been a curiosity. The particulars of the descent have never been clear. My reading would follow the sketch recommended by L. Robin and Hermann Lind.[3] Socrates and Phaedrus leave Athens southwardly from a point slightly less than parallel with the Olympieum. They head in the direction of Megara, as Socrates explicitly suggests they are doing.[4] The reference to Megara evokes recollection of a course Lysias had taken years before when, from a distance in Megara, he helped plot the democrat overthrow of Athens.

Socrates playfully assumes the role of Lysias often in *Phaedrus*, yet only to do the opposite of what Lysias would intend. Here Socrates volunteers to retrace Lysias's steps; but in doing so Socrates would generate a contrary coup. Socrates would turn Phaedrus away from the Lysian, democrat decadence Phaedrus had embraced since his return from exile. So, next time, after this benign exile in the company of the Zeus-inspired Socrates, Phaedrus might finally make a good return to Athens to help Athens return to a course nobler than that offered by democrats like Lysias.

Phaedrus and Socrates descend away from the Olympieum, all the way outside the city. Yet, Plato's pointed reference to the Olympieum suggests that, after descending, Socrates and Phaedrus carry on their discourse in the virtual, if not actual, shadow of the temple of Zeus. Indeed, it is not long before Phaedrus himself recalls, if perfunctorily, that "Zeus [is] the god of friendship."[5]

Phaedrus knows the moniker of Zeus, god of friendship. That famous moniker should not have been hard to recall, as, in the very first line of the dialogue, Socrates calls Phaedrus "friend." But Phaedrus does not know the true meaning of friendship because he has been corrupted. It falls to Socrates to reveal the true nature of the god of true friendship, Zeus, to

3. Lind, "Sokrates am Ilissos," 18n.
4. *Phaedrus*, 228a.
5. Ibid., 234e.

Plato's Rehabilitation of Zeus

correct the confounding theology of the city. Outside the city, yet in the virtual shadow of the temple of Zeus, Socrates has occasion to rehabilitate Zeus.

Even though Socrates did not believe in the literal figure of Zeus as Olympian god, he knew what the character of a god should be: noble, profound, consistent, and willing to suffer. Jaded Phaedrus, however, enthralled by the work of sophists and demythologizers, had abandoned even the slightest reckoning of divine character.

As Phaedrus had almost entirely abandoned even the slightest reckoning of divine character, it would be hard for him to appreciate the Zeus-inspired labor Socrates would be performing for Phaedrus. Socrates's Zeus-inspired work would generate a depiction of the true lover: the lover who has character traits the opposite of those of Phaedrus and Lysias.

Indeed, Phaedrus and Lysias—male-homosexual, competition-based, honor-lovers—adopt the title Typhonic lovers precisely because they challenge Zeus-inspired love. Typhon was the enemy of Zeus. The true, Zeus-inspired lover, as Socrates sees it, is not always wealthy, healthy, handsome, and socially connected like the Tyhponic lover is supposed to be. On the contrary, the true lover, the *Zeus*-inspired lover, is willing to assume some suffering for the betterment of the beloved. The true, noble, Zeus-inspired lover operates with the premise that self-sacrifice is necessary to improve the beloved's lot. The true lover, of course, is Socrates.

Socrates is willing to suffer; and that very fact is evidenced in Socrates's willingness to descend outside the city on Phaedrus's behalf. For reasons difficult for us to understand, Athens was essentially the center of Socrates's universe. So, Socrates's descent outside the city was almost a voluntary act of impiety, given Socrates's status as the god's gift to Athens. Socrates's descent was also, metaphorically, a descent approximating a descent to Hades itself, or at least a place inferior.

Socrates's descent with Phaedrus outside the city was an act of condescension, in the proper meaning of the word. The grove at which Socrates and Phaedrus arrive is depicted as quite beautiful. So, metaphorically understood, the descent of Socrates and Phaedrus was not a full descent into Hades. Yet, as the grove's god was Pan (who owed his divinity to Hermes, who owed his divinity to Zeus), the Zeus-inspired Socrates's descent to a grove associated with Pan was an act of condescension; a state once, or twice, removed from the god most proper, Zeus. The grove is engaging in its natural beauty, but vastly inferior to the temple of Zeus to which Lysias should have, *qua* lover, led Phaedrus.

Who Is Phaedrus?

Socrates descends with Phaedrus out of Athens, physically, to see to the ascent of Phaedrus's soul. This ascent/descent motif mirrors the dialectical elements of ascending and descending *dianoia* in *Republic*.[6] Thus even more of Plato's dianoetic poetics: after leaving Lysias's company, Phaedrus was in a tenuous position; a position resembling the tenuous position of the soul engaged in *dianoia*. When the soul is engaged in *descending dianoia*, it risks remaining mired in the realm of the merely sensuous, where the soul might stay steeped in the rankly superficial. On the other hand, when the soul is engaged in *ascending dianoia* it achieves *episteme*, the realization of its divine nature.

Phaedrus should have been led upward by Lysias to the temple of Zeus for the consecration of their love. Yet, in the pretext of *Phaedrus*, Lysias had left Phaedrus to descend, alone, to a very low point; so low as to suggest a pending descent into Hades.

Thus more *CO*: as an ironic dianoetic Zeus-like hero, Socrates has to proceed in the direction opposite to the ascending course taken by Zeus in the myth in the *PL*. Zeus elevates mortals to the height of heights, to the supreme contemplation of Essences in the Essence Wheel. The ascent Socrates achieves for Phaedrus is obviously not an actual ascent to the Essence Wheel in a chariot train. Only a god could do that, much as only a god could teach dialectic. Socrates, in effect, teaching dialectic in both word and deed, would have Phaedrus recall his original heavenly trek to the Essence Wheel. Then Phaedrus might make a good return to Athens itself, a good return marked by the ability to discern all kinds of identity and difference, similarity and dissimilarity, truth and deceit, none of which distinctions Phaedrus has learned from his new lover, Lysias.

The ascent/descent motif in *Phaedrus* is a key to the appreciation of the dialogue. Indeed, the subtext of *Phaedrus* suggests an ascent/descent motif. Sallis notes that before the action of the dialogue begins, Lysias himself would have ascended to Athens, as Lysias lived in Pireus, the port at the base of Athens.[7] After that first ascent to the city, Lysias would have made a second ascent within the city, to the house of Epicrates.

We can take Sallis's observations about the pretext of *Phaedrus* further. Since the action of the dialogue takes place in the virtual, if not actual, shadow of the temple of Zeus, Plato is implying that if Lysias truly loved Phaedrus, Lysias would have taken the lead, like Zeus (or Socrates), and

---

6. Cf., chapter 3, "The Line On Dialectic, Part 2," and chapter 1, "Situating *Phaedrus*."
7. Sallis, *Being and Logos*, 107.

Plato's Rehabilitation of Zeus

led Phaedrus on yet another ascent. Lysias should have led Phaedrus from the house of Epicrates up higher to the temple of Zeus. There Lysias might have consecrated his love for Phaedrus, if Lysias really loved Phaedrus. Yet, Lysias did not love Phaedrus.

Lysias ascended only as far as Lysias wanted. So Socrates, Lysias's opposite, has to take the Zeus-like lead for Phaedrus in a half-comical *CO*: by following. Socrates ascendingly leads Phaedrus in *logos* after descendingly following Phaedrus outside the city. From that vantage point, outside Athens, Phaedrus might learn how to make a proper return to Athens.

Lysias was not a proper lover or leader. Lysias—democrat, naturalist, and veritable atheist—was not inclined to enter the temple of Zeus. Typhonic, *Schadenverbesserung eros* lovers such as Lysias consciously rebelled against all things associated with the spirit of Zeus. Yet, even if Lysias wished to consecrate his love for Phaedrus in the temple of Zeus, extenuating circumstances might have suggested Lysias reconsider such a move; and Lysias was nothing if not calculating.

First, there was the possible desuetude of the temple. Perhaps the Olympieum was no longer housing services. Yet, secondly, even if services were still being held at the temple of Zeus, Phaedrus, and anyone with him, might not have been allowed in the temple, or even the temple's grounds. Lysias could have been incriminated even if Lysias had chosen to make a consecrating move with Phaedrus.

According to Douglas MacDowell, entry of a sacred setting by anyone prosecuted for impiety, such as Phaedrus had been, and anyone accompanying such a person, would be in violation of the Decree of Teisamenos.[8] MacDowell has argued plausibly that the Decree of Teisamenos would still be in effect in 407, even if the decree had undergone revisions between 410 and 403. Following temporal clues from *Phaedrus*, *Symposium*, and other historical material, Rhodes concludes that the chronological setting of *Phaedrus* would likely be, or is supposed to be, the summer of 407.[9] Alkibiades, who had also been banished for his participation in the *MH* and the *PEM*, had returned to Athens from exile in 407. As Phaedrus seems to have been a clinger in Alkibiades's cult, it is likely Phaedrus returned to Athens at or about the same time Alkibiades did. So, given the Decree of Teisamenos, criminals such as Phaedrus, and anyone in the company of such a person,

---

8. MacDowell, *Andocides, On the Mysteries*, 194.
9. Rhodes, *Eros, Wisdom, and Silence*, 414–15.

Who Is Phaedrus?

could be charged with impiety for entering just the grounds of a sacred place.

The calculating Lysias surely would stay away from the temple, at least in the company of Phaedrus, for that reason alone. While not an Athenian, Lysias was first and foremost a businessman. He surely wished to maintain a decent reputation in and around Athens. Even if Lysias desired to accompany Phaedrus to the temple of Zeus, he would do so at the risk of his reputation.

Socrates, the veritable opposite of Lysias, was instinctively religious. Vlastos reminds us that Socrates manifestly accepted the existence of the supernatural; a point that deserves repeating, even if it is "so embarrassing to modern readers."[10] As Vlastos says of Socrates:

> He subscribes unquestioningly to the age-old view that side by side with the physical world accessible to our senses, there exists another, populated by mysterious beings, personal like ourselves, but, unlike ourselves, having the power to invade at will the causal order to which our own actions are confined, effecting in it changes of incalculable extent to cause us great benefit, or, were they to choose otherwise, total devastation and ruin.[11]

So, assuming the temple of Zeus was still operating, and assuming Socrates knew of the Decree of Teisamanos, would Socrates have risked the charge of impiety by leading Phaedrus up to the temple?

Virtually all of *Phaedrus* deals with Socrates's task of impressing upon Phaedrus the importance of a Zeus-inspired love of wisdom. In the stipulated theology of *Phaedrus*, a Zeus-inspired love of wisdom is the necessary condition for true love. Surely it would be easier to stress the importance of Zeus-inspired love if Socrates could lead Phaedrus to Zeus's very temple.

Yet, would Socrates have repudiated the Decree of Teisamenos to save Phaedrus? It is doubtful Socrates would have repudiated the Decree, given what we know from *Crito*. For Socrates, even the unjust laws of the city had to be obeyed, until the legislators could be persuaded that their human laws did not measure up to divine law. As it turns out in *Phaedrus*, the momentum of Phaedrus's descent out of Athens carried Socrates and Phaedrus down and away from the temple anyway.

Yet, given Socrates's alternatives in the moment, and our understanding of the Decree of Teisameinos on the one hand, and our understanding

---

10. Vlastos, "Socratic Piety," 214.
11. Ibid.

Plato's Rehabilitation of Zeus

of Socrates's relationship with Athens on the other, in Socrates's very descent with Phaedrus all the way outside the city, we see Socrates as a tragic figure. In his willingness to save Phaedrus, Socrates has no good choice.

Socrates's divine post was in the city. So, simply by leaving Athens, even if to save Phaedrus, Socrates was committing impiety, or was on the cusp of doing so. On the other hand, if Socrates were to ascend to the temple with Phaedrus to consecrate his friendship with Phaedrus more immediately, and instruct Phaedrus in the ways of Zeus-inspired love, Socrates would violate the Decree of Teisamenos. Either way, Socrates would violate his own ethical principle about duty to the civil law, and therefore divine law. Like the priest in another tradition, who must, by his position, violate the Sabbath by working on it so others might observe it, Socrates, in his relationship with Phaedrus, has to offend the divine, one way or another.

So, as Socrates cannot lead Phaedrus to the temple of Zeus to consecrate their friendship in Zeus, Socrates does the next best thing. He follows Phaedrus to a sacred grove, outside the city limits, where the Decree of Teisamenos would not apply.

Yet, even then, the grove is sacred mainly due to the descendents of Zeus, especially Pan. So, in *Phaedrus*, virtually throughout the dialogue, Socrates plays the role of Zeus as far as a mortal can; and his deeds match his words. Socrates, the Zeus-inspired hero, is doing all he can in *Phaedrus* to save Phaedrus. Socrates must condescend, suffer, to serve as the Zeus-inspired wisdom lover, distinct from the Typhonic lover, or non-lover, that Lysias is.

There have been other allusions to Socrates as divine or heroic guide in *Phaedrus*. Following a hermeneutical line established by Zdravko Planinc, Rhodes notes in detail how Socrates's many words and even minute actions reveal Socrates to be a kind of shaman figure like Odysseus.[12] Yet, more pertinent in *Phaedrus* is the way Socrates is a Zeus-like hero, especially given the dialogue's multiple, and glowing, references to Zeus, and the dialogue's rehabilitation of Zeus's reputation.

One might even see Plato's rehabilitation of the reputation of Zeus in *Phaedrus* as the primary reason for the dialogue's being. James Hans claims the very "primary" purpose of Plato's work is the perfection of the images of the gods:

> Once Socrates has straightened out the gods, he has achieved his primary goal. The rest is window dressing, but it is important

12. See Planinc, *Plato through Homer*.

Who Is Phaedrus?

> enough for Socrates to go to some lengths so we can see what follows from his earlier arguments. Most pertinently, if the gods have been simplified and corrected, it follows that humans must likewise adhere to a new standard. They have been created in the gods' image, which was a problem when the gods were evil, protean, and dissolute, but now that the gods are only good and only one thing, humans can brush up their own image. So Socrates sets out to mend us as well.[13]

Hans does not refer to *Phaedrus* in particular; but what he says obviously applies to *Phaedrus*. Plato's rehabilitation of Zeus is primary relative to Phaedrus's particular problems as a Typhonic lover. Socrates is clearly trying to transform Phaedrus, and, as will be demonstrated in the end, that to which Phaedrus is to be transformed is indeed the "simple," the antidote to all things Typhonic.

β) Zeus's and Socrates's Double Duty

The focus on Zeus in *Phaedrus*, indeed Plato's rehabilitation of Zeus, reinforces another connection between *Phaedrus* and the *Republic*. What operates over the course of *Phaedrus*, but especially in the famous first half, is a poetic dissertation on relationships in *Phaedrus* that corresponds with the presentation of the types of love in the soul formulated in the *Republic*.

Hence the following parallels:

In the *Republic*, wisdom-love (*philosophia*) is the highest, or is supposed to be, the highest form of love. In *Phaedrus*, wisdom-love takes the form of Zeus-inspired love that willingly suffers so the beloved can attain wisdom.

In the *Republic*, honor-love (*philotimia*) is second-highest. In *Phaedrus*, the problematic form of honor-love that receives the most focus is *Schadenverbesserung eros* in which lovers compete with one another and threaten to shame one another should one not attain physical, social, or economic success.

In the *Republic*, money-Love (*philochrematia*) is the lowest form of love. In *Phaedrus*, pederasty is the form of money-love that receives the most focus.

In the *Republic*, the best individual soul maintains as far as possible the hierarchy in the three types of love: wisdom-love over honor-love;

---

13. Hans, *Socrates and the Irrational*, 160.

honor-love over money-love. The same psychology applies in *Phaedrus*. In *Phaedrus*, Socrates offers a list of the nine vocations found in the city, 1) philosopher, or lover of beauty, or one of a musical and loving nature; 2) law-abiding king, or military man, or ruler; 3) politician, or businessman, or financier; 4) gymnast or physician; 5) prophet or conductor of the mysteries; 6) imitative artists; 7) craftsman or husbandman; 8) sophist or demagogue; 9) tyrant.

The best human souls can be found in three triads that correspond to wisdom-love, honor-love, and money-love:

> Wisdom-love — philosopher; lover of beauty; or a musical and loving nature;
> Honor-love — law-abiding kings; a military man; or a ruler;
> Money-love — politician; man of business; financier.[14]

Rhodes is correct to note that there are surely many subtle critiques of Athenian democracy at work in the offering of the list of nine professions overall, as the list even bothers to mention the demagogue.[15] A study of those details is not the purpose here.

The point here is that Plato does not deny that money-love and honor-love are necessary elements of the human soul. However, there is good love of honor and bad love of honor; rational money-love and irrational money-love. The right-thinking soul does not resort to perversions of honor-love and money-love, which perversions in *Phaedrus* take the form of Typhonic *eros* and pederasty respectively.

Plato's presentation of the three types of relationships in *Phaedrus* that correspond to the three types of loves in the soul in the *Republic* reinforces his claims about the flaws of democracy in the *Republic*. The backdrop of *Phaedrus* is a feverish, shallow, democrat-dominated Athens that gives greater recognition to a strange form of money-love, pederasty, and a crass form of honor-love, *Schadenverbesserung eros*, than it does to wisdom-love. The essence of Socrates's position in *Phaedrus* is that Typhonic, *Schadenverbesserung eros*, that sells itself to Athens as a form of honor-love, is really a collective exercise in vanity; little more than money-love in disguise. Also, pederasty, a disguised form of money-love, and love of everything money can buy, seems to condition young men to become no more than Typhonic lovers over time.

---

14. *Phaedrus*, 248d.
15. Rhodes, *Eros, Wisdom, and Silence*, 304–5 and 493–94.

Who Is Phaedrus?

In Typhonic, *Schadenverbesserung eros*, male homosexual lovers compete with one another openly and socially. Ostensibly they compete with one another for the betterment of one another. The unspoken contract between the "lovers" is that, should one of the two fail to attain and maintain, physical, intellectual, or sexual perfection, the other is allowed to dishonor, to shame, the failing party.

Such ostensible honor-love is really just a disguise for money-love promoted as a virtual religion most beneficial to the welfare of the city. Hence Phaedrus's claim in the *Symposium*: "if there were some way of arranging that a state or an army could be made up entirely of pairs of lovers, it is impossible to imagine a finer population."[16] When Phaedrus argues that Typhonic love should be the only form of love authorized by the state, he is arguing that shame-improvement love is what will maintain a spirit of competition that is good for the society on the whole because it forces individuals to strive for financial, social, and sexual perfection.

One of Socrates's problems with the premise of Typhonic, *Schadenverbesserung eros* is that such an attitude unduly reduces honor-love to a type of money-love *sans* recognition of the superseding form of love, wisdom-love. Indeed, early in *Phaedrus* Socrates says openly that he realizes when he is talking to Phaedrus he is engaging in "business." The "business" in question is the rhetoric business in which Lysias and Phaedrus are engaged. Lysias wrote speeches as clever commodities, not as vehicles for the revelation of truth.

In turn, the *erastes* of *L'/P'*, the elder male who hires out the sexual services of a boy, allegedly for the improvement of the boy, claims to be merely an honest businessman of a sort, simply seeing to the needs of both parties. Yet, the *erastes* has ulterior motives. The *erastes*'s alleged education of the boy is not really for the realization of the *boy's* desires. Rather, the implication in the contract is that the boy will take the *erastes*'s money and training, and then proceed as a man into greater society to do the *erastes*'s bidding. The man uses the boy as an instrument by which to shape the city in the man's image, for the man's vanity. Socrates is bringing to Phaedrus's attention that Zeus-inspired wisdom-love is the antidote to both Typhonic honor-love and pederastic money-love.

Also, in the stipulated theology of *Phaedrus*, the Zeus-led lords of commerce are supposed to see that their fair love of money is legitimized to the extent to which they are genuine lovers of wisdom. In the *Republic*,

---

16. *Symposium*, 178e.

Plato makes a similar point with a play on the term οὐσία.[17] Οὐσία is a feminine active participle that has a variety of meanings, one of which is the "active being" of something, or Essence, as in the Essence Wheel. (The term οὐσία is later crucial for Aristotle's system; and a derivate is crucial later yet for the Christian Gospels.) Yet, οὐσία also has a slang meaning akin to the Italian *soldi*, "money," and somewhat akin, in usage if not etymology, to the English "substance." "Substance" could mean Essence, or money/property, or depth. To call someone a person of "substance" could mean that the person has significant wealth or so-called *gravitas*. This *double-entendre* on οὐσία can also be found in *Theaetetus*.[18]

This play on *ousia* in *Phaedrus* is part of Plato's rehabilitation of Zeus. Zeus does double divine duty in *Phaedrus*. Zeus is not only the god of friendship and leadership, both of which are necessary for success in commerce, Zeus is also the god who takes the lead in the attaining of wisdom.

This is why Socrates's wording early in *Phaedrus*, when he quotes Pindar, is such that "that which is even greater than business" is what Socrates is eager to discuss with Phaedrus.[19] Yet, Socrates has to assume, to some degree, the role of businessman in *Phaedrus*. Socrates quickly discerned that if Phaedrus came from a meeting with Lysias, the shield-making businessman who had turned rhetoric into a business, then Socrates, to some extent, was going to have to talk business. Zeus does double divine duty in *Phaedrus* as the god of wisdom and commerce. Socrates must do the same, as Zeus-like hero.

So, in light of the double meaning of οὐσία or "substance" (or Essence), toward the ultimate transformation of Phaedrus, Zeus-inspired Socrates must help Phaedrus recollect the Essence Wheel *via* the *PL*. The indigent and seemingly worthless Socrates has to be a better businessfriend to Phaedrus than Lysias is. While Lysias had turned rhetoric into a business, Socrates, at least according to Socrates's thesis, could even be a better business friend to Phaedrus than Lysias is because Socrates can "teach" Phaedrus dialectic, the means by which Phaedrus might master rhetoric.

Here we see a further irony. Given the dynamics of *Schadenverbesserung eros*, Socrates would even be a good friend to his enemy, Lysias. If Phaedrus and Lysias were to remain *Scadenverbesserung eros* lovers, a

17. *Republic*, 329e.
18. Polansky, *Philosophy and Knowledge*, 41.
19. *Phaedrus*, 227b.

relation Socrates thinks Phaedrus should disown, Socrates's improvement of Phaedrus by dialectic would make Phaedrus that much better at rhetoric, and therefore more competitive. Thanks to knowing dialectic *per* Socrates, Phaedrus would be able to think better and challenge his *Schadenverbesserung eros* lover, Lysias, that much more, allegedly thereby making for more improvement of Lysias in the Typhonic competition-test. That would mean Socrates, the indirect improver of Lysias, loves his enemy, even or at least in accord with his enemy's premise.

Here we see yet another instance in which Phaedrus would be *epamphoterious*, torn between two ways. Zeus's dyadic leadership, which Socrates is undertaking in his heroic effort, operates on the level of both wisdom-love and money-love at the same time. Between those two loves is honor-love. Honor-love, however, is the most problematic type of love in the soul: a) because it can be directed in two ways; and b) because honor-love has no or few objects toward which it is immediately directed. Wisdom-love has a domain of "objects" at which it can aim, at least in the images offered in *Phaedrus*. In the imagery of *Phaedrus*, the domain of "objects" at which wisdom-love aims is comprised of all of the Essences in the Essence Wheel to which the mortal is led by Zeus. Similarly, money-love has obvious objects at which it can aim: the beautiful things money can buy such as human bodies and grand houses like that of Epicrates, etc.

Yet, honor-love is problematic. Honor-love is *de facto epamphoterious*. It must direct itself, ultimately, toward objects associated with either wisdom-love or money-love. In the warrior ethic, for example, the honor-love that motivates the just warrior makes him aim not at spoils of war he can possess for personal gratification; not even the garlands or medals he might display as evidence of his honor. Rather, the just warrior, the supreme honor-lover, aims at something not immediately visible, namely, the realization of just states and just laws.

In descending direction, the unjust warrior reveals he is not a true honor-lover when he betrays that he is fighting for mere possessions. The unjust warrior is really only a money-lover in disguise. As Socrates says of such misguided honor-lovers in *Phaedo*, such honor-lovers only appear courageous: they are really fighting from fear; fear of being without certain material goods.[20] That is why in the ranking of the best souls in *Phaedrus*, the term "warrior" is predicated with the attribute "law-abiding;" and why Socrates is ultimately criticizing Phaedrus's speech in the *Symposium* that

---

20. *Phaedo*, 68b.

argues that pairs of Typhonic lovers would make the best soldiers because they would fight all the more to defend the beloved in the trench. The proper soldier does not exist to fight for his beloved in the trench but for laws that reflect divine wisdom.

For Socrates, Typhonic, *Schadenverbesserung eros* is just a form of money-love in disguise. That is why, in the *PL*, when describing a situation that could apply to Phaedrus and Lysias, Socrates hedges his compliment of some lovers by saying that some lovers "probably" are motivated by honor-love.[21] Socrates's point is that *Schadenverbesserung eros* lovers are not motivated by true honor when they problematically preach social success as a sign of honor.

The phenomenon of the problematic nature of honor-love also makes a profound appearance in *Phaedrus* in Socrates's underappreciated *HH*. When Socrates dutifully cancelled *P'/S'* with his *HH*, he offered a quote from Ibycus who feared being shamed for "buying honor among men."[22] Socrates, when delivering *P'/S'*, was playing the role of Lysias. So, when Socrates halted *P'/S'* and quoted Ibycus, Socrates was informing Phaedrus that Lysias was not a true lover because Lysias was not even a true honor-lover. Lysias was a money-lover in disguise.

In the terms and images of *Phaedrus*, only Zeus-inspired love grounded in the contemplation of the Essence Wheel is a guarantor of true love. There is, however, an element of honor-love, and therefore shame, involved even in the love of wisdom. The lover of wisdom would be ashamed for basing his love on something less than recognition of the divine.

γ) The Lisper contra Zeus

The myth in the *PL* is not the only case in which Plato rehabilitates Zeus in *Phaedrus*. After the *PL,* when the discourse degenerates into the more banal discussion of rhetoric, Socrates generates another myth within that degeneration. The topic turns to the problematic nature of writing. During that discussion, Socrates's myth-making displays a comical but ultimately serious point. Again Zeus is at the center.

Much, perhaps too much, has been made of Plato's ironic criticism of writing in a written dialogue, *Phaedrus*. Commentators have written virtual folios on the issue. Ferrari, for one, argues that Jacques Derrida, Ronna

21. *Phaedrus*, 256c.
22. Ibid., 242d.

Who Is Phaedrus?

Berger, and many others have taken the topic too seriously. But, by an irony perhaps inextricable from the issue, Ferrari himself spends pages saying (or writing) that too much has been said on the subject.

One of the best summary statements on the issue is that of Ernst Heitsch: "Obviously [Plato] sees in language primarily an instrument not of *presentation* but of *mediation* . . ."[23] Both writing and speaking are capable of presentation (*Darstellung*), but not necessarily mediation (*Vermittlung*). A written work does not know the context in which it appears. Therefore a written work cannot properly or fully play the role of mediator.

Erring perhaps on the side of brevity, I shall enter and exit the question of writing quickly, as the focus here remains the question of Plato's rehabilitation of Zeus.

The issue of the problematic nature of writing appears in the context in which Socrates presents the myth of Theuth, the demi-god who allegedly invented writing. It is not accidental that the myth of Theuth appears in this dialogue in which Zeus is the dominant god. Relative to Theuth, Zeus's attributes as lord and leader are rather, pun intended, pronounced. Of the many points of the myth of Theuth, the key point, perhaps, is best and summarily appreciated in the very verbalization of the names involved.

Thus one of those marvelous moments in which Plato educates by jest: via some cheap humor, Plato's main point about the myth of Theuth and writing is best expressed in the actually spoken word. Say out loud (not silently as in writing), "Zeus." Then say out loud "Theuth." Then ask yourself: which of these two would I follow into battle: Zeus or Theuth?

With a cheap joke about lisping, Plato makes several points at once. Socrates would quickly close his case about many forms of superiority: of speech to writing; of Zeus to pretenders; of the Greek to the Egyptian; of Socrates to Lysias; of dialectic to rhetoric.

Phaedrus is indignant at Socrates's Theuth myth. Perhaps Phaedrus was offended because he himself had a lisp, or a feigned one. Perhaps Phaedrus had a feigned lisp because his former hero and perhaps lover, Alkibiades, was famous for a lisp. According to Wohl, Alkibiades's lisp was actually an affectation: "The younger Alcibiades also lisps, an affectation he gets from his father, whose own lisp, says Plutarch, 'gave his speech a persuasion that brought pleasure.'"[24]

---

23. Heitsch, "Τιμιότερα," 278. "Offensichtlich sieht er [Platon] in der Sprache primär ein Instrument nicht der *Darstellung*, sondern der *Vermittlung* . . ."

24. Wohl, *Love among the Ruins*, 133.

Plato's Rehabilitation of Zeus

Wohl notes just how famous Alcibiades's lisp was. "Alcibiades' lisp was parodied throughout Aristophanic comedy."[25] Here is another possible reason Plato made a cheap joke about lisping. Plato was competing yet again with the poets, and, this time, beating Aristophanes at his own game.

Perhaps Phaedrus was also annoyed at Socrates's lisping myth because it reminded Phaedrus of Alkibiades. Any memory of Alkibiades might have been a reminder of yet another way Phaedrus had been *epamphoterious*, "torn between two ways." Phaedrus had surely been a joiner in the cult of Alkibiades, and was possibly Alkibiades's lover. Yet, Phaedrus's new lover, Lysias, despised Alkibiades and Alkibiades's whole family: "Lysias, speaking against Alcibiades' son, paints the entire family with a broad brush as prostitutes and imagines the son (imitating his father by showing himself a 'most depraved young man') spending his youth lying under a cloak with his lover, drinking."[26]

Perhaps Alkibiades's lisp had helped to seduce Phaedrus to join in Alkibiades's version of the *PEM* that had led to Phaedrus's banishment from Athens. The cheap joke about the lisp may have reminded Phaedrus of Phaedrus's own shallowness and perhaps lingering love of Alkibiades because at this time, Phaedrus, enamored of Lysias, almost had to be one of Alkibiades's sworn enemies because Lysias was. Yet, here is Socrates suggesting that Phaedrus is choosing badly again, as the writer, Lysias, *qua* writer, is as bad as the lisper, Alkibiades; and arguably worse.

Perhaps Phaedrus was offended by Socrates's lisp humor for yet other reasons. That is, Plato's cheap but telling joke is important relative to Socrates's claims about rhetoric. We recall Socrates in *Gorgias* categorizing rhetoric as a species of pandering along with grooming, cooking, and sophistry.[27] Even if rhetoric were an art, according to Socrates in *Phaedrus*, that art would be problematic indeed. The art of speaking might depend on a highly mutable or fortuitous precondition, the gift of eloquence, a point with which even Phaedrus agrees. So, no matter how intelligent, morally determined, or politically astute a person might be, a lisper, perhaps by a fluke of physiognomy, might be a failure *a priori* in the art of speaking; or a success if the audience happens to find a fluke of nature charming.

Even if a lisp, like Alkibiades's father's, were somehow endearing, the effect would owe more to a permutation in nature than to a real art. More

---

25. Ibid., 133n.
26. Ibid., 131.
27. *Gorgias*, 465a.

yet, there might be something worse for the art of rhetoric. If Alkibiades's rhetoric, for example, succeeded because of a fake lisp, the absurdity would be that the art of rhetoric depended on the mastery of a prior art, the art of lisping.

δ) Dodona Devotionals

Toward a final attempt at the rehabilitation of the image of Zeus, Socrates suggests Phaedrus consider "the holy place of Zeus at Dodona."[28] The bumpkins at Dodona were the virtual opposites of the likes of Lysias. The bumpkins at Dodona were illiterate and did not meddle in the affairs of the city. Yet, to Socrates, those bumpkins who listened to Zeus through stones were wiser than *literati* who got their words written by a sophist, Lysias. Who would really want the title logographer?

---

28. *Phaedrus*, 275b.

8

Triads and Dyads of Speeches

a) Lysias's/Phaedrus's Pederasty Speech

AS A THOUGHT-EXPERIMENT EXTENSION of the dialectical dynamics from the *Republic*, *Phaedrus* is veritably laced with triads that reduce to telling dyads. The Morychus-*Epicrates-Lysias triad reduced to significant pair-permutations; as do Epicrates-Lysias-Phaedrus; Lysias-Phaedrus-Socrates; the triad of the arts of contention in speech; the triad of Homer-Solon-Lysias; and Lysias-Socrates-Isocrates at the end. The famous triad of speeches in *Phaedrus* allows of similar reduction and assessment.

The first half of *Phaedrus* is dominated by three speeches:

(1) *L'/P'*: Lysias's speech in praise of the non-lover; composed by Lysias; read to Socrates by Phaedrus.

(2) *P'/S'*: Socrates's first speech, yet not a speech endorsed by Socrates; really just *L'/P'* rendered differently; a speech against the lover. Socrates delivers *L'/P'* upon Phaedrus's challenge to Socrates. The challenge is to deliver the very same thesis of *L'/P'* but differently, and somewhat improved.

(3) The *PL*: Socrates's second speech. Phaedrus requested that Socrates give a speech that would complete *P'/S'* after Socrates abruptly terminated delivery of *P'/S'*. But the *PL* differs from *P'/S'*, and indeed *opposes P'/S'* and *L'/P'*. The *PL* praises love and madness, provided the issue is *divine* madness, not merely human madness associated with erotic obsession and immediate gratification.

So, more particularly, what is *L'/P'*?

L'/P' is a speech for an elder man, an *erastes*, to deliver to a teen "boy" (*pais*) verging on manhood: hence pederasty (*pais-erastes*). Hardly

Who Is Phaedrus?

common to all classes in Athens, the pederasty relationship was approved in upper classes as a way for male elders to shape future generations, and therefore Athens, in their own image. A "boy," the *pais*, a teen on the verge of becoming a man, would be partially adopted by the *erastes* and therefore influenced by the *erastes*. Allegedly a kind of "love" relationship would be established between *pais* and *erastes*, as the *erastes* probably provided the former clothing, a stipend, and introduction into social circles in Athens. The boy would provide the *erastes* moments of intercrural sex, at least, in a kind of shaming rite-of-passage. With the boy dressed as a girl, the *erastes* would achieve ejaculation by rubbing his penis, *sans* penetration, between the boy's thighs.[1]

The idea was that once the boy became a man, the boy-man would spend his career trying to shape Athens in the image of his *erastes*, out of allegiance to his homosexual sugar-daddy who showed so much "love" for the boy. Public shaming of many kinds, especially in courts, was common in Athens: so, better for the boy/girl to learn early how to deal with shame, and learn it in private before facing various forms of shame in public for the rest of his life.

L'/P' is therefore novel and clever. *L'/P'* recommends dropping any pretense to an affectionate relationship between *pais* and *erastes*. *L'/P'* promotes an entirely contractual, utilitarian relationship between the *erastes* and boy. *L'/P'* even denigrates love. It offers a list of numerous self-inflicted ills that befall those who actually fall in love.

In a sense, *L'/P'* is a timeless, if cynical, speech that applies to heterosexual circumstances as well as homosexual. With minimal tweaking, *L'/P'* can come across as the greatest "single's bar" speech ever written: the ultimate apology for sexual relations between parties with no emotional or personal commitment.

L'/P' argues, in essence, that no one should be a lover because lovers are insane. Evidence for lovers' insanity can be found in a long list of foibles: wasting time and money, being prone to jealousy, being subject to the fickleness of the other, writing really bad poetry, etc.

Phaedrus reads *L'/P'* aloud. Socrates then poses his critique. Socrates regards *L'/P'* a rhetorical mess. *L'/P'* is ostentatious, repetitious, and, worst of all, it begins with a peroration. *L'/P'* begins with its conclusion. That last

---

1. Nicholson, *Plato's Phaedrus*, 111.

Triads and Dyads of Speeches

critique, seemingly trite, is actually very significant, as it does double-duty later in Socrates's criticism of the "Eleatic Palamedes," Zeno.[2]

In Socrates's view, *L'/P'* is not only a rhetorical mess, it is a *moral* mess. For Socrates, it is wrong to denigrate love, certainly unequivocally. The speaker of *L'/P'* is a kind of moral fraud. Rosen displays the sense in which the non-lover behind *L'/P'* is really a disguised lover at the same time. The speaker of *L'/P'* is actually a non-lover of the beloved, because he is really a self-lover.[3]

Rosen makes that case at length to challenge Nussbaum's argument that there is practical wisdom to be gleaned from *L'/P'*.[4] Nussbaum argues that *L'/P'* offers some prudent advice, especially for young women, in a highly complicated and competitive social world. Rosen disagrees at length; but Rosen did not have to exercise so much ingenuity to counter Nussbaum. Socrates had already done so. Socrates had already suggested that many persons might find utilitarian virtue in *L'/P'*. In Socrates's provocative terms, those who might find utilitarian virtue in *L'/P'* do so because such are the morals of the "common folk" who preach utilitarianism as rule.[5]

Phaedrus is upset by Socrates's criticisms of *L'/P'*. Phaedrus demands that Socrates's criticisms be justified. Indeed, Phaedrus challenges Socrates to give essentially the same speech as *L'/P'* but differently and improved.

Socrates pretends to be uninterested in the challenge. Yet, Socrates is faking. The occasion for Socrates to offer a *CO* in the form of identical but different speeches is just what Phaedrus needed so Phaedrus could engage, if unconsciously, in *dianoia*, and dialectic. What Phaedrus needed most were lessons in dialectic; and he would soon be swimming in dialectical dynamics once Socrates offered a speech, *P'/S'*, that was essentially the same as *L'/P'* yet different; and then delivered *PL* that was different from both *L'/P'* and *P'/S'*. The *PL*, different from both *L'/P'* and *P'/S'* because nobler, did hold a premise in common with *L'/P'* and *P'/S'*, that lovers are insane. Yet, the *PL* is about *divine*, not human, madness.

After some silly coyness on Socrates's part, and some exceedingly artificial banter between Socrates and Phaedrus that imitates the silly playing-hard-to-get language of courters, Socrates complies with Phaedrus's request that Socrates present *L'/P'* but differently. Socrates seizes the opportunity to

2. Cf. chapter 11β, "Countering Zeno and Lysias."
3. Rosen, "The Non-Lover in Plato's Phaedrus," 435.
4. Cf. chapter 5, "Phaedrus's Middle Whence: Was Phaedrus Bi-Rebellious?"
5. *Phaedrus*, 256e.

engage in the rhetorical exercise of improving *L'/P'* with a speech that is essentially the same: thus *P'/S'*, the same speech as *L'/P'* in thesis, but rendered in an opposite fashion, and improved.

β) Phaedrus's/Socrates's Pederasty Speech

How are *L'/P'* and *P'/S'* the same but different?

L'/P' tallies the foibles that might befall the lover. By contrast, yet similarly, *P'/S'* reveals the harms involved in the passive side of love, that is, the suffering the beloved would endure at the hands of a lover.

In *P'/S'* the beloved would suffer the state of being at the lover's every beck and call. The lover would want the beloved poor, so the beloved could not flee; ignorant, so the beloved could not espy the lover's deceits; isolated from friends and family, so the beloved would be defenseless; and pale and effeminate.

Not accidentally, most, if not all, of these attributes of the abused beloved apply to Phaedrus. When Socrates encounters Phaedrus after Phaedrus's encounter with Lysias, Phaedrus is alone, abandoned by no less than Lysias, his "lover." Phaedrus is also about as ignorant as ever. He is also pale from being shaded and seeks out the shade when arriving at the grove with Socrates. Finally, Phaedrus is effeminate, or at least enfeebled: he seeks out the softer roads for his therapeutic walk.

Phaedrus was supposed to see that *L'/P'* was clever indeed, as it praised the rational non-lover; and that, *via L'/P'*, Lysias, in his absence as a writer, was basically saying to Phaedrus's face that Lysias did not really love Phaedrus.

What then are the rhetorical improvements Socrates makes to *L'/P'* via the same but different speech, *P'/S'*? The improvements are minimal; but that is the point. *L'/P'* was so bad it took little to improve it.

Socrates's first improvement upon *L'/P'* in *P'/S'* is a better beginning. Socrates complained that *L'/P'* began with a closing, a peroration. So, to improve upon *L'/P'*, Socrates opens *P'/S'* with a clear beginning. Yet, comically, it is the most token of openings: "Once upon a time . . ." The words "Once upon a time . . ." evoke recollection of the simplest of tales, Aesop's fables.[6] Socrates's comical improvement suggests that *L'/P'*, over which Phaedrus fawns, was so unsophisticated it was barely better than a fable by Aesop.

---

6. *Phaedrus*, 237b.

Triads and Dyads of Speeches

Socrates then offers another token improvement. Socrates's opening continues: Once upon a time there was a "boy" (*pais*) ... or rather a "young man" (*meirakiskos*). Socrates qualifies his terms. It is not just any "boy" or lad to whom Socrates refers, but a *meirakiskos*. A *meirakiskos* is the more precise term for "boy" within the practice of pederasty.[7] By distinguishing "boy" from *meirakiskos*, Socrates was employing one of the rhetorical "principles" he posits later in the dialogue. Socrates was distinguishing ambiguous terms from unambiguous ones. So, with the qualification of at least one term, *P'/S'* offered a *de facto* improvement upon *L'/P'* because *L'/P'* was altogether lacking in definitions.

Yet, soon in *P'/S'*, Socrates reverts to the use of the broader term, "boy." Nicholson argues that Socrates reverts to the term "boy" in *P'/S'* simply to revert to a looser idiom because "Socrates does not want to be fussy and technical."[8] Yet, Nicholson's claim here, for all of his excellent work otherwise, is not tenable. When was the last time Socrates did not want to be fussy or technical? It is better to claim that, in this case, Socrates was inconsistent on purpose. Socrates's point was to make Phaedrus aware of the sense in which *pais* and *meirakiskos* are possibly identical though different. So, when Socrates otherwise calls Phaedrus himself "boy" (*pais*) at a telling point, later at the end of the *PL*, Phaedrus is supposed to realize that he, Phaedrus, was in some sense a *meirakiskos*. That is, Socrates is suggesting that Phaedrus is really being treated by Lysias as a mere "boy" in a rather bizarre form of pederasty, which, for Socrates, was strange enough already. That is, while Lysias was likely younger than Phaedrus, Lysias's high social position, and Phaedrus's low social position as a former exile, made Lysias, oddly, the *erastes* to Phaedrus as *pais*.

Socrates was delivering the message that Phaedrus, a man, was being treated by Lysias as a mere boy in a pederasty relationship. That is also why, in part, Socrates delivers *P'/S'* with a wrap on his head. The *erastes* wore a wrap on his head when making love to the "boy" or *meirakiskos*. So, Socrates is signaling to Phaedrus, by the very mode of delivery of *P'/S'*, in a silly but ultimately serious way, that Socrates is playing the role of *erastes* and the role of Lysias, as *P'/S'* is essentially the same as *L'/P'*. Phaedrus is supposed to become aware of his status accordingly. Phaedrus, a man, deluded into thinking he is in a competitive, Typhonic, *Schadenverbesserung*

---

7. Nicholson, *Plato's Phaedrus*, 111.
8. Ibid., 111.

Who Is Phaedrus?

eros relationship with Lysias, is being treated by Lysias as little more than a boy in a non-love pederasty affair.

Phaedrus was unaware of his pathetic status as boy relative to Lysias, not only because Phaedrus and Lysias were likely the same age, or Lysias was actually younger; but also because Phaedrus was unaware of the nature of true love.

So, on the rhetorical front, to cite Ronald Levinson, who cites a part of *Phaedrus* (263a–e): "if Lysias's speech is to pass muster, he must have compelled us 'at the beginning of his discourse on Love . . . to conceive it as a certain definite entity, with a meaning he had himself decided upon.' In these unambiguous terms Plato had declared the necessity, for a responsible rhetoric not less than for dialectic, of unambiguity."[9] When Socrates distinguished *meirakiskos* from *pais*, he was slightly improving upon *L'/P'* by employing at least a minimum of dialectic, the means by which one arrives at definition, or compelling discernment, to register all manner of identity and difference, similarity and dissimilarity.

Further, as *L'/P'* offered no definitions whatsoever, Socrates offered rhetorical improvement by *P'/S'* by offering at least a classification of love. Of course, this is an intentionally problematic improvement because *P'/S'* remains essentially *L'/P'*. Thus Socrates's further intentionally problematic improvement: Socrates classifies *eros* as a species in the genus "desire" (*epithumia*). As desire involves the passions, Socrates claims there are two ruling principles of the passions, a kind of *CO* relative to the passions. On the one hand, there is an "innate desire for pleasure (*hubris*)" as opposed to an "acquired conviction for virtue (moderation)."

As *P'/S'* is essentially just *L'/P'*, this opposition, "innate desire for pleasure" as opposed to an "acquired conviction for virtue," is not an operating premise in Socrates's worldview. In his view, moderation, as a part of virtue, is natural, not acquired. For Socrates, indeed, all four components of virtue—namely, wisdom, courage, moderation, and justice—are in the soul naturally. If wisdom, courage, moderation, and justice do not emerge as operative in a person on a regular basis, it is because that person's soul has been corrupted. That is why one of the formal charges brought against Socrates in the *Apology*, corruption of the youth, had such a sting to it. Socrates's accusers knew Socrates's stance on virtue: that it cannot be taught or "acquired." And Socrates's accusers knew that Socrates was trying to de-corrupt the young on a regular basis. Socrates's accusers knew, actually, that

---

9. Levinson, "Language, Plato, and Logic," 273.

they were the corruptors of the youth, not Socrates; but they were masters of concealing the fact.

It is important to recall that the *P'/S'* CO, an "innate desire for pleasure" as opposed to an "acquired conviction for virtue," is stipulated in *P'/S'* merely for the sake of Socrates's token improvement of *L'/P'*. It is a mistake to conclude that this stipulated CO is Socrates's position. However, some otherwise astute readers have done just that. Kenneth Dorter, for example, is for the most part correct when he provides a considerable list of dualities, seven all told, he finds in *Phaedrus*. One of those seven is, on the one side, "a natural tendency to hubris" and, on the other side, "an effort to acquire self-control."[10]

Dorter is quite right to concentrate on so many CO in *Phaedrus*; and Rosen offers a list of CO found in *Phaedrus* that could augment Dorter's list: "Light and shade, heat and coolness, reclining humans and a flowing stream, feminine nature and masculine logos: the setting takes on the character of a harmony of opposites (229a1–c3)."[11] Yet, it is important to see those dynamics in the right light and context.

Dorter misses the context for Socrates's claim about "a natural tendency to hubris" vs. "an effort to acquire self-control." Dorter seems to think the stipulated CO of the ruling principle of the passions in *P'/S'* is a position Socrates himself maintains. Dorter does not note, or forgets, that in *P'/S'* Socrates is speaking not as himself but as, in effect, Lysias, or any sophist who would promote the dubious thesis of *L'/P'*.

Moreover, Dorter offers the rather baffling claim that Socrates's stipulated claim about the dualism of "a natural tendency to hubris" vs. "an effort to acquire self-control" provides the very key to the dyadic format of *Phaedrus*: "this dual species [the duality of the innate desire for pleasure which is *hubris* and an acquired conviction for virtue which is moderation] gives rise to the two halves of the dialogue."[12] This is a very problematic claim. Dorter never defends this claim in any detail; not, at least, in the piece in which the claim appears. How do Dorter's terms operate? Is the first half of *Phaedrus* the "innate" half; the second the "acquired"? Or is it *vice versa*? In what sense is the one "the innate" and the other "the acquired?" Dorter never establishes how the CO of the ruling principle of the passions in *P'/S'* reflects the operating structure of the dialogue. Besides, the dyadic consti-

---

10. Dorter, "The Method of Division and the Division of the Phaedrus," 263.
11. Rosen, "The Non-Lover in Plato's Phaedrus," 431.
12. Dorter, "The Method of Division and the Division of the Phaedrus," 263.

tution of *Phaedrus* could clearly be the case without Socrates's concocted claims in *P'/S'*.

Such confusion regarding *P'/S'* almost justifies Donald Levin's otherwise extreme claim about *Phaedrus*. Levin claims that in *Phaedrus* there is "one central Platonic insight, viz., the value of contextual definition."[13] I hardly agree with Levin summarily when he says that "contextual definition" is the "one central" insight Plato delivers in *Phaedrus*. Yet, Levin's claim about "contextual definition" certainly applies to Socrates's classification of *eros* in *P'/S'*. Socrates's definition of love in *P'/S'* is sacrificed entirely to context.

Socrates's pseudo-definitions of love in *P'/S'* are consciously problematic and so are the derivatives of it. The proof they are consciously problematic for Socrates is evidenced by Socrates's abrupt halting of *P'/S'*. Rhetorical improvement upon *L'/P'* aside, Socrates cannot long deliver *P'/S'*, a speech with which he disagrees.

Socrates's *P'/S'* definitions, really just provisional classifications, are minimal and flawed; but at least they approach definitions. Lysias offered none in *L'/P'*, much as Phaedrus did not offer a definition of love in his *Symposium* speech, as Pausanius was quick to note.[14] Even though the definitions and principles in *P'/S'* are not positions Socrates maintains, they have a reason for being beyond the rhetorical improvement of *L'/P'*. Socrates's posing of two opposed ruling principles of the passions was to force Phaedrus to reckon with a considerable, thought-provoking *CO*, the better for Phaedrus to engage in *dianoia* at least.

As ascending *dianoia* moves the mind beyond the merely sensuous order, Phaedrus's forced engagement with *dianoia* here is especially appropriate in this context with so many sexual overtones. By ascensional *dianoia* the mind moves manifestly beyond the sensuous; and the very issue surrounding the *P'/S'*, at least for Socrates, concerns precisely moving beyond the merely sensuous, in this case the sexual. This is why Phaedrus, in his self-ignorance regarding his status as Lysias's "boy," is so very pathetic.

The notion of suffering for the beloved is utterly foreign to the likes of Lysias and Phaedrus, which is why they really are non-lovers when love is properly defined. Socrates knows that real love involves suffering, so in this circumstance he has allowed himself to be led outside the city, solo, where he could easily be abused. Indeed, Socrates notes explicitly that he has let

---

13. Levin, "Some Observations Concerning Plato's Lysis," 270.
14. *Symposium*, 180c.

Triads and Dyads of Speeches

Phaedrus lead him outside the city in a demeaning manner, by the nose like a pack animal.[15] Further, Socrates draws a most appropriate analogy: Phaedrus wants to try new rhetorical moves on Socrates the way a bad lover might try new sexual moves on the beloved, against the beloved's will.[16]

Phaedrus's veritable abuse of Socrates stands opposed to the way Socrates treats Phaedrus. Phaedrus is supposed to see that Socrates is suffering on Phaedrus's behalf because in true love, as Socrates says, "the beloved receives all service from his lover as if he [the beloved] were a god."[17] Ironically, Socrates treats Phaedrus, the virtual atheist, as if he, Phaedrus, were a god.

Phaedrus has much to learn, and discern, in this circumstance rife with opposites and dyads. There is a comical dyad, a kind of dialectical but edifying farce, even in the very circumstance when Phaedrus delivers *L'/P'* to Socrates, and when Socrates, in turn, delivers *P'/S'* to Phaedrus.

L'/P' was written as a speech to be delivered by an older, wealthy man, to a "boy." There is a farce of opposites when Phaedrus delivers *L'/P'* to Socrates. During *L'/P'*, Phaedrus speaks as the elder, but is much younger; and, on the receiving end of that pederasty speech, Socrates is old and legendarily ugly, the opposite of a beautiful boy or *meirakiskos*.

The dialectical farce continues when Socrates speaks to Phaedrus in turn via *P'/S'*. Socrates lacked entirely the key qualification for an *erastes*. Socrates was not only ugly; he was indigent, far too poor to be a serious *erastes*. It is no accident Socrates refers to his own poverty in the dialogue's opening stages in which pederasty is established as a backdrop.[18]

Moreover, Socrates had no desire to be an actual *erastes*. Socrates did not really assume individual charges the way a sophist or an *erastes* did.

The comical but poignant element in Socrates's delivery of *P'/S'*, however, can be seen on the receiving end of *P'/S'*. Phaedrus, perhaps approaching forty, was young compared with Socrates, but hardly young enough to be pursued by a typical *erastes*. No boy or *meirakaskos* would be complaining about his waning health, and taking therapeutic strolls, as Phaedrus was. (Rhodes even bothers to note, regarding Phaedrus's age, that when Socrates calls Phaedrus "young man" at one point, that term is not to be taken literally but as a term of endearment *per* the vernacular. Rhodes explains with a

15. *Phaedrus*, 230d.
16. Ibid., 236e.
17. Ibid., 255a.
18. Ibid., 227d.

Who Is Phaedrus?

contemporary example: when he, Rhodes, wrote *Eros, Wisdom, and Silence* in his sixties, he still had greater elders who would call him "sonny" by comparison.[19]) Phaedrus was no "boy," so it would be absurd for him to be on the receiving end of an actual pederasty speech. Yet, Socrates's message between the lines to Phaedrus is that Phaedrus is actually being treated like a "boy" by his alleged "lover," Lysias, in a pederasty relationship in which Lysias holds all the social priorities.

There is something else very serious, moreover, in Plato's dyadic farce when Socrates and Phaedrus address one another in the guises of *erastes* and *meirakaskos*. It would not be idly comical for Phaedrus to practice *L'/P'*. Phaedrus might be practicing *L'/P'* with the aim of using that very speech someday as an *erastes* himself. If Phaedrus could ever connive his way into another fortune, as he apparently did once when he married his cousin, he might become an *erastes* himself in just a few years.

This is surely yet another, and perhaps the primary, reason why Phaedrus is so excited about *L'/P'*, not primarily because of the "devious and illicit nature of the nonlover's proposition," as Eva Buccioni suggests.[20] If Phaedrus were to become an *erastes*, something Socrates would prevent, that would mean an exacerbation of the corruption of the youth of Athens, as Phaedrus is the prototypical corrupted youth come of age. Thus Socrates's attempt to de-corrupt Phaedrus the man: a still corrupted Phaedrus at forty could do far more harm to Athens than the young Phaedrus who joined in the *PEM* ever did.

The really important point in Socrates placing a bag over his head when he delivers *P'/S'* is that this hooding appears to have been the custom of the *erastes* during the sex he committed on the boy, or *meirakiskos*. In this hooding protocol in pederasty, perhaps the idea was that the boy, shamed enough already by being dolled up as a girl and mounted by the man, need not also witness the disturbing distortions of the man's face during the sexual act. So, when Socrates is delivering *P'/S'*, a pederasty speech, Socrates plays the *erastes* but he does so as a physically distant *erastes*; a kind of benign paragon, as Socrates disapproved of actual pederasty in which undue shame falls to the boy.

Scully has a good measure of Socrates's estimation of the function of shame and domination in pederasty, a domination cleverly concealed in *L'/P'*, which Socrates finds undignified: "Much of the talk about love in

19. Rhodes, *Eros, Wisdom, and Silence*, 521.
20. Buccioni, "Keeping It Secret," 19.

the *Phaedrus* conforms to this asymmetrical model. From this perspective, Lysias's argument that a boy should grant favors to a non-lover appears to offer a radical, and witty, departure from convention, but Socrates's vision in the Palinode of erotic reciprocity between man and boy would be a much deeper challenge to Greek same-sex eroticism."[21] Socrates understood why a man would want to shape Athens in his own image, and to do so via young surrogates. Yet, according to Socrates, pederasty was one weird way to go about it. For Socrates, the erotic reciprocity between man and boy need not involve sex at all; just a dual regard for wisdom, as only a population of wisdom-lovers will generate a great society.

Yet, the most serious point in Socrates's playing the *erastes* in *P'/S'* is Socrates's effort to make Phaedrus aware of the bizarre case of Phaedrus's own relationship with Lysias. Despite Phaedrus's age, Phaedrus is being treated by Lysias as little more than a boy, or *meirakiskos*, in a pederasty relationship. Lysias, like the more typical *erastes*, held all the money, power, and station. Phaedrus was not a boy in age; yet, as a former exile who had lost his property, he was barely better than a boy in a social sense. Phaedrus was surely dependent upon his lover, Lysias, for just about everything, the way a boy was dependent upon the *erastes*, especially for introduction into greater society; or, in the case of Phaedrus as former exile, re-introduction.

Socrates tries not to disabuse Phaedrus, the man, too quickly about Phaedrus's rather pathetic status as a mere "boy" to Lysias as *erastes*. Phaedrus fancied himself in a Typhonic, *Schadenverbesserung eros* relationship with Lysias. But Phaedrus had been self-ignorant before. What David Levine says of Charmides, another troubled figure in Plato's work, can be said of Phaedrus, even if Charmides's and Phaedrus's situations are not exactly identical: "He is debilitated as much by his own failure of self-knowledge as he is by those around him."[22] Phaedrus did not realize that his "lover," Lysias, was really a "non-lover," and did not have Phaedrus's best interests in mind.

Worse, Phaedrus continues in the delusion precisely because he is so clueless about that which he is actually so passionate about and that at which his deceptive "lover" is a master: rhetoric. Phaedrus is fascinated by how clever *L'/P'* is in its praise of the non-lover. Yet, if Phaedrus really considered the content of *L'/P'* (and *P'/S'*) and actually applied it to his real life circumstance in the moment, Phaedrus would see that *L'/P'* was more

21. Scully, *Plato's Phaedrus*, xi.
22. Levine, "The Tyranny of Scholarship," 68.

clever yet. By *L'/P'*, Lysias tells Phaedrus to Phaedrus's very face that his lover, Lysias, does not love him.

γ) Socrates's Half-Comical Halting

Love is the one subject Socrates claims to know rather well.[23] So, having met the challenge of rhetorically improving upon *L'/P'*, Socrates could not long deliver *P'/S'*. He disagreed with the thesis of *P'/S'* which was identical to that of *L'/P'*. Given that *P'/S'* was so awful, morally and rhetorically, Socrates had to halt it.

Socrates halts *P'/S'* abruptly and half-comically. In part, Socrates is seriously ashamed for having denigrated love in his delivery of *P'/S'*. Yet, too, in part, Socrates suggests comically that he is being overtaken by a nymph-inspired, erotic madness that might move him to accost Phaedrus sexually on the spot, as all of the talk of non-love in *P'/S'* was causing Socrates to repress his love instincts. Socrates half-comically claims he might burst out in a fit of passion. Socrates's *HH*, more deed than speech, is crucial. It reveals that Socrates himself is the locus of a *CO* relative to *L'/P'* and *P'/S'*, and the pending *PL*.

In his *HH* of *P'/S'*, Socrates is both non-lover and lover at the same time, if in different respects. Denying himself a nymph-inspired passion for Phaedrus, Socrates reveals he is a non-lover but in a very narrow sense; a non-lover of the merely sexual. Yet, therewith, Socrates reveals he is the opposite, a lover; i.e., a lover of the divine, especially the noble Zeus, who inspires the true lover to treat the beloved as if the beloved were a god. A Zeus-inspired lover/non-lover knows not to succumb to the gratification of the moment.

Socrates's *HH* serves to reveal that the speaker of *L'/P'* was a lover and non-lover at the same time, if in different respects. The speaker of *L'/P'* was a lover of himself and a non-lover of the other. Yet, when Socrates performs his *HH*, he reveals that he, as Zeus-inspired lover, is also a lover and non-lover at the same time, if in different respects; but in a way categorically superior to the lover/non-lover in *L'/P'*.

Socrates's *HH* shows that Socrates loves Phaedrus's *soul*, which is ugly, and does not love his body, which is handsome or "beautiful." It is Socrates's dyadic, lover/non-lover deed that effects the transition from the speech dyad of *L'/P'*//*P'/S'* to the superseding speech, the *PL*.

23. *Symposium*, 177e; *Phaedrus*, 257a.

Triads and Dyads of Speeches

Yet, more, Socrates's *HH* does not merely move the action to the *PL*. Socrates's *HH* functions structurally with the three speeches, *L'/P'*, *P'/S'*, and *PL*, in such a way that the structure's image anticipates the image of the soul that emerges in the *PL* itself.[24] Yet, how does the triad of speeches, *L'/P'*, *P'/S'*, and the *PL*, reduce to dyads; and how are those speeches in pairs identical and different?

δ) Divining the Palinode

L'/P' is identical to, yet different from, *P'/S'* to the degree to which *L'/P'* and *P'/S'* are identical in thesis. *L'/P'* and *P'/S'* both argue that it is better to be a non-lover than a lover because lovers are insane: in the former, the lover is at a disadvantage; in the latter, the beloved is. That dyad, *L'/P'* and *P'/S'*, is/are really one speech: *L'/P'//P'/S'*. How then is/are *L'/P'//P'/S'* both identical to, yet different from, the *PL*?

L'/P'//P'/S' and the *PL* are identical as all three, or both, would eliminate the detriments caused by human love. The difference between/among them is that *L'/P'//P'/S'* would eliminate the foibles that befall humans due to human madness by negating human love, while the *PL* would eliminate foibles that befall humans by affirming love, provided it is love involving divine madness.

There are other triad-dyad dynamics between and among *L'/P'*, *P'/S'*, and the *PL*. There is a very narrow identity and difference between *P'/S'* and the *PL*. *P'/S'* and the *PL* both have a myth function. The Zeus myth in the *PL* is obvious and famous. But in his rather bizarre fashion, Socrates also referred to *P'/S'* as a "myth" (μύθου).[25] As Scully notes of *P'/S'*: "Socrates will call this speech a fable (*mythos*) again at 241e, but he uses the same word to characterize the story of the charioteer and the two horses in the Palinode (253c)."[26] So, *P'/S'* and the *PL* are identical as they both contain the mythical. Yet, they are different, too. The whole of *P'/S'* is a myth; but only a part of the *PL* is a myth: the soul's ascent to the Essence Wheel.

At 241e, then, Socrates was benignly equivocating with the word "myth" for pedagogical reasons. Socrates was suggesting that *P'/S'* is a "myth" in the sense of being a kind of traditional falsehood. *P'/S'* argued that love is bad because the beloved always suffers. That "myth" makes for

---

24. Cf., chapter 9, "Images of the Image of the Soul."
25. *Phaedrus*, 237a.
26. Scully, *Plato's Phaedrus*, 15, n38.

facile jokes about love, and about marriage in particular. Yet, it is not always true that the lover makes the beloved miserable. That is why Socrates disowns *P'/S'*. The genuine lover does not make the beloved miserable. The genuine lover treats the beloved "as if he were a god."

L'/P' and the *PL* have their own identity/difference dynamic. The most profound sense of identity and difference between *L'/P'* and the *PL* lies in the way Lysias's "cleverness" in *L'/P'* is like but unlike Socrates's "sportiveness" in the *PL*. The "sportive" turns out to be a crucial notion in *Phaedrus*, as when Socrates says of the *PL*: "In some way, though I can't say exactly how, we offered an image of erotic experience and perhaps touched upon a truth in some instances and in others were wide of the mark, blending together a not totally unpersuasive account in a playful [or sportive] way . . ."[27]

Scully's note in his translation is significant here: "The verb *propaizo* has two meanings: 'to do something in a playful manner' (as at 262d2) and 'to sing in praise of.'"[28]

From Socrates's mouth, the "sportive" can suggest the playful or clever, and yet, also, the "reverent." The *PL*, after all, has no shortage of reference to the divine. So, we can clarify further the identity/difference triad-dyad reduction of the three speeches: *L'/P'* is clever rhetoric; *P'/S'* is clever myth; *PL* is sportive myth.

The key point is that there is a categorical difference between/among *L'/P'//P'/S'* and the *PL*. *L'/P'//P'/S'* blames love whereas the *PL* does the opposite: it praises love, provided the love involves divine madness. Appropriately, upon concluding the *PL*, the speech in praise of love and divine madness, Socrates prayerfully worries that the gods might be offended by so much that preceded Socrates's *HH*. So, Socrates says directly to the divine, and indirectly to the attending naturalist and virtual atheist, Phaedrus: "blame Lysias." Lysias, Phaedrus's lover, or non-lover, is to blame for writing a blameworthy speech; blameworthy because it blames love for ills while never defining love in the first place.

---

27. *Phaedrus*, 265b.
28. Scully, *Plato's Phaedrus*, 51.

9

Images of the Image of the Soul

a) Images of the Soul in the Palinode

THE SIGNIFICANCE OF SOCRATES's *HH* did not immediately occur to Phaedrus. Perhaps it never did. If it ever did, it was not until much later when Phaedrus returned to Athens.

Even then, the significance of Socrates's *HH* would not dawn on Phaedrus until Phaedrus engaged in some long and rigorous thinking; not only about the particulars of his discourse with Socrates, but about the very course of that discourse.

One of the effects of Plato's creative non-fiction is that the reader (or re-reader) has the advantage over the *dramatis personae* in the dialogue. In *Phaedrus*, at a crucial point, the reader can see how, within the closed world of the dialogue, Socrates offers Phaedrus the opportunity to conceive of the significance of the very course of the discourse, and therefore of Socrates's *HH* as well. Yet, Socrates almost has to call special attention to his *HH* precisely because it is a deed more than a speech. Phaedrus, a man obsessed with speeches, is not inclined to appreciate deeds.

To appreciate fully Socrates's *HH* in particular, Phaedrus needs to contemplate the imagery Socrates offers in the discourse, and more. Phaedrus needs to appreciate various images of that imagery. In sum, Phaedrus needs to consider how double-imaging itself has a message about the work Socrates was doing on Phaedrus's behalf.

The functional significance of Socrates's *HH* is that it spurs the discourse beyond the *L'/P'//P'/S'* dyad. To make the more seamless transition to the *PL*, Socrates's *HH* had to be something like and unlike *L'/P'* and

Who Is Phaedrus?

P'/S', which the *HH* succeeded, and like and unlike the *PL*, which the *HH* preceded.

Of *L'/P'* and *P'/S'*, Socrates says the two speeches were "really very funny . . . while they were saying nothing sound [or 'healthy', ὑγιὲς] or true."[1] In one sense, Socrates's *HH* is like *L'/P'//P'/S'*: it, too, is very funny, in part. Socrates did not mean a word of his suggestion that he had to halt his delivery of *P'/S'* lest he accost Phaedrus. Yet, on the serious side, Socrates's *HH* moves the action from the *L'/P'//P'/S'* dyad to its/their opposite, the *PL*. The *PL* addresses elevating madness, divine madness, not the silly, pseudo-divine madness of the nymphs under whose sway Socrates pretends to operate in the *HH*.

Socrates's *HH* involves, in itself, a *CO*, but without a violation of the principle of non-contradiction. In his *HH*, Socrates is a non-lover and lover at the same time, but in different respects. It was the "non-lover" of the merely sensuous that prevented Socrates from accosting Phaedrus; and, therewith, it was the "lover" of the divine in Socrates that propelled the discourse toward the *PL*: thus the movement of the discourse toward the appreciation of the true, the divine, and the eternal in the *PL*.

It was nigh impossible for Phaedrus to appreciate how Socrates's *HH* moved the action from *L'/P'//P'/S'* to an opposing discourse, the *PL*, without Socrates violating the principle of non-contradiction. Along with the fact that the principle of non-contradiction had never been promulgated as such, and as Phaedrus had never sufficiently engaged in dialectic (the condition for the very conception of the principle of non-contradiction in the first place) Socrates's actions and words that would impart the recognition of dialectic comprised the kind of instruction Phaedrus needed.

So, Socrates's *HH* does more than merely move the discourse. Socrates's *HH* has a crucial function relative to all three speeches that dominate the first half of *Phaedrus*. Socrates's *HH* is ultimately situated as a part of that which emerges as an image of the discourse; an image key to Phaedrus's ongoing tutorial in dialectic.

Many are familiar with the famous image of the human soul depicted in *Phaedrus*. A charioteer in a chariot supersedes a winged-horse dyad: one horse dark and unruly, the other horse light and obedient.

---

1. *Phaedrus*, 243a.

Images of the Image of the Soul

The Image of the Human Soul

Charioteer

↕

Chariot

↕

Dark, Unruly Pegasus ↔ Light, Obedient Pegasus

The obedient, noble Pegasus is always ready to forego mundane pleasures, and fly to the heavens' pinnacle where, hovering, below the level of the gods, the charioteer can engage in the sometimes troubled contemplation of Essences in the Essence Wheel. That contemplation is troubled at times because the wings of the winged horses are not always in tandem, the result being that the head of the charioteer cannot always rise to the same level as the Essence Wheel to behold the Essences with the consistency of a god.

To the extent to which the charioteer can maintain attention to the Essences in the Essence Wheel, he comes to appreciate Beauty especially. Beauty, in a sense, is the Essence of Essences, as it perpetually shines Truth through every other Essence. Hence, again, the subtitle of *Phaedrus*: *On the Beautiful: ethikos*.

The unruly, obstinate Pegasus, however, is preoccupied with mundane pleasures, especially sexual. It refuses, aggressively, to fly to the heights. That refusal on the part of the unruly horse to fly to the heights causes a rupture in the activity of the dyad of winged horses. One horse is always poised to fly to the heights; the other is happy merely to tramp about the earth in the pursuit of immediate gratification, especially sexual. It takes both winged horses flying in conjunction, and even then in conjunction with a charioteer who has grown wings of his own, after suffering pain to gain them, to fly off the earth to the heights to behold, again, the Essence Wheel.

Many see here another parallel with the *Republic*, especially Hackforth, who says it is "obvious that the charioteer with his two horses symbolizes the tripartite soul familiar to us in *Republic* IV."[2]

With minor qualifications, that is certainly true. In terms of the myth, the discord in the soul caused by the inability to harmonize money-love and honor-love causes, in turn, the whole soul to remain on the level of the mundane. The result is the deprivation of the charioteer's sublime

---

2. Hackforth, *Plato's Phaedrus*, 72.

contemplation of the Essence Wheel. That is the worst deprivation of all, being the deprivation of the soul's relationship with its ultimate whence as a thinking being.

The image of the human soul is compared and contrasted with another image of a soul in the *PL*, the soul of a god (in this case, Zeus, the signature god of *Phaedrus*):

The Image of the Divine Soul

Zeus

↕

Winged Chariot

↕

Noble Pegasus ↔ Noble Pegasus

The soul of Zeus is also portrayed as a charioteer superseding a winged-horse dyad. The difference between the soul of the god and the human soul, however, is that both of Zeus's winged horses are obedient and noble, and, remarkably, Zeus's very chariot is animated with wings. Even the god's chariot is ever-ready to fly to the height of heights.

With no mundane impediments, the god flies with ease to the height to behold the Essence Wheel. The human soul struggles. The human charioteer must rein in the dark Pegasus, lest that unruly horse tramp its way across the merely mundane plane seeking immediate satisfaction. More, even when the winged elements in the human soul are harmonized and take flight, the human soul still has to do the heavy lifting of the wingless chariot.

Socrates's image of the human soul serves to reveal the role of a very important phenomenon in *Phaedrus*: shame. When the dark horse hinders flight by pursuing immediate sexual gratification, it has a dyad of critics: "the other horse and the charioteer oppose all this with modesty and reason."[3] The noble horse and charioteer have a superior sense of shame. They know the cost of pursuing immediate and superficial satisfaction: the loss of contemplation of Essences, in which contemplation the human soul recoups its awareness of its likeness to a god.

The nobler elements in the human soul are ashamed when they fall short of that divine status. Via this imagery, Socrates locates genuine shame

---

3. *Phaedrus*, 256a.

Images of the Image of the Soul

in a domain relative to a divine standard. This is different from Phaedrus's sense of dishonor. Phaedrus, a Typhonic, *Schadenverbesserung eros* "lover," locates shame relative to Lysias's opinions or the latest fashion, far removed from the standards that are the Essences in the eternal, unchanging Essence Wheel.

Socrates's conception of an *eros* grounded in the love of wisdom, signified by the soul's concern for contemplation of Essences, would undermine the problematic shame *ethos* Phaedrus and his Typhonic friends embrace as a kind of civic religion. The Zeus-inspired lover, a wisdom-lover, does not shame his beloved for falling short of financial, physical, and sexual perfection. Socrates's view of love is expressed in the crucial line that always bears repeating. The true lover cares for the beloved "as if he were a god." The true lover, a lover of wisdom, is willing to suffer for the beloved, so the beloved may realize the beloved's divine nature: "And therefore it is just that the mind (*dianoia*) of the philosopher only has wings, for he is always, so far as he is able, in communion through memory with those things the communion with which causes the divine to be divine."[4] That which causes the divine to be divine is Beauty that even the gods love to behold, as Beauty shines truth through all of the other Essences.

When the dark horse dominates the desires, the soul, to that extent, is benighted. Such ignorance is the state of Phaedrus's soul when Phaedrus encounters Socrates in *Phaedrus*. Phaedrus's soul has been corrupted, and for a long time. Phaedrus's soul is stuck in pursuits motivated entirely by a problematic form of honor-love; problematic for many reasons, not the least of which is that his honor-love is really only a form of money-love.

In the *PL*, therefore, Socrates tries to call attention to the problems that arise when two dark-horse-dominated lovers meet: "ruled by a love of honor, probably, when they have been drinking, or in some other moment of carelessness, the two unruly horses, taking the souls off their guard, will bring them together and seize upon and accomplish that which is by the many accounted blissful; and when this has once been done, they continue the practice, but infrequently, since what they are doing is not approved by the whole mind."[5]

Socrates is being generous. Putting the best face on *Schadenverbesserung eros* that he can, Socrates suggests that Typhonic lovers like Phaedrus, not motivated by the love of wisdom, are "probably" motivated by some

4. Ibid., 249c.
5. Ibid., 256c.

Who Is Phaedrus?

sense of honor; but not necessarily. Phaedrus's only sense of honor-love, Typhonic love that shames the beloved into physical and sexual perfection, is really only a form of money-love, meaning money and everything money can buy: sex, improved appearance, social connection, etc. Phaedrus, with Lysias, personifies money-love dominated, superficial Athens.

Phaedrus only gives lip-service to the divine, if he recognizes it at all. That is why Socrates begins the *PL* with three accounts of divine madness (and closes the *PL* with a fourth), which three accounts are followed almost immediately by a "proof" of the inherent immortality of the soul: If "All Soul" (ψυχὴ πασα, or "the whole soul," singular) is always in motion, it must be self-moving; if "All Soul" is always self-moving it must have no agency outside itself; if "All Soul" has no agency outside itself, it must be uncreated. Therefore, if "All Soul" is uncreated, it is inherently immortal.[6] The argument here is not just that soul survives the demise of the body at death. This is an argument for the inherent immortality of the soul: that the soul exists even prior to its present embodiment because soul simply *cannot* not-be.

Plato knows this proof is problematic. The proof's problematic nature has been analyzed by various commentators from many angles.[7] One of the problems with the proof is that it is not clear what the reference to *psuche pasa* really intends. Does it refer to a single cosmic soul? Does "All Soul(s)" imply also all individual souls: rational, passionate, or vegetative? Another problem with the proof pertains to the question as to whether, and how, soul as such, which is not a body, can be said, *propter se*, to be in motion. Yet, the point of Socrates's delivery of this consciously problematic proof is to challenge Phaedrus to conceive of something not merely beyond the conditions of the mundane order, but indeed of something that has no genesis whatsoever.

Socrates is countering Phaedrus's view of the problematic whence promulgated in Phaedrus's speech from the *Symposium*. There Phaedrus argued that *eros* was, in a sense, its own prime origin. Yet, according to Phaedrus's other premises, *eros* was not at all its own prime origin. *Eros* was derivative of Earth, and Earth was derivative of Chaos.

So, as problematic as the *PL*'s proof of the inherent immortality of the soul may be, it is not absurd like Phaedrus's claims about *eros* in the

---

6. This is a summary statement of *Phaedrus*, 245c–d.
7. Sallis, *Being and Logos*, 136–49; Rhodes, *Eros, Wisdom, and Silence*, 476–81.

Symposium. The *PL*'s proof, while problematic, at least has a moral that matters relative to Phaedrus's problems. If the soul is inherently immortal, then a person is a god or is like a god. And if a person is a god or is like a god, then that person's lover should care for the beloved "as if he were a god," as Socrates has been saying all along. That is the moral about love that matters most to Socrates. That is why Socrates says the proof is not for the merely "clever," like Lysias, who scoff at the idea of suffering for the beloved.

Socrates surely wishes Phaedrus would challenge the *PL* proof of the inherent immortality of the soul. Yet, did Phaedrus have the wits to do so? The rub is this: to complain about the proof, Phaedrus would have to engage in dialectic. And that, above all, is what Socrates *wanted* Phaedrus to do. It would take dialectically-charged discernment for Phaedrus to realize how problematic Socrates's proof might (or might not) be and to realize how Lysias is not treating Phaedrus as if he were a god.

To complain about the proof, Phaedrus would have to admit he was arguing from a position borne of dialectic, from "collection and division." On the "collection" side, Phaedrus would have to admit that the condition for the possibility of a refutation of the proof lay in his dialectical conception that all souls, or "parts" of all souls, might be "collected" in the singular "All Soul." On the "division" side, to complain about the proof, Phaedrus would have to conceive of the first division of all, the first *CO* of all: the division of the metaphysical from the physical. Socrates says in the *PL*, after all, that he resorts to an image of the soul because the soul, not being a body, has no image. Socrates was all but hinting as to the way Phaedrus might object to the proof. Only upon the greatest division of all, the metaphysical from the physical as such, could Phaedrus object (like Aristotle does later) that soul *propter se* could not be in motion because it is not a body. But for Phaedrus to make that very objection, Phaedrus would have to acknowledge the metaphysical: and once even an iota of the metaphysical is admitted, then the otherwise thoroughgoing naturalist, Phaedrus, would have to admit the limits of his naturalist worldview.

Further, the proof of the inherent immortality of the soul intimates to Phaedrus a consequence of conceiving of an uncreated nature. If the subject, as it were, the soul, is inherently immortal, with no mundane origin, it would surely find ultimate satisfaction only in "objects" that are eternal. Thus the Essence Wheel in the *PL* where there is no "genesis" (γένεσις) in knowledge, or genesis of the "objects" of knowledge: "In the revolution it [the soul] beholds justice, temperance, and knowledge, not such knowledge as has a beginning [*genesis*] and varies as it is associated with one or another of the things we call realities, but that which abides in the real eternal absolute..."[8]

Thus, again, a kind of epistemological tether between the *Republic* and *Phaedrus*: In the *Republic*, *dianoia* is a kind of knowing that has a genesis. *Dianoia* is activated in the encounter with a CO in the sensuous order. So, in *Phaedrus*, ascending *dianoia* moves higher to *episteme* to note especially how the uncreated, imageless Essence *par excellence*, Beauty, shines Truth through all other imageless Essences. As Bruce Gottfried has said of the PL: "in Socrates's second speech, we are told that earthly beauty has the ability to inspire a lover of truth to divine madness because it is a closer likeness of true beauty. If a lover of truth combines this madness with temperance (*sophrosyne*), so that reason is not abandoned to appetite, then earthly beauty can act as an aid to memory. Perceived beauty does not lead to knowledge; it induces the act of *anamnesis*... which then leads to knowledge."[9]

Knowledge of Beauty is stressed in *Phaedrus* because Phaedrus's own *Symposium* speech tied *eros* to beauty. There, however, Phaedrus's sole concern was merely physical beauty. Socrates tries to move Phaedrus to the original: the operation of Beauty in the Essence Wheel. Phaedrus, corrupted, has all but removed himself from true Beauty in his preoccupation with physical beauty; mostly his own.

It would be easy for Socrates merely to moralize about Phaedrus's ignorance; but Socrates does not. Indeed, Socrates tries to spur Phaedrus to recognition of the divine even by suggesting, in the PL, that Phaedrus might find consolation from the gods for acting upon love in some sense of the word, even if not the noblest sense: "when they [dark-horse motivated lovers' souls] depart from the body they are not winged, to be sure, but their wings have begun to grow so that the madness of love brings them no small reward; for it is the law that those who have once begun their upward progress shall never again pass into darkness and the journey under the earth, but shall live a happy life in the light as they journey together..."[10]

In this portion of the PL in which Socrates displays patience with Phaedrus, it is clear that Socrates is the one who truly loves Phaedrus. Socrates is acting upon the fourth kind of divine madness delineated in the PL,

---

8. *Phaedrus*, 247d.
9. Gottfried, "Pan, the Cicadas, and Plato's Use of Myth in the *Phaedrus*," 189–90.
10. *Phaedrus*, 256d.

possession by a god, in this case Zeus, because it is said of Zeus-like lovers that "by persuasion and education they lead the beloved to the conduct and nature of the god, so far as each of them can do so; they exhibit no jealousy or meanness toward the loved one, but endeavor by every means in their power to lead him to the likeness of the god whom they honor."[11] Socrates, as Zeus-like lover, treats Phaedrus "as if he [Phaedrus] were a god." Lysias does not.

β) The Image Superseding the Palinode

This Zeus-like concern that Socrates has for Phaedrus returns us to Socrates's *HH* in which Zeus-like love was first made manifest: when Socrates refused to accost Phaedrus in the heat of the moment. That function of the *HH* brings us to the very image of the discourses in *Phaedrus*, an image of the image(s) of the soul.

Socrates has in mind an image of the discourses that Phaedrus should entertain. Consider how, almost immediately after the *PL*, Socrates pointedly tries to make Phaedrus aware of how the discourse proceeded. In one of the most crucial lines of the dialogue, Socrates suggests that Phaedrus observe how the discourses in the first half of *Phaedrus* made a transition from one opposite to another: "Here let us take up the point and see how the discourse succeeded in passing from blame to praise."[12] This line about the transition of the speeches from blame to praise is entirely ignored by many commentators, or addressed only minimally.[13]

It is especially remarkable that Hegel in particular passed over this almost literal appeal to "Observing Reason," to put the matter in terms of Hegel's own *Phenomenology of Spirit*. Thus my earlier criticism of Hegel's claim that the image of the soul in Plato's *Phaedrus* "teaches us nothing:"[14] In the closed world of *Phaedrus*, which is a very large world nonetheless, the image of the soul teaches us very much, both in and beyond itself.

The significance of the image of the soul, beyond itself, lies with lines such as Socrates's post-*PL* line about the procedure of the discourses. The structure of the relations of the discourses, a structure that includes Socrates's *HH*, is an image of the image of the soul:

11. Ibid., 253b.
12. Ibid., 265c.
13. Scully, *Plato's Phaedrus*, 52.
14. Cf. chapter 1, "Situating *Phaedrus*."

Who Is Phaedrus?

The Image of the Human Soul

Charioteer

↕

Chariot

↕

Dark, Unruly Pegasus ↔ Light, Obedient Pegasus

Hence:

The Image of the Discourses

PL

↕

Socrates's *HH*

↕

L'/P' ↔ *P'/S'*

When we consider that the image of the soul occurred in the *PL*, and the *PL* is the capital in the image of the discourses, an image of the image of the soul depicted in the *PL*, a new question emerges. Which comes first: the image of the discourses or the image of the soul?

Again we are to appreciate the significance of Socrates's *HH*. That *HH*, as something like and unlike both *L'/P'//P'/S'* and the *LP* was the transition between the mundane speeches about love and the sublime metaphysical speech about love. The structure of the discourse is such, then, that the triad of speeches resolves in an image that works as an image of the soul, which image appears in the very capital of the discourses, the *PL*.

Here we see Plato's ingenious synthesis of form and content in *Phaedrus*, a synthesis arguably without parallel in any other work of literature. The very course of the discourse that led to and included the *PL* was itself already a working image of the image of the soul presented in the *PL*. Phaedrus, of course, could not appreciate these dynamics in the moment. He did not note how, in the image of the soul, and in images of the image of the soul, he might see the very key to Socrates's Zeus-inspired labor on his behalf.

γ) The Stymied Image

Were Phaedrus more attuned to dialectic, he could more readily grasp that the image of the structure of the discourses, an image of the image of the soul in which the image of the soul appeared, was similar in structure to yet another image Phaedrus could conceive from the dramatic setting.

In the dialectically-charged images of the image of the soul, we see relations of identity and difference in each root. In the image of the human soul, the root was the identity and difference between the winged-horse dyad. In the image of the discourses, the root was the identity and difference between L'/P' and P'/S'. There are actually two other root-dyad relations to consider from the dialogue's very opening: one between Lysias and Phaedrus; another between Phaedrus and Socrates.

We have noted the various modes of identity and difference between Phaedrus and Lysias. Lysias and Phaedrus are alike as promoters of rhetoric. Yet, the most disturbing difference between Lysias and Phaedrus, that Phaedrus did not yet realize, is that while Lysias and Phaedrus are both Typhonic lovers, Lysias really is a virtually self-confessed non-lover (via no less than L'/P' itself), while Phaedrus really seems to love Lysias; or, at least, Phaedrus thinks he is in a Typhonic relationship with Lysias, equal competing with equal, when the reality is more that Lysias is using Phaedrus essentially as a boy in a pederasty relationship.

Similarly, *via* Plato's dramatic devices, we have seen how Phaedrus and Socrates were identical and different: both were lovers of speeches, if for very different reasons.

So, *per* an image of the image of the soul, and from awareness of the image of the discourse to which Socrates calls Phaedrus's attention, Phaedrus is supposed to see, *via* the dramatic setting and the recent action in his immediate whence, that Phaedrus's relationship with Lysias is flawed by way of a distorted, or aborted, image of the image of the soul.

The Stymied Image in the Dramatic Setting

Friendship in Zeus

↕

Olympieum (The Temple of Zeus)

X

Lysias ↔ Phaedrus

Who Is Phaedrus?

Lysias did not lead Phaedrus to the temple of Zeus where, as Socrates more than implies, Lysias and Phaedrus could, and should, engage in "a blessed chorus-dance . . . in Zeus's entourage."[15]

Thus the failure, X, in the image of the structure of the Lysias-Phaedrus relationship. Lysias did not lead Phaedrus up to the temple of Zeus to consecrate their love. So, Socrates had to lead Phaedrus to the temple in spirit, yet, via the opposite course, a descent away from the temple, all the way, in fact, outside the city. Socrates had to provide an ascent to the temple in the only way he could, and yet in the best way, in *logos*.

In this analysis of the images of the image of the soul, we can lend more precision to Zwicky's claim about *Phaedrus*: "The dialogue is not merely a statement of doctrine; it is an attempt to elucidate grounds for any thinking that aims at genuine understanding. Not only does it raise and attempt to respond to objections about its own theses regarding the roles of love, sex, rhetoric, and dialectic in the pursuit of a meaning-filled life: it attempts to display the roots of its own methodology—respect for myth and the practice of dialectic—so that we may begin to think through these questions, and Socrates' answers, for ourselves."[16] I would add that the *dianoetic* function within dialectic is also on display in *Phaedrus*, even if in a way Phaedrus cannot appreciate at once.

The images of the image of the soul reveal a peculiar "methodology" at work in *Phaedrus*. The image of the soul and the images of that image are not functions of cutesy poetry. They provide nothing less than a vehicle by which the titular figure might see a solution to his very personal, and profound, problems.

In the stymied image of the image of the soul, Phaedrus could see that, and how, Lysias did not lead Phaedrus in a way ascending. Socrates, descending, did.

---

15. *Phaedrus*, 250b.
16. Zwicky, "Philosophy as Dialogue with the Dead," 34.

10

Phaedrus
Inverse Cicada

α) Noon

As *Phaedrus* is famous for its two different halves, a consideration of its midpoint is a must.

The dialogue reaches its middle with an obvious metaphor for a midpoint: noon. It was "almost noon" when Socrates performed his *HH*.[1] By that timing in the dramatic particulars, Plato is offering a clever inversion. Socrates's mystery philosophy would compete with, and supersede, the mysteries of the city, even the impressive Eleusinian mysteries. So, Socrates's mystery philosophy emerges at noon, the antithesis to the setting of the Eleusinian mysteries that were held "at full moon," and likely midnight, as that is when Demeter went looking for the lost Kore.[2] In the present case, Socrates is saving or finding the lost boy/girl, Phaedrus.

If Socrates's *HH* is close to noon, the *PL* is the noon speech, making or marking the transition from the first half of the day to the second. So, what occurs as the day and dialogue move to the other half?

After the *PL*, Socrates recommends he and Phaedrus reflect on the three speeches: *L'/P'*, *P'/S'*, and the *PL*. There is a doubling in self-awareness at this time. Socrates and Phaedrus reflect upon whether or not they should reflect; but Socrates finally suggests he and Phaedrus continue their conversation. They should reflect on the transition from *L'/P'//P'/S'* to the *PL* lest

---

1. *Phaedrus*, 242a.
2. Zeruneith, *The Wooden Horse*, 95.

the cicadas above, messengers of the gods, consider Socrates and Phaedrus lazy. Socrates is avoiding shame. He does not want to be deemed a slavish soul, as only a slavish soul naps at "mid-day."[3]

For the second time in minutes Socrates aims to avoid shame. In his *HH*, Socrates was ashamed to deliver *P'/S'* any further because *P'/S'* was a speech that denigrated love. During noontime, Socrates would avoid shame once again. The cicadas, messengers of the gods, might give the gods a bad report about Socrates and Phaedrus if Socrates and Phaedrus proved derelict in their pursuit of wisdom and truth.

Socrates's noontime actions reveal the extent to which, and in what manner, Socrates exercised no mean amount of *philotimia*, love of honor. The flip-side of honor is shame; but Socrates makes manifest to Phaedrus, a self-proclaimed honor-lover, that Socrates's sense of honor-love is properly guided by Socrates's respect for the divine. Socrates's sense of honor-love is subordinate to his love of wisdom and that which Socrates associates with the divine, the eternal.

Socrates is also trying to instill more than a little self-reflection in Phaedrus. Socrates's reference to the myths of the cicadas fits, ironically, his reflection upon reflection.

β) The Cicada Transformation

The myth of the cicadas is very much about self-awareness, or a lack of self-awareness of being transformed. The myth of the cicadas is about transformation from one nature to another, yet the parties transformed were not even aware of their transformation.

In the myth, the cicadas were once humans, the first ever to hear music. They became so enamored of beauty they slipped into a state of extreme negligence: they forgot to eat and drink. Entirely distracted by beauty, those first humans to hear music shriveled up and became cicadas. They died and did not know it.

Socrates does not describe the pre-enchanted state of the first humans to hear music, and die. But their rapture is easy to imagine: persons going about their daily affairs in machine-like fashion; then comes the music, out of nowhere. An entire city comes to a standstill, gazing rapt into open air trying to visualize tones never heard before. Eventually those humans die

---

3. *Phaedrus*, 259a.

and do not know they have been transformed into cicadas, messengers of the gods.

Bruce Gottfried is right to criticize Hackforth for calling the myth of the cicadas merely "a charming little myth"; right again when he criticizes De Vries for referring to the myth as a merely "relaxing intermezzo."[4] The myth of the cicadas is *crucial* in the rather literal sense of the word crucial. The myth not only occurs at the crux of the dialogue, the myth poses the crux of the dialogue: Phaedrus is to emerge from this conversation transformed; as an inverse cicada. Phaedrus is to come to life, especially with his reflection on the first half of *Phaedrus*; but, unlike the cicadas, he is supposed to be aware of his transformation.

The radical transformation of the cicadas pertains to self-consciousness, or lack of it; a theme Phaedrus needs to hear. Phaedrus's realization of his transformation might occur only in the post-text, and long after his return to Athens. But the transformation of Phaedrus is supposed to occur; and perhaps in actual history, it did. Perhaps then, and only then, did Phaedrus become one of Plato's favorites.

So, what was the main moral of the myth of the cicadas?

In Ferrari's reading of *Phaedrus*, the myth of the cicadas has two morals, in a sense opposed.[5] On the one hand, a life lacking in beauty is not a properly human life. On the other hand, there is a cautionary moral to the myth. Those first humans to hear music became too enthralled; so much so they shriveled up and died. An obsession with beauty might invite self-destruction.

In Ferrari's reading, the myth seems to recommend moderation. But is that Socrates's ultimate point? If that is so, then Socrates is offering a partial affirmation of the prudential morals of the "common folk" he criticized when he criticized L'/P' for blaming love for so many modes of self-destruction. Surely that is not Socrates's final point about the myth.

γ) The Transformation of Phaedrus

The most important point of the myth is the point about self-awareness, or lack thereof. Phaedrus is supposed to come to see himself as an inverse cicada. Thanks to Socrates, Phaedrus is supposed to move from being dead, morally and intellectually, to alive, and know as much. In terms of

---

4. Bruce Gottfried, "Pan, the Cicadas, and Plato's Use of Myth in *Phaedrus*," 189.
5. Ferrari, *Listening to the Cicadas*, 26–30.

Who Is Phaedrus?

the myth, when Phaedrus returns to Athens this time, after his benign exile with Socrates, Phaedrus may not exactly be a messenger of the gods, but he is supposed to serve as the next best thing, a messenger of Socrates, the divine gift to Athens.

In light of a subtext of *Phaedrus*, the city-influencing function of pederasty, Socrates is serving as a different kind of *erastes* (as Alkibiades said of Socrates in the *Symposium*). Like any other *erastes*, Socrates would influence Athens indirectly through the young also; but in the case before him in *Phaedrus*, not through a youth, and not by the unusual practice of pederasty (which Socrates never practiced), but by the late de-corruption of a corrupted youth come of age, the inverse cicada, Phaedrus.

Plato invites us almost explicitly to view Phaedrus as an inverse cicada. Socrates claims outlandishly, for example, that the PL is something "no human poet" has ever sung before.[6] Like the cicadas, humans who had never heard music, Phaedrus would hear something the likes of which he had never heard. Then, thanks to Socrates, Phaedrus might come alive and not know it; not, at least, until the post-text, after Phaedrus returns to Athens, and maybe a long time after that. Phaedrus would come alive and see how paltry Athens was, especially an Athens dominated by democrats like Lysias and Epicrates.

Other elements of Plato's terms and text recommend this inverse cicada, coming-to-life conclusion. In the course of the dialogue, Phaedrus does not see, or certainly does not appreciate, the difference between dead-letter Lysias and living-speaking Socrates. The written word, at least in *Phaedrus*, is dead compared with the "living and breathing word" of the one who has knowledge in his soul.[7] In the second half of *Phaedrus*, Phaedrus is coming alive (or is supposed to be). But, as future inverse cicada, in the moment, Phaedrus was not fully aware of such.

Socrates knows this coming-alive phenomenon is supposed to happen. So, somewhat as the gods send the cicadas to mortals, at the end of the dialogue Socrates sends Phaedrus back to Athens to gauge who is engaging in the love of wisdom or beauty. Socrates sends Phaedrus back to Athens to address a triad: Homer, Solon, and Lysias, and everyone who practices the arts associated with these famous men.[8] Appropriate to the myth of the cicadas, the former two had been long dead, but Lysias is alive. Yet Lysias,

---

6. *Phaedrus*, 247c.
7. Ibid., 265a.
8. Ibid., 278b–c.

for Socrates, is essentially dead, while Homer and Solon are alive. Phaedrus is supposed to realize that he, Phaedrus, should die unto his "lover," Lysias, because Lysias is basically dead as a "non-lover."

Socrates's cicada myth was occasion for Phaedrus to reflect on how philosophically dead Phaedrus and Lysias were. When Phaedrus acknowledges he had never even heard of the myth of the cicadas, Socrates says something jolting: it was "improper for a lover of the Muses never to have heard of such things."[9]

When Socrates uses a term as loaded as "improper," with sexual connotations appropriate to the context of *Phaedrus*, one has to take note. Phaedrus had indeed been "improper" for much of his life, certainly in his participation in the *PEM* and probably in the *MH*. Socrates also thinks Phaedrus has an "improper" relationship with Lysias because Lysias is not a true lover, as Lysias is treating Phaedrus, a man, as if Phaedrus were just a boy in a pederasty relationship.

Socrates's accusation that it was "improper" that Phaedrus had never heard of the myth was to make Phaedrus self-aware of how "improper" Phaedrus had been in many ways.

Phaedrus, as improper muse-lover, is supposed to awaken to the discourse itself. When Socrates calls Phaedrus an improper muse-lover, Phaedrus is supposed to realize he has been simultaneously insulted and complimented. Phaedrus was called improper; and yet, given Socrates's earlier ranking of the best human souls, when Socrates called Phaedrus a muse-lover, Socrates was placing Phaedrus's soul in the highest rank: 1) a philosopher, or a lover of beauty or one of a musical and loving nature, as compared with 2) a law-abiding king, a military man, or a ruler, as compared with 3) a politician or man of business or a financier.

If a muse-lover is on a par with the Beauty-lover and philosopher, and Phaedrus has been placed there by Socrates himself, surely Phaedrus is supposed to ask himself: why would I, Phaedrus, assume an inferior status to Lysias, a "man of business," who is third on the list?

Here again is an appeal to Zeus. Recall Socrates saying he realized in this context he was going to have to talk business to some extent. In *Phaedrus*, Zeus is the bridge between philosopher and businessman. So, if Phaedrus could see some identity between himself, as muse-lover, and Lysias as businessman, it would be an identity realized in a friendship inspired by Zeus. With that realization, Phaedrus, as a kind of inverse cicada,

---

9. Ibid., 259b.

Who Is Phaedrus?

would be transformed. He would change from Typhonic, anti-Zeus lover, to Zeus-like lover who bases his honor-love in the love of wisdom, not the social honors dictated arbitrarily by democrat society.

So, the further question is this: does Phaedrus really fit in the top ranking of souls? If Phaedrus were a true lover of Beauty, he would not have fawned so absurdly over a speech as bad as *L'/P'*. That insipid fawning over *L'/P'* betrayed the fact that if Phaedrus was a lover of the Muses, he was a lousy lover indeed; "improper" at the very least.

When Socrates places Phaedrus in first place in the ranking of the souls that is the moment Phaedrus is to be transformed, even if Phaedrus did not know it. That status might occur to Phaedrus when Phaedrus returned to Athens to see that it was Socrates who placed Phaedrus in a higher position relative to Lysias than the position Phaedrus had assumed for himself relative to Lysias. As a Typhonic lover, Phaedrus had fancied himself an equal in competition with Lysias on the level of honor-love. That status, in Socrates's eyes, would be bad enough. Yet, Phaedrus was actually in a worse position relative to Lysias. Lysias had been treating Phaedrus like a mere boy in a pederasty relationship. Socrates inverts Phaedrus's status when he puts Phaedrus in the first rank of souls and makes Phaedrus Lysias's superior.

δ) The Typhonic Violation of Nature

When Socrates suggests that Phaedrus had indeed been "improper," that accusatory term was tame compared to another indirect reference to Phaedrus as one who:

> is not newly initiated, or who has been corrupted, [who] does not quickly rise from this world to that other world and to absolute beauty when he sees its namesake here, and so he does not revere it when he looks upon it, but gives himself up to pleasure and like a beast proceeds to lust and begetting; he makes license his companion and is not afraid or ashamed to pursue pleasure in violation of nature.[10]

Socrates delivers another very provocative phrase here: "violation of nature." Even beyond "improper," the phrase "violation of nature" could be taken as yet another of the age-old criticisms of homosexuality.

10. *Phaedrus*, 251a.

Socrates would not resort to such a seemingly common critique without some greater aim. Phaedrus is supposed to be jolted, and he is ultimately to realize that while Socrates is not denigrating Phaedrus for his homosexuality, Socrates is recommending a "simple," probably ascetic, life for Phaedrus.

Yet, Socrates has to jolt his audience at times. As Marina McCoy has stated of Socrates's "method" more broadly: ". . . Socrates's questions are sometimes designed to get his interlocutors to experience certain emotions, such as shame or confusion. . . . Socrates's practice suggests that certain sorts of emotional or thumotic state, such as shame, self-doubt, and confusion, are part of what it means to be in a state of greater self-knowledge. . . . These non-logical dimensions to Socratic questioning are crucial because Socrates is interested not only in how to *do* philosophy but how to *be* a philosopher."[11]

Socrates suggests that Phaedrus's *Schadenverbesserung eros* relationship with Lysias is a "violation of nature." Yet, Socrates means more by the phrase "violation of nature" than someone speaking like the "common folk." Socrates uses the terms "improper" and "violation of nature"—usual condemnations of homosexuality—to stun Phaedrus into at least a new mode of self-reflection.

Yet, Socrates was no mere moralizer. Given the phrase "violation of nature," it is important to recall another reference by Socrates to "nature" in the *PL*. There "nature" had a narrow sense relative mainly to the Essence Wheel. Socrates declared that it was a "law of destiny" that the human soul traverse the limits of the mundane plane and ascend to engage in the heavenly contemplation of Essences.[12] While Socrates clearly deemed both pederasty and *Schadenverbesserung eros* shameful and problematic, the real violation of nature Socrates had in mind was the violation of nature relative to dialectic. Dialectic is natural, and necessary, for an inherently immortal soul to return to a state like that when it beheld the eternal Essence Wheel. Phaedrus's lack of attention to dialectic was a violation of nature. According to Socrates, a rational soul would deem dialectic the first law of nature, as without it there is no reason. A proper lover of speeches or anything else, would first love what is truly natural, dialectic, the very means to systematic thought in the first place.

---

11. McCoy, *Plato on the Rhetoric of Philosophers and Sophists*, 84.
12. *Phaedrus*, 248c.

Who Is Phaedrus?

The notion that dialectic is natural is difficult to fathom, as dialectic seems artificial, especially to those weaned on so many linguistic artifices concocted by sophists and rhetoricians. Yet, the numerous instances of *CO* in *Phaedrus* anticipate one of the classic questions associated later in the history of philosophy with Hegelian dialectic: how can a person fully note the work and fruits of dialectic while enmeshed in them?[13] Such a question has made Hegel's "Preface" to the *Phenomenology of Spirit* almost a study unto itself, as *per* Derrida.[14] It is remarkable that Hegel in particular missed a similar quandary in Plato. But many commentators, with more time and distance to observe the same than even Hegel had, have missed this issue issuing from *Phaedrus*.

Socrates realizes that persons, enmeshed in so many confounding particulars that life brings, have a difficult time with dialectical discernment. So, sometimes Socrates has to shock them out of their confused immediacy. It should not be shocking to see Socrates use a combination of provocation and sublimity to get Phaedrus to focus. To quote Russell Bentley, Socrates operates on the premise that there is "an imperative to be self-critical through interaction with others."[15] Socrates knew that the vain and valetudinarian Phaedrus had little capacity for self-critique.

To quote Bentley further: "we should read Socrates's commitment to self-knowledge as more than a Delphic commandment. Knowing oneself is necessarily an exercise in self-reflection and, ultimately, self-transformation."[16] Phaedrus, however, resists transformation.

Ian Leask provides insight into Phaedrus's resistance to personal transformation. In his analysis of the many roles of statues in *Phaedrus*, Leask highlights a key moment before Socrates delivers P'/S'. After Phaedrus challenges Socrates to deliver a speech superior to L'/P', Phaedrus volunteers that if Socrates is able to deliver a speech that does not merely borrow the thesis of Lysias's speech but surpasses it in every way, then "Phaedrus will follow the *archontes* and dedicate statues of both Socrates and himself."[17]

According to Leask, this is a peripheral reference to Solon's moral-political reforms. (Recall that Socrates, knowing Solon is dead, sends

13. Hegel, *Phänomenologie des Geistes*, 9–59.
14. See Hyland's critique of Derrida in *Questioning Platonism*, 86–122.
15. Bentley, "On Plato's Phaedrus," 230.
16. Ibid., 247.
17. Leask, "Statuary Presence," 97.

Phaedrus

Phaedrus back to Athens to address Solon.) Solon commanded that if any of the *archontes*, chief magistrates, were to transgress any of the laws of the state, they would have to do penance by dedicating a golden statue at Delphi. In a twist on the penance-statue phenomenon, if Socrates were to surpass Lysias, Phaedrus would place two statues as an act of penance, one to honor Socrates and another of Phaedrus, presumably inferior, to call shame upon Phaedrus's reputation. (Is Plato informing us here that the statue of Socrates erected in Athens after his death, and after the voluntary resignation of the democrats, was funded in part or in whole by the eventually transformed Phaedrus or Phaedrus's family?)

Leask observes the peculiar mixture of knowledge and ignorance in Phaedrus's offering to build two statues thusly. In the competition in rhetoric between Socrates, the dirt-poor aristocrat, and Lysias, the wealthy democrat, Phaedrus does not really want Socrates to win: "Phaedrus has, unthinkingly, delineated the broader political movement—from Solonic virtue and *sophrosyne* to Cypselidean *hybris*. In doing so, he betrays the degenerate lineage of sophistry."[18]

As it became clear that Socrates would not substantially alter the thesis of *L'/P'* in *P'/S'*, Phaedrus was relieved; considerably. Leask acutely sees the cause of Phaedrus's relief in that moment: Phaedrus was spared some disabuse regarding Lysias.

We can take Leask's insight a step or two further. Phaedrus, the honor-lover, does not want to lose. Also, Phaedrus would actually celebrate if Socrates could not both duplicate and transform *L'/P'* because then Phaedrus would not have to transform himself into something different.

Yet, quite soon, even in the first half of *Phaedrus*, Socrates would lay the basis for the transformation of *L'/P'* and therefore the transformation of Phaedrus. Socrates's *HH* would repudiate the thesis of *L'/P'* and move the discourse to the *PL*, the antithesis of *L'/P'*.

Phaedrus, corrupted and therefore not aware of any need for transformation, needed Socrates to do Phaedrus's transforming for him. Only later, in the post-text, might it dawn on Phaedrus, as inverse cicada, that he had participated in a rather remarkable violation of nature indeed: he would come to life and not initially know it.

---

18. Leask, "Statutary Presence: *Phaedrus* 235d–236b," 98.

11

Confounding Rhetoric

a) Phaedrus the Artless

SOCRATES'S EMPHASIS ON DIALECTIC in *Phaedrus* bears repeating. Socrates himself, in effect, repeats it. There are suggestions of the priority of dialectic to all other arts in the first half of *Phaedrus* and expressions of the priority of dialectic in the second half. The point relative to Phaedrus's interests is that if rhetoric were an art, then Phaedrus should become attuned to dialectic, the fundamental science as the means by which almost any art is mastered. Heidegger has "nicely summed up," as Hyland says, the Platonic issue of dialectic's priority over rhetoric in this case:

> In *Phaedrus*, Plato does not retain the negative attitude toward rhetoric expressed in the *Gorgias*. We must keep in mind that Plato does not intend to develop a rhetoric, as Aristotle did later. And indeed, it is not simply that Plato does not in fact care to do so, but he even considers it unnecessary, since dialectic occupies a different position within his concept of science than it will later for Aristotle. Plato sees his dialectic as the only fundamental science, such that in his opinion all other tasks, even those of rhetoric, are discharged in it.[1]

Actually, Heidegger is a bit generous here. In *Phaedrus*, Socrates is still hesitant to say unconditionally good things about rhetoric. The most affirmative thing he says about rhetoric, really, is that it might function as "soul-leading." But that leading could be misleading.

---

1. Hyland, *Questioning Platonism*, 49.

Phaedrus, of course, woefully ignorant about dialectic, is also therefore ignorant about rhetoric itself and its status as an art, or non-art. Early in *Phaedrus*, via a play on one word in particular, Plato humorously addresses Phaedrus's ignorance of the status of rhetoric. Responding to Phaedrus's excessive fawning over *L'/P'*, Socrates says: Θειός γ᾽ εἶ περὶ τοὺς λόγους ὦ Φαῖδρε καὶ ἀτεχνῶς θαυμάσιος.[2] Fowler translates this line: "Phaedrus, you are simply a superhuman wonder as regards discourses!" This is not a bad translation. But there is a telling pun in the Greek no translator can easily pose.

The pun lies with the word ἀτεχνῶς which can mean "simply" or "utterly." Yet, ἀτεχνῶς also resonates like ἄτεχνος, a term Socrates uses in the context of discussing rhetoric explicitly, which suggests "artless."[3] By the pun, Socrates is saying that Phaedrus is an "utter" wonder given Phaedrus's ability to prompt speeches from almost any source; and Socrates is saying Phaedrus is an "artless" wonder. Phaedrus, in spite of his obsession with speeches, and despite having begun to teach rhetoric side-by-side with Lysias, remains ignorant as to rhetoric's very status as an art.

The play on ἀτεχνῶς/ἄτεχνος in the first half of *Phaedrus* anticipates the discussion of rhetoric in the second half. That earlier play on words anticipates another play on essentially the same word regarding rhetoric. The later play on words relates to rhetoricians' attempts to codify rules of rhetoric in "manuals" (τέχνας) or "technique books."[4] Socrates's main criticism of such manual writers is that such "artists" do not present, prior to the specifics of their "art," a body of thought that justifies their claim to any kind of systematic knowledge in the first place. These pseudo-artists cannot name the "necessary preliminaries" of their "art" because they do not consciously exercise dialectic; or if they do exercise dialectic, even though they may not know the name, they do not call attention to their knowledge of dialectic because to do so would only serve to expose their sophistry.

One of the crucial and most complex parts of *Phaedrus* therefore comes when Socrates questions the nature and worth of rhetoric "manuals" (τέχνας), none of which is well-grounded. When it comes time to entertain discourse about Phaedrus's favorite entertainment, speechifying, or rhetoric, Socrates reveals that he does not take rhetoric as an art seriously except to the extent to which it can damage: "When the orator (ὁ ῥητορικὸς) who

---

2. *Phaedrus*, 242a.
3. Ibid., 260c.
4. Ibid., 261b.

Who Is Phaedrus?

does not know what good and evil are undertakes to persuade a city which is equally ignorant . . . what harvest do you suppose his oratory will reap thereafter from the seed he has sown?"[5]

In brief and in sum, Socrates tries to impress upon Phaedrus the point that without an underlying love of wisdom, philosophy, Phaedrus will never be able to speak well about anything. Socrates says as much literally, if in a playful prayer to the powers in the grove. The prayer is playful because he calls upon divinities to "persuade" Phaedrus (by some kind of divine rhetoric with Socrates as the medium?) that unless Phaedrus pays attention to "philosophy, he will never be able to speak properly about anything."[6]

What ensues is Socrates's presentation of a rather absurdly complicated list of arts relative to speech. This list is presented as a way to "examine," as Phaedrus himself says, the hypothetical arguments that would make the case that rhetoric is not an art. This procedure comes after Socrates, playfully again, speaks for the "art of speaking."[7] Knowing she is about to undergo judgment, the art of speaking tries to defend herself in light of the fact that there have been so many bad and deceptive speeches delivered from perpetuity. The art of speaking says it is not her fault; she compels no one to speak without knowing truth first.

Socrates is exceptionally playful further when he says: "'I seem' (δοκω) to hear some arguments approaching and protesting that she [the art of speaking] is lying and is not an art but a 'craft devoid of art' (ἄτεχνος τριβή)."[8] This reference to seeming, as distinct from appearing, (how distinct?!) will come into play quite soon in the discourse when Socrates refers to how public assembly speaking can make things "seem" (δοκειν). In that context, Socrates omits any reference to public assembly speaking as an art because, in essence, Phaedrus, who thinks there is such an art, clumsily omits any commitment that such speaking actually is an art. As we will see, that is, Socrates presents some confounding challenges about rhetoric that Phaedrus would be incapable of answering.

Socrates then proceeds to a rather ridiculous treatment of rhetoric, the idea being that Phaedrus, who does not consciously engage in dialectic or philosophy, does not stop to consider sufficiently, or well at all, how

5. Ibid., 260c.
6. Ibid., 261a.
7. Ibid., 260d.
8. Ibid., 260e.

quickly the discussion of rhetoric degenerates into one confusion after another because rhetoricians are not grounded in dialectic.

In the engagement of the question as to whether or not rhetoric is an art, Socrates offers his quick definition of rhetoric as "soul-leading with words."[9] Then Socrates proceeds to astonish Phaedrus by claiming that, whatever else rhetoric is, it may be employed everywhere: not just in courts or public assemblies, but even in private.

Phaedrus volunteers that he was unaware that rhetoric extended even into the realm of the private. This would explain, accordingly, why Phaedrus was not on his guard when he was reading *L'/P'*. On the one hand, Phaedrus did not think of the written word alone as a case of rhetoric, and on the other hand, Phaedrus did not realize that the content of *L'/P'* might apply to his own private life. Phaedrus did not realize that *L'/P'*, a speech in praise of the non-lover, was telling Phaedrus to his face that his lover, Lysias, was a non-lover and did not love Phaedrus.

Phaedrus proceeds, then, actually unwittingly, to engage in a division of rhetoric broadly defined as "soul leading with words." Phaedrus always thought there were two subsidiary arts that intersect: a "writing and speaking art for courts" (περὶ τὰς δίκας λέγεταί τε καὶ γράφεται τέχνηι) distinct from a "speaking [the term 'art' omitted and therefore only implied] for public-assemblies" (λέγεται δὲ καὶ περὶ δημηγορίας).[10]

What Phaedrus does not realize is that, in his very wording, he does not repeat the word τεχνηι in the second clause in his distinction. Phaedrus merely implies that rhetoric is an art. By the omission, however, Phaedrus is actually introducing into the conversation the opposite of that which he would defend. His intention would be that rhetoric is an art; but his wording, operating only with the implication, does not make manifest that public assembly speaking is anything more than just speaking. He, himself, is allowing that a branch of the art of speaking is somehow not an art.

What we see here, applied to Phaedrus, is an instance of that to which Socrates will refer quite soon in this context: "He who is to deceive another and not be deceived himself must know accurately the similarity and dissimilarity between things."[11] Left to his own devices, and, of course, without dialectic, Phaedrus renders in speech, and about speech, the very opposite of his operating premise.

9. Ibid., 261a.
10. Ibid., 261b.
11. Ibid., 262a.

Who Is Phaedrus?

The discourse becomes even more complicated. Given the limited scope Phaedrus has in mind for rhetoric, courts and public assemblies, Socrates assumes that Phaedrus makes that problematic and limited distinction because Phaedrus has only heard of the "manuals of the audible word" (τέχνας ... περὶ λόγων ἀκήκοας) composed by Nestor and Odysseus, but not "that by Palamedes" (τῶν δὲ Παλαμήδους).[12] Phaedrus concedes he has not heard of the manuals by Nestor and Odysseus, but infers those names may be disguises for names he does know: Gorgias, and Thrasymachus and Theodorus (paired) respectively.

Clouding the issue further, yet clarifying some by qualification, Socrates acknowledges he might be using those very disguises Phaedrus notes. Yet, Socrates states: "Perhaps ... but never mind them."[13] But what is Socrates dismissing or qualifying? Overall, he is not concerned with the issue of disguises at this point; not, at least, relative to those areas in which Phaedrus thought rhetoric applied exclusively (namely, court speech and speaking in public assemblies). Yet, Socrates proceeds at once to narrow the question as to what people do in lawsuits in courts; never mind, for the moment, public assembly speaking.

Socrates proceeds to ask a, well, rhetorical question relative to the narrower topic of speaking in courts: what do the "contenders" (ἀντι-δικοι) in a lawsuit do? They obviously "contend in speech" (ἀντι-λεγουσιν). Those terms really define themselves, as does the obvious element about which they contend: the just versus the unjust.

Then Socrates uses language that makes things tricky again, tricky to the point of the ridiculous. Socrates would reveal to Phaedrus how convoluted the issue of rhetoric is without an understanding of truth in the first place.

Relative to court speech, Socrates refers to ὁ τέχνηι, which could mean either "the one proceeding by way of the art" or "the one proceeding by use of the manual." There is a lack of clarity in this duality, especially as in this case Socrates does not explicitly refer to the art of "speaking." Socrates merely implies he is referring to an art, any art it seems, by use of a word, τέχνηι, that could mean indeed "by the art" or "by the manual."

Assuming there is such an "art" or "manual use" for this ability "to make the just appear at one time to the same person at another time unjust,"

---

12. Ibid., 261b–c.
13. Ibid., 261c.

Confounding Rhetoric

there is a perplexity in this duality that Phaedrus himself actually introduced.[14] In Phaedrus's own terms, there is really a dyadic art for courts: a writing and speaking art; or writing/speaking art; or some such. But what is it? The question Socrates exposes but does not actually express is a question that would destroy Phaedrus's notion that there is a clear art is this case. Is there one art or two?

If there are two arts, or one dyadic art, in court speaking, are they both operative at the same time, in the same way, and in the same respect? Or is the writing element prior to the spoken? Or, does one proceed "by the manual" so as then to proceed "by the speaking art?" Or, is it that the manual is composed by virtue of a study of artistic speeches? If that is the case, is the writing part really an art, or just a way to inventory? (That question is what seems to drive the tedious tally of rhetorical devices later; a mostly uninformative tally.[15]) Phaedrus cannot concentrate enough to answer, and the damage to the claim that rhetoric is an art is all but done already. Yet, Socrates continues his intentionally confounding inquiry.

Socrates moves to the issue of public assembly speaking and its nature. In Phaedrus's own clumsy wording previously, Phaedrus merely implied there was an art involved in public assembly speaking. He did not expressly use the word "art," or a variation of it. Likewise, here Socrates does not refer to an art when he raises the question as to the nature of public assembly speaking. He simply addresses the nature and content of such speaking: such a speaker will, at one time, make that which seems good to the city at another time seem "the opposite."

Even though it is left to the reader to see as much, here, again, Socrates is being both awkward and picayune for a reason: to expose to Phaedrus even further the myriad of confusions rhetoric seems to entail when there is no prior dialectical treatment of it.

For one, when, during the discussion of the nature of public speaking, Socrates refers merely to the "good" and its "opposite," his very lack of clarity with the word "opposite" makes his case about the confounding nature of rhetoric. Phaedrus does not dispute Socrates's description of public assembly speaking here. But what, for Phaedrus, or the art of rhetoric, is the opposite of the good? Evil? Bad? Corrupt? It is unclear, and surely Phaedrus, *qua* rhetorician, would have no immediate and obvious answer.

---

14. Ibid., 261c–d.
15. Ibid., 267a–e.

Who Is Phaedrus?

Phaedrus lets Socrates's premise pass; but the premise cries out for clarity, and it is not obvious that Phaedrus, *qua* rhetorician, could offer any. Indeed, perhaps that is the very point: the rhetorician may be entirely pleased with an obtuse premise.

To complicate matters further, and therefore to challenge Phaedrus's belief that rhetoric is an art even more, Socrates notes that in the use of speech in courts, the "art" there, if it was one, (or perhaps it was just the use of a manual?), was such as to be able "to make [the just] appear" (ποιήσει φανηναι) unjust. Socrates is showing Phaedrus how ridiculously obtuse Phaedrus would appear, or actually be, were Phaedrus really to pursue even more the argument that rhetoric is an art because then Phaedrus, by the very terms to which he has agreed, would have to explain the difference between "seeming" and "appearing." That is, in courts the issue appears to be making things "appear" (φανηναι) just or unjust, whereas in public assembly speaking the aim is to make the good "seem" (δοκειν) to the city at one time good and at another time the opposite.

Will, or can, Phaedrus really establish, in artistic detail, the difference between "seeming" and "appearing"? And will, or can, Phaedrus even begin to explain why "appearing" more properly applies to issues in courts, and why "seeming" more properly applies to speeches in public assemblies? If the rhetorician is really supposed to be able to address, with all artistic clarity, every subject possible in courts or public assemblies, how does the rhetorician begin with the first step of all, distinguishing "appearing" from "seeming"?

This appearing/seeming perplexity would be baffling enough to explain; yet, Socrates complicates the topic even further.

When Socrates refers to "the Eleatic Palamedes"—who is almost certainly assumed to be Zeno, and who apparently proceeded talking "by the art" (τέχνηι) (or by the manual?!), in such a way that the same things "appear" (φαίνεσθαι) to his hearers "to be like and unlike, one and many, in motion and stationary"—Socrates is expanding the field of references for rhetoric, and therefore increasing the areas that Phaedrus, *qua* rhetorician, would have to explain.[16] So, if Phaedrus wants to pursue rhetoric, or the art of speaking, this far, he will find himself in areas that philosophy would handle: ontology, epistemology, metaphysics, etc.

Yet, that obvious point aside, *qua* rhetorician, Phaedrus would have to answer even more, for example: why is the issue of "seeming" (δοκειν)

---

16. Ibid., 261d.

unique to issues in public assembly speaking? Also, why is "appearing" (φαίνω) common to both writing/speaking for courts, and ontology/epistemology/metaphysics, but not a function of public assembly speaking? Moreover, the hilarious Socrates, who is about to move the discourse to the issue of "resemblances," is challenging rhetoricians to explain if "seeming" only seems to be different from "appearing" or if it really is so.

It seems that Socrates's challenges, albeit unspoken in this context, could not get more bizarre; but they do. Given the terms used here by Socrates, and assumed by Phaedrus, the rhetorician would also have to explain how and why there is also a subtle difference in the kind of appearing that happens in speeches for courts and speeches for ontology. In the former, that is, the one who has the art has an almost aggressive undertaking: he "makes" the unjust appear just, and *vice versa*. Yet, somehow, by contrast, the use of the art (the same art?) by Zeno is such that the same things, apparently of themselves, "appear" (φαίνεσθαι) to the hearers to be opposites without being "made" to appear so. Can Phaedrus explain this difference?

Socrates then continues to pseudo-clarify. There would apparently be, somehow, one something, "antilogic" (ἀντιλογικὴ), that, "if it is an art at all," would somehow be one and yet do triple duty in court-speaking, public assembly speaking, and ontology. Moreover, in that triple duty, antilogic would have a dual function that always had to do with resemblances: a) to produce a resemblance between all things in which a resemblance can be made; and b) to reveal resemblances produced and disguised by others. How many products of these variables are there?

Surely this is not what Phaedrus intended in the effort to establish that rhetoric is an art. Indeed, at this point Phaedrus finally admits he is flummoxed: "What do you mean by that?" The time for Phaedrus to ask that question was well before Socrates managed to go so far from, or with, the original issue: whether or not rhetoric is an art. In this absurd course, during and after which Phaedrus was supposed to be flummoxed, and he was, Socrates is clearly showing Phaedrus that Socrates does not think rhetoric is an art; and if it is an art, rhetoric still gains whatever clarity it has or might have only by virtue of dialectic.

Thus the clincher, not only for this particular part of *Phaedrus* but essentially for the remainder of the second half that addresses rhetoric in particular: when Socrates began with rhetoric, which is allegedly the art of persuasion, did he not actually end with an art that is the opposite?

With what art does Socrates here terminate? It is the art of a) producing resemblances, and b) exposing resemblances. Is this strange two-fold art pertaining to resemblances, not really, in effect, the art of dissuasion? That is, in producing a resemblance, is not the producer in some sense dissuading the audience from, or distracting the audience from, the original? And in exposing a resemblance, is not the revealer dissuading the audience from, or distracting the audience from, the copy or image? So, all told, is rhetoric—allegedly the art of persuasion—not also its own opposite, the art of dissuasion? Or is rhetoric an inevitably dyadic or dianoetic art?

Here we see Plato the poet generate yet another of those remarkable moments in which the action of the dialogue is reflected in the discourse and *vice versa*, or what Polansky calls the mirroring of discourse and action: "In nearly all the dialogues, Plato manages to contrive the conversation such that what the characters are arguing about connects directly to their own conversational situation. Where this occurs the drama of the dialogue enacts exactly what the interlocutors are inquiring about, so the matters at issue are displayed as well as discussed. The conversation may accomplish in deed (*ergon*) through action, what is sought in words (*logos*)."[17]

Here, the reflexivity is such that Socrates proceeds at once to address the phenomenon of making "a transition by small steps from a thing to its opposite," and that is precisely what Socrates has done by moving the discourse through all types of arts of speaking, beginning with the art of persuasion, and ending by degrees with the art of dissuasion.[18] Further, this demonstrates Socrates's position that, to the extent to which rhetoric might be an art, rhetoric would owe its basis to dialectic. That is, Socrates can achieve this dianoetic feat of antilogic, performed in discourse about rhetoric itself, precisely because he possesses that which even supersedes antilogic, dialectic.

β) Countering Zeno and Lysias

In the foregoing, Socrates did not deny he might be using disguises for certain figures. For all of his obscurity on those points, he did at least isolate where his focus was, if negatively. For the discussion of rhetoric initially at least, he dismissed all of the figures originally mentioned other than the

---

17. Polansky, *Philosophy and Knowledge*, 22.
18. *Phaedrus*, 262a.

Confounding Rhetoric

Eleatic Palamedes, whom he mentioned soon after he mentioned mere Palamedes. We have then, at least, a Palamedes dyad.

The assumption that the Eleatic Palamedes is a moniker for Zeno has been the assumption of commentators for centuries, apart from "negligible exceptions" such as the position of Nietzsche who thinks the Platonic text should have read Ελαιτικον instead of Ελεατικον, thus suggesting the reference was to Alcidamas, since Quintillian insists there is a reference to Alcidamas in *Phaedrus*.[19] Yet, while it is possible that there is a reference to both Alcidamas and Zeno by the reference to the Eleatic Palamedes, it is hard to deny that the Eleatic Palamedes is supposed to be Zeno, given the dichotomies mentioned (motion *versus* rest, etc.) and the association of those dichotomies with Parmenides and therefore Zeno. More, as Vlastos has argued, Plato does not hesitate to couple Parmenides and Zeno: "Parmenides, in his arguments for monism, and Zeno, in his arguments against pluralism, were maintaining 'virtually the same thing;'"[20] and "in the opening lines of the *Sophist* . . . Plato couples Zeno's name with that of Parmenides for the purpose of identifying the philosophical group with which the Stranger has had friendly association."[21]

Our previous analysis bore out the notion that the highest form of rhetoric might be "antilogic." That analysis confirms Vlastos's claim, and those of others, that Zeno seems to Socrates to be a promoter of "*antilogic*; a mode of philosophical debate in which antithetical positions are held by the participants in an exchange of questions and answers . . . to expose contradictions in the position of the adversary and cause him to reject his own position or to accept both his and the other person's position."[22] Cornford concludes that Socrates considers Zeno a "mere sophist," an *antilogikos* to be classified "with the demagogue and the forensic orator, who can make the same action seem right or wrong as they please."[23]

It is difficult to pinpoint the tenor of Socrates's criticism of Zeno on this front, if in fact there are degrees. Vlastos, for his part, does not find the Socratic disdain for Zeno that Cornford finds. Vlastos does agree with Cornford, however, that Socrates considers Zeno, in the sum of things, an antilogician. But Vlastos argues further that there is nothing in Plato's other

---

19. Dušanić, "Alcidamas of Elaea in Plato's *Phaedrus*," 349.
20. Vlastos, "Plato's Testimony Concerning Zeno of Elea," 137.
21. Ibid., 153.
22. Barrett, *The Sophists*, 56.
23. Vlastos, "Plato's Testimony Concerning Zeno of Elea," 153.

work—for example, the *Sophist*—that suggests that Socrates had deep disdain for Zeno.

Vlastos concludes further that if Socrates were to label Zeno an antilogician that would not necessarily mean Socrates considered Zeno a rank sophist. Socrates may have regarded Zeno a promoter of "an honest, though small-minded and unproductive, species of philosophical debate."[24] The problem is that we do not know precisely the sources by which Plato knew Zeno. We tend to identify all of Zeno's thought with paradox; but there must have been more that Plato knew. It is probably more accurate to say, at least relative to *Phaedrus*, that any vitriol Cornford finds in Socrates for Zeno more properly applies to Alkidamas, student of Gorgias.

Further, we have to consider the suggestion from Aristotle that Zeno was the inventor of the dialectical method.[25] While Socrates surely saw his own treatment of dialectic as a radical improvement over what Zeno meant by the term dialectic, *Phaedrus* presents us in part with a lover's quarrel over dialectic. Socrates sees dialectic as the divine science, and therefore apparently playfully balks at even using the term dialectic because: a) "only God knows" if that is the right term for the most fundamental mode of thinking; and b) the term may have had currency in the residual influence of Zeno.

Here Vlastos's reference to antilogic as an unproductive mode of discourse applies well. What Zeno called "dialectic" was mere antilogic that left the listener suspended between two sides of an issue. Thus my emphasis on Socrates's summary critique of Phaedrus as *epamphoterious*, "torn between two ways": Phaedrus was not alone in always being *epamphoterious*. Any and all of the "hearers" of the antilogician Zeno became, by the design of the rhetorician himself, *epamphoterious*. Socratic dialectic, that must weigh so many *CO* in its course, must seem like antilogic along the way. Socratic dialectic, however, is "productive" in the end. It takes a direction and leads to definitions and/or discernment of similarities and dissimilarities, of identities and differences, between and among multiplicities, triads, and dyads.

On the whole, it seems Socrates admired Zeno for at least one reason: for being capable of any form of philosophical discourse at all in the daunting wake of Parmenides. The only philosophical course of action after Parmenides that would defend Parmenides almost had to be negative: there

---

24. Ibid., 154.
25. Barrett, *The Sophists*, 56.

was little or nothing one could say concerning particulars to promote Parmenidean metaphysical monism. After Parmenides's sublime emphasis on Being, all that seemed left to Parmenideans was the role of critic; pluralism critic.

Yet, more, for Socrates life extends beyond courts and politics. Phaedrus's training in the art of contention in speech should lead him to consider what is problematic about the art of contention in speech in the broadest issue of all, ontology itself: thus Socrates's reference to the "Eleatic Palamedes" who had mastered the way to confound others about basics: the like *versus* the unlike; the one *versus* the many; rest *versus* motion.

Phaedrus was to appreciate especially how Socrates's critique of Zeno was hiding in plain sight. According to one Zeno paradox, the "racecourse," no complete transition from one point to a goal is possible because the mover "cannot reach the end of the course until reaching the halfway point; but the distance from the beginning to the half-way point can also be divided in half, [etc.]"; and something "similar" is the case in the "Achilles" paradox, in which the swifter Achilles can never overtake the slower opponent who is given even the slightest advantage.[26] For Zeno there can be no development to an end; no accomplishment; no truth other than static, unqualified Being. A thing might as well not move at all; and, in principle, does not. In that light, the "Eleatic Palamedes," Zeno, is himself a disguise for the Being-obsessed Parmenides: thus Socrates's reference to the One and the Many, terms usually associated with Parmenides.

Yet, we see refutations of Zeno in *Phaedrus*. Socrates moved the discourse not only to a goal, but from one opposite to another: *L'/P'* to the *PL*. Some of the second half of *Phaedrus* therefore involves a critique of Zeno and even Parmenides, albeit delivered in part humorously and between the lines. But Plato, or Socrates, while appreciating the sublime simplicity of Parmenides's emphasis on Being, certainly had a problem with Parmenides. R. E. Allen writes: "Plato faced a Parmenidean problem, that of reconciling the sensible world with criteria of reality it cannot satisfy. To be real is to be intelligible, not qualified by opposites, self-identical, and unchanging. The sensible world is none of these things, and it therefore cannot be real."[27]

Allen writes further:

> But an unreal world is a philosophical embarrassment, especially when it happens to be a world in which we live. To say that it is in

26. Stumpf and Fieser, *Philosophy*, 17.
27. Allen, "The Argument from Opposites in *Republic V*," 165.

> *no* sense real is impossible; for it must in some sense exist even to be illusion. The alternative is to suppose that there are degrees of being and reality, and this alternative Plato chose: There are objects of opinion; they are qualified by opposites; and they are *not* fully real. Plato held true what Parmenides had held impossible, that "things that are not are." The objects of opinion are intermediate between full reality and complete unreality.[28]

Perhaps what is underappreciated in encounters with paradoxes on the whole, ancient or contemporary, but especially Zeno's, is what we might call the facility principle. It takes Zeno little time, as it were, to pose a counterintuitive paradox. But note the lengths to which critics go to refute those virtual non-arguments that are so counterintuitive. Regarding Zeno in particular, note how many pages Joseph Mazur devotes to a presentation of Aristotle's even more voluminous work devoted to refuting that which, in Zeno's literary economy, is briefer than an Aesop fable.[29]

Especially regarding the question of the One and the Many, with very little rhetorical effort the Eleatic can facilely attack his enemy as superficial. How could anyone be so superficial as to recognize anything other than Being? Almost any protest against the extreme ontology of Parmenides makes Parmenides's enemy seem a defendant of the merely contingent, the unreal. Yet, for Plato, at least in *Phaedrus*, Parmenides's and Zeno's mastery of the art of contention in speech, or writing, can be regarded as problematic, as their philosophy might serve as the basis of an unwarranted, extreme, and even dangerous form of skepticism. This is why Plato aimed at formulating a view of dialectic as the means by which to reconcile opposites, or to see, in some sense, the identity of opposites, and/or to reveal, if not explain, the transition from one opposite to another.

In *Phaedrus*, therefore, there are many little critiques of Zeno and Parmenides between the lines. Indeed, in one sense there is a major critique of Zeno in the accumulation of all the lines. *Phaedrus*, as such, offers a *de facto reductio ad absurdum* of the Eleatic position. *Phaedrus*, after all, is famous, or infamous, for being presented in two opposed halves. Yet, anyone who has read *Phaedrus* from beginning to end must acknowledge he has achieved what the "Eleatic Palamedes" suggests one cannot, a transition from one opposite to another. Any reader of the whole of *Phaedrus* has accomplished a successful traversal of at least one mid-point, if not many.

---

28. Ibid., 165.

29. See Mazur, *The Motion Paradox*, 34–42.

Here we have, in one peculiar case at least, an answer to the sometimes tiresome question as to why Plato wrote dialogues. In *Phaedrus*, the medium itself is part of the message. The book itself is a critique of one of the thinkers criticized therein. Read the whole, and the "Eleatic Palamedes" is refuted.

Another critique of Parmenides and Zeno comes in the presentation of the Zeus myth in the *PL*. In the dynamic of the contemplation of Essences in the Essence Wheel, Plato offers a view of the reconciliation of supreme opposites, the One and the Many. Beauty is not merely one Essence among many. Beauty alone shines Truth through each and all of the other Essences: hence, again, the subtitle of *Phaedrus*, *On the Beautiful: Ethical*. Beauty even "causes" the divine to be divine; or, referring to Parmenides, Beauty would "cause" the Being of Being to be intelligible in the first place. So, Parmenides would have to acknowledge that the ultimate state is not a mere One, Being as such. Never mind that Being having a name suggests a dyad of beings at least, Being and its signifier: even a nameless Being would be intelligible only in cooperation with something else, the Beauty of its being better than everything contingent.

Plato's dialectically charged poetry criticizes Zeno's paradoxes otherwise. Consider Zeno's paradox that contends that nothing can ever reach its target because it must be, at some point, halfway between its origin and the mark. Consider then, too, the many references to mid-points in *Phaedrus*. For example, Phaedrus was frustrated when Socrates ceased delivery of P'/S'. In particular, Phaedrus complained that Socrates stopped "in the middle."[30] In his complaint about that midpoint termination, the otherwise skeptical Phaedrus betrayed that he actually desired a hearing of the whole. He betrayed, unwittingly, that he really hoped the likes of Zeno were wrong, and argued, unknowingly, that the likes of Zeno must be wrong. He betrayed that he thought an achievement of a whole was possible.

There are other midpoint references in *Phaedrus*. When Phaedrus complained about Socrates halting P'/S' "in the middle," appropriately Phaedrus's complaint occurred at another "halfway" point, "noon." Plato's poetic devices answer Zeno's paradoxes. Noon comes and noon passes. Nature, or the "real nature of things," as Socrates says, traverses midpoints to arrive at targets all the time. So, naturally, Socrates would attempt to articulate a philosophy with a logic, dialectic, that could address becoming, development, and consummation. To pose the issue in both ontological

---

30. *Phaedrus*, 241d.

Who Is Phaedrus?

and sexual references as *Phaedrus* often does, if Zeno is correct we live in a world constituted by universal onanism. But that is unreal.

For Socrates, Zeno's clever paradoxes are indeed clever, but they do little to promote a foundational understanding of reality as a lived phenomenon. Clever paradoxes would be of no aid to Phaedrus in coming to better self-understanding. The key issues in Phaedrus's life certainly did not center on clever paradoxes. Clearly, contrary to a Zeno paradox, Phaedrus made it to a limit, a border. In fact, Phaedrus exceeded the border when he was banished from Athens. He exited entirely, lest he be imprisoned.

Moreover, no paradox held an answer as to why Phaedrus exceeded the boundaries of good taste and good sense in the first place; why Phaedrus participated in the *PEM*. Socrates had a remedy, Zeno did not. It would take a second return for Phaedrus, after this second exile in the company of Socrates, to return to Athens properly. And part of that good return is to see the cleverness of Zeno and cleverness of Lysias for what they are: idle, at best, and harmful respectively.

In *Phaedrus* all roads lead back to Athens and the problem of Lysias. Even the critiques of Zeno may be regarded, in part, as critiques of Lysias. Note Phaedrus's unconsciously ironic complaint when Socrates introduced the complex case of the Palamedes dyad. When Socrates referred to Palamedes and the Eleatic Palamedes, Phaedrus complained that the conversation had suddenly turned "too abstract."[31] The rather clueless Phaedrus did not realize that and how he was both right and wrong at the same time. The "abstract" point about which Phaedrus complained lay in Socrates's claim about the person who might have the "art of making his hearers pass from one thing to its opposite by leading them through intervening resemblances."[32] Phaedrus did not realize that what he considered "abstract" was being played out right before his very nose.

When Phaedrus complained that matters had become too "abstract," Socrates recommended the antidote: look for examples. Socrates suggested he and Phaedrus "look in the speech of Lysias . . . and in what I said, for something which we think shows art and the lack of art."[33] In Socrates's suggestion that something there was done "without art" (ἀτέχνων) by Lysias, and "with art" (ἐντέχνων) by Socrates, we have more Socratic language play that is serious nonetheless. While Socrates claims he does not possess the

---

31. Ibid., 262c.
32. Ibid., 262b.
33. Ibid., 262c.

"art of speaking," he allows here that he has performed an art, the "art of making his hearers pass from one thing to its opposite by leading them through the intervening resemblances." But Socrates's peculiar admission to possessing an art is only part of the point.

The full significance of Socrates's claim here lies with a compelling play on words *via* the term ἐντέχνων. Not only does ἐντέχνων mean "with art," it can also mean "poured in." "Poured in" recalls the image of the flowing fluids associated with the lovers in Socrates's *PL*. In that image, love, like overflowing water, flows from the eyes of the lover into the eyes of the beloved. That flow is so profuse it produces a gushing overflow, into the beloved's eyes and out his ears; in, through, and out; all over his entire body.

There is another sense of ἐντέχνων Socrates may intend: εντεχνων also suggests being "given over wholly" to something. In *Phaedrus*, it is Socrates who is given over wholly to love, not Lysias. Socrates is given over wholly to the highest love of all, the love of wisdom. And Socrates's overflowing love of wisdom is better than the cleverness of Lysias (and Zeno). Indeed, Socrates's love of wisdom provides the basis for right perspectives on Zeno and Lysias.

We see then, also, an ingenious critique of Lysias and Zeno at the same time when Socrates suggests that Phaedrus look in *L'/P'* for an example of a transition from one opposite to another. Recall Socrates's early, seemingly picayune, criticism of *L'/P'*. *L'/P'* was rhetorically flawed for many reasons; but one flaw in particular stood out. *L'/P'* began with a peroration. *L'/P'* was rhetorically awful, as it began with its end. Now, after so many lessons in dialectic, Phaedrus is supposed to appreciate this especially clever critique of Zeno, which is also a critique of Lysias.

When Socrates is trying to tutor Phaedrus in the "art of making his hearers pass from one thing to its opposite," and to discern that *L'/P'* was done "without art," Socrates has Phaedrus re-read Lysias's speech. Socrates recommends, in fact, that Phaedrus read the opening of Lysias's speech twice.[34] When Socrates says to Phaedrus: "Read me the beginning of Lysias's discourse" he is saying really, also: "Read me the end of Lysias's discourse," as *L'/P'* began with its peroration.

So, *L'/P'* serves as an example of rhetoric that could, if comically, both confirm and refute none other than the antilogician, Zeno, who argues that a beginning cannot reach an end. *L'/P'* does reach its end. But it reaches its end because its end is the beginning. So, Zeno is refuted. Yet, too, as

34. Ibid., 262e; 263e.

Who Is Phaedrus?

the end of *L'/P'* is the beginning, where Phaedrus stops, the speech does not really proceed at all. So, Zeno, comically, is confirmed: maybe nothing really moves. By dialectic Socrates out-antilogics the antilogicians, and for a purpose. Socrates is moving Phaedrus to realize, most importantly, that Phaedrus needs a transformation; one Phaedrus can actually achieve.

γ) The Triad of Speakers

We noted how Socrates moved the discourse from one topic, rhetoric, to its opposite, or its apparent opposite. As a rhetoric-superseding dialectician, he did so without Phaedrus even noticing. Socrates in turn makes manifest that such a move, if made by increments, can proceed almost without detection. A drastic move from one opposite to another would be noticed; would call attention to the sophistry involved.

There were subtle moves within that overall subtle move, as Slobodan Dušanić has recognized. When Socrates referred to both Palamedes and the Eleatic Palamedes, Zeno, both of whom allegedly employed rhetoric and either wrote or used rhetoric manuals, Socrates used the term τέχνηι twice accordingly:

> Thanks to Plato's skillful formulation of the phrase—intentionally ambivalent, as the word in question could and probably would have been omitted otherwise—the *technei* permits of two translations: "scientifically" (the dative of manner) and "with his manual" (the instrumental dative . . .). The ambiguity was necessary to make the transition from the political theme of "law courts" and "public harangues" (261a–e) to the philosophical theme of "resemblance and dissimilarity" (261e) less abrupt.[35]

Dušanić's point is well taken, but his more important contribution on this topic is his identification, as far as there can be one, of the more contemporary figure for whom Palamedes is a disguise.

We observed how Socrates allowed that he might have been using the names Nestor and Odysseus as disguises for more contemporary rhetoricians such as Gorgias and Thrasymachus. We also noted that Socrates said "never mind them." That dismissal still left another figure to consider: Palamedes. For whom was Palamedes a disguise?

---

35. Dušanić, "Alkidamas of Elaea in Plato's *Phaedrus*," 351–52.

Confounding Rhetoric

Dušanić argues that Palamedes is a disguise for Alkidamas of Elaea, pupil of Gorgias, who wrote at least one manual on rhetoric. That plausible conclusion will be reinforced here.

Why Alkidamas? There is a quote from Quintillian that compels readers to seek out Alkidamas in *Phaedrus*: "... et, quem Palameden Plato appellat, Alcidamas Elaites."[36] Alkidamas is never mentioned by name in *Phaedrus*, so he must be disguised, and the choice of Palamedes as the disguise is certainly as good as any. This conclusion might be considered erroneous, however, given the fact that Alkidamas wrote a work called *Odysseus* that attacked Palamedes. That work seems contrary to his teacher, Gorgias, who wrote an *Apology of Palamedes* that defended Palamedes.[37] This seeming discrepancy might be explained easily: what better way for a sophist to pay homage to his teacher than by writing a work that is a sophistical opposite?

More proof that Palamedes is a disguise for Alkidamas may be seen in the fact that the work of Alkidamas suits perfectly the context in question: "Alcidamas refers constantly to the courtroom, to lawsuits and the Assembly..."[38] Alkidamas's treatises on rhetoric are very much in the mode of Gorgias on that front. They presume to show anyone how to win any argument on any topic whatsoever, but especially where it matters: in courts and assemblies. Socrates, of course, is above such.

There is, however, an element of Alkidamas's work with which Socrates agrees: a commitment to the ability to speak extemporaneously. Of course, Socrates does not like spontaneous sophistry any more than he does written. But Alkidamas's emphasis on speaking over writing is compelling and accrues to another triad for dyadic reduction and dialectical discernment. We are to consider in what way or ways Alkidamas, Zeno, and Socrates are alike yet different.

The first thing to consider is that Socrates almost stresses that Zeno was essentially a speaker. This point Vlastos makes, if for reasons different from ours at present: "we are entitled to put on them [Plato's words about Zeno at 261c] a different accent: *ouste phainesthai tois akouousi*, that is to say, take them to mean that it was to his hearers—who thought Parmenides' doctrine preposterous, not to all, including the enlightened, who knew better—that Zeno made it 'appear' that the same things are both

---

36. Ibid., 347.
37. Ibid., 348, n15.
38. Van Hook, "Alcidamas versus Isocrates," lines 77–78.

like and unlike."[39] Socrates's reference to Zeno's "hearers" could be taken to suggest that Zeno was every bit as emphatic of the importance of speaking as Socrates was. What we see in this Palamedes section of *Phaedrus*, then, is occasion for Phaedrus to perform yet another triad/dyad comparison of three influential figures who, if for different reasons, stressed the importance of speaking over writing.

Zeno and Socrates had this much in common: they were concerned with ontology, unlike Alkidamas who cared only about political or legal expediency. Zeno and Alkidamas, however, were more alike in one way in particular: Zeno's paradoxes work by antilogic to promote skepticism about universal matters; Alkidamas uses antilogic to baffle persons regarding judicial and policy matters. By contrast, Socrates's philosophy is the one that uses dialectic, which supersedes its own use of antilogic, to see to the superseding of the difference between the universal and the individual, and to overcome any form of cheap skepticism.

Zeno and Socrates are alike in another way: they both claim to promote dialectic. Otherwise, Alkidamas and Socrates are alike insofar as both claim to be lovers of wisdom. Yet, Socrates's dialectic would supersede what Zeno calls dialectic, which is really only antilogic. And what Socrates means by philosophy is an activity that couples contemplation and discernment, while Alkidamas's philosophy is only antilogic with a social/political twist.

Enter, then, Socrates. While Socrates was suspicious of Isocrates's emphasis on writing, Socrates would agree in part with Isocrates's summary critique of Alkidamas and Gorgias: "These teachers are accused of dishonesty and stupidity; it is maintained that they are dishonest in their pretentious infallibility to produce eloquent orators from any human material, whether the pupil possesses capacity or imagination, or not. Such charlatanism tends to discredit all in the profession."[40]

Of course, Socrates did not care about the rhetoric "profession." Operating with an essentially religious element in his philosophy, Socrates thought rhetoricians, mainly, were rather pathetic souls who could not see that Socrates's philosophy superseded the rhetoricians' antilogic tailored to conditions. In a sense, that is, Socrates and Alkidamas are quite alike, as Alkidamas, like his teacher Gorgias, apparently claimed to be able to teach anyone about everything conceivable, and, as Socrates has to admit by his own words, he, the dialectician, holds a similar premise: "Can

---

39. Vlastos, "Plato's Testimony Concerning Zeno of Elea," 151.
40. Ibid., 47–51.

there be anything of importance which is not included in these processes [i.e, collection and division operative in dialectic]?"[41] Yet, there is a difference between Socrates and Alkidamas, certainly regarding the claim to universality.

The Socratic critique of Alkidamas suggests that Alkidamas could only instruct his students in the ability to engage in every topic conceivable by resorting to the most tedious skeptical strategy found in later pamphlets in skepticism: simply counter the premise of the other party with an opposing proposition and let the propositions hover in intellectual abeyance. Then the hearer will think that one proposition is as plausible as the other. That way the student of Alkidamas could appear expert on any and every issue.

However he operated in detail, as Alkidamas's writings are less revelatory of his teaching method than they are critical of other rhetoricians, Alkidamas apparently drew inspiration from the skepticism borne of Zeno's paradoxes, themselves borne of Parmenidean ontology. If Being, alone, is what is, and is the same, and remains the same, fixed within the bonds of necessity, then all other ways of being, and thinking, are *de facto* participants in non-being and therefore participants in error. In more modern terms, Alkidamas's rhetorical system would find ways to impress unreasonable doubt in the mind; especially in the minds of jurors. That is the antilogician's goal: to cause the hearer to be suspended between two seemingly equal alternatives. As Zeno's thought existed to cast a wary eye on all pluralism, Alkidamas apparently found a way, as a most unusual, indirect disciple of Parmenides, to cast all manner of suspicion on all forms of testimony about every conceivable particular.

δ) An *Apologia* for Phaedrus

So, finally, what are we to make of the man whose name appears twice in this context, Palamedes? Socrates speaks glowingly of Palamedes, among others, at the end of the *Apology*.[42] Aside from serving as a disguise for Alkidamas, is there more Phaedrus might infer from the reference to Palamedes in this context?

If Palamedes, whom Socrates reasonably praised, was a disguise for Alkidamas, whom Socrates mostly would criticize, that was a most unusual disguise indeed. Yet, relative to the topics at hand, court and public

41. *Phaedrus*, 266d.
42. *Apology*, 41b.

Who Is Phaedrus?

assembly speaking, Alkidamas's rhetorical bailiwick, as distinct from ontology and metaphysics, Zeno's bailiwick, the idea that Palamedes is a disguise for Alkidamas is at least plausible if not utterly compelling.

Yet, what is the point relative to Phaedrus and Phaedrus's circumstance?

In this context which contains references to court speaking, surely Phaedrus was to recollect the case of Palamedes in the Trojan War. Palamedes found himself in a court martial. The court martial case of Palamedes offers a synthesis of the first two forms of the art of contention in speech: the just *versus* the unjust in lawsuits; and the good *versus* the bad for the State on the whole.

Palamedes was a superb commander; but he had a nemesis, Odysseus. Odysseus was envious of Palamedes's extraordinary talents. During war, Palamedes was framed. Someone, possibly Odysseus himself, surreptitiously placed an envelope of money in Palamedes's tent, allegedly a payoff from the enemy for spying.

Palamedes was tried for treason; and the case became fodder for rhetorical exercises. Gorgias composed a *Palamedes* that became famous almost immediately. Indeed, some consider Gorgias's *Palamedes* the rhetorical model upon which Plato based his *Apology* for Socrates. As Marina McCoy notes: "Commentators such as Seeskin, and Feaver, and Hare view the *Apology* as a 'parody' of the *Palamedes*. Seeskin sees Plato as concerned with the truth, while Gorgias cares only about probability. Along similar lines, Feaver and Hare argue that Socrates's use of rhetoric is ironic."[43]

McCoy proceeds to present the details of Palamedes's probabilistic defense in Gorgias's fictive *Palamedes*. McCoy does not agree with others that Plato's whole *Apology* is a satire based on Gorgias's *Palamedes*, but those particulars are not material here. What is material here is that Socrates's very raising of the question of Palamedes surely has some bearing on Phaedrus's future.

Phaedrus had been found guilty for involvement in the *PEM*. Given the nature of Athens's courts, it was quite possible Phaedrus could be tried, at any time, for involvement in the *MH* also. If Phaedrus were tried for participation in the *MH* also, that would mean Phaedrus would need a dyadic defense. So, perhaps Socrates raised the Palamedes issue so Phaedrus could consider the dyadic nature of Palamedes's own dyadic defense in Palamedes's trial for treason.

---

43. McCoy, *Plato on the Rhetoric of Philosophers and Sophists*, 40.

Palamedes's defense, with its essentially dyadic counter to Odysseus, might compel Phaedrus to engage in *dianoia*, and therefore dialectic. Phaedrus would need dialectic to construct a dyadic defense of his own as, given the litigious fever in which Athens almost always found itself, someday Phaedrus might undergo a kind of double jeopardy for his involvement in the *PEM*, along with a trial for being involved in the *MH* also. Phaedrus could become a second Pherakles, "involved in both."

When Palamedes was accused by Odysseus of taking a bribe from the enemy, Palamedes offered essentially a dyadic defense. Palamedes argued, in essence, that Odysseus's charge violated the principle of non-contradiction (before there was a manual in logic to give the principle a name). To do that of which he was accused, Palamedes argued, he would have to be both sane and insane at the same time and virtually in the same respect. (Ironically, of course, Odysseus was originally angry with Palamedes because Palamedes realized Odysseus himself was only feigning insanity to avoid service in the war into which Palamedes would draft him.)

Palamedes was at least once removed from communication with the enemy. He would therefore have to be extraordinarily clever, and therefore sane, to arrange payment of a bribe from an enemy from that distance. Yet, at the same time, knowing the mortal consequence of treason, Palamedes would have to be quite insane to collude with the enemy.

Not only was Palamedes's defense dyadic, his use of the "art of contention in speech" was two-fold. Given Palamedes's status as a prominent commander, his was a case of debating the just *versus* the unjust in a court (martial); and of debating the good *versus* the bad for the state on the whole. The state should not lose a man of Palamedes's talents.

So, who knows? Phaedrus was no Palamedes; but Phaedrus might someday find himself in a position in which he needed a dyadic defense, and maybe from charges brought by none other than his own lover. Someday, were Phaedrus ever to cross Lysias, Lysias might bring charges of impiety against Phaedrus for participation in the *MH* also. Lysias, the democrat, could bring that charge with relish, as Lysias had before against others charged in the *MH*. Lysias might bring the charge of Phaedrus's participation in the *MH* as a vindictive lover, or non-lover, if Phaedrus ever threatened to leave Lysias, or if Phaedrus ever repudiated the democrat leanings he had adopted since his return to Athens from exile. Lysias, as champion of democracy, might easily accuse Phaedrus of being a "crypto-oligarch" in much the same way Andokides had been accused.[44]

44. Missiou, The Subversive Oratory of Andokides, 1992.

Who Is Phaedrus?

Such possible charges were always in the air, especially given the loose meaning of terms such as "democrat" and "oligarch" at the time:

> What do we mean by "oligarchic" and "democratic" in Athenian politics? There were no official parties, no written manifestoes, no functioning party-political systems. Cases such as Alkibiades and Peisandros show individuals changing their political allegiances as circumstances demanded; oligarch and democrat are indeed labels which the Greeks used themselves to classify public figures, but they should not be pressed too far: Athenian politics seems to have been to a very considerable degree a question of individual personalities and their following, rather than conflicting ideologies to which the individual was subordinate.[45]

Given the whimsical nature of Athenian politics and prosecutors, Socrates was trying to make Phaedrus aware that Phaedrus was subject to prosecution at almost any hour, and by no less a person than his own lover, Lysias. We have already seen, *via L'/P'*, how clever Lysias could be. By a kind of rhetorical sin of omission, since he never defined love in *L'/P'*, Lysias could proceed with all kinds of presuppositions about lovers and non-lovers. So, who could easily stop Lysias in a court if he played fast and loose with terms such as democrat, oligarch, or aristocrat?

There is an exceptionally subtle point behind this unspoken juridical forewarning on the part of Socrates. Perhaps in a brief homage to Isocrates, Socrates is referring here to Isocrates's approach to rhetoric that, in principle, is nobler than Alkidamas's, for whom victory in court meant everything. In Isocrates's *Antidosis*, Isocrates introduces his view of *philosophia* through an artifice: "he constructs the fiction of his own trial."[46] So, while Isocrates uses the idea of a trial to introduce his greater philosophy, at least he does not reduce philosophy entirely to the task of winning arguments in courts like the sophist Alkidamas. Alternately, curiously, while Socrates's philosophy is also not reducible to winning arguments it courts, such victories might come more often from Socratic dialectic than by Isocrates's pragmatism or Alkidamas's sophistry.

So, Phaedrus is to consider Palamedes. If the essence of Palamedes's defense was that he would have to be both sane and insane at the same time and in the same respect to take a bribe from the enemy, Phaedrus would have to make future accusers ask: how could anyone be so sane and insane,

---

45. Furley, *Andokides and the Herms*, 61.
46. McAdon, "Plato's Denunciation of Rhetoric in the *Phaedrus*," 29.

Confounding Rhetoric

at the same time, as to take part in both the anti-democrat *MH* and the anti-aristocrat *PEM*?

Phaedrus might even develop a derivate dyadic defense. Phaedrus might answer charges of participation in both the *MH* and the *PEM* by saying he was simply caught up in the frenzied activity of Alkibiades. Alkibiades was surely a man insane enough, and calculating enough, to participate in, or instigate, actions as opposed as the *MH* and the *PEM*. Phaedrus could claim his only crime was that of being a sycophant in the cult of Alkibiades.

In that regard, Phaedrus could argue he was no worse than Athens itself. Athens, especially democrat-dominated Athens, had once banished Alkibiades and then had given him a hero's welcome on his return. If Athens itself could not decide what it wanted; if Athens itself was so pathetically *epamphoterious*, how could it accuse Phaedrus of worse?

12

Phaedrus's Whither

a) Another Return to Athens

PHAEDRUS, AS WITH ALL other persons who encounter Socrates, is to be transformed. Broadly, those who encounter Socrates are to be transformed from ignorant to wise. Many, if not most, who meet Socrates do not think they need transformation. Many not only resist change, they seek Socrates's demise.

Phaedrus is to be transformed; but from what to what? *Phaedrus* offers a very specific term regarding the nature of the transformation Socrates intends. What is Phaedrus's key flaw? He "epamphoterizes"; he seems to want everything both ways. So, Phaedrus is to be transformed from *epamphoterious* to "simple."[1]

When Plato uses a form of ἁπλόος or "simple" to describe the state to which Phaedrus would be transformed, Plato certainly did not choose a simple word. Plato's detractors who detest wordplay in philosophy cannot be pleased with the word ἁπλα (or, in context, even the adverbial ἁπλως).

The term, ἁπλα, suggests numerous meanings: "simple," "single-minded," "not ambivalent," "frank," "straight-forward." In the vernacular regarding the simple, perhaps there was also a suggestion of "single" or, especially, "ascetic" or "celibate." Many, such as Catherine Zuckert, argue that Socrates, despite having three sons, had always recommended an almost

---

1. *Phaedrus*, 257b. Socrates uses the adverbial ἁπλως as in "with singleness of purpose."

entirely ascetic life: "Socrates urges human beings to suppress their bodily desires in order to attain greater and more lasting psychic intimacy."[2]

The term, ἁπλα, simple, or the adjectival derivative, also has a moral sense as a linguistic opposite of πολύπλοκος, which, applied to persons, can mean "crafty" or "cunning."[3] We have noted that Socrates intimates, with Socrates's play on the word ατεχνως, that Phaedrus was rather naïve.[4] In that context, Socrates was implying that, compared with the crafty Lysias at least, Phaedrus was, indeed, guileless given the extreme cunning in Lysias's rhetoric.

In one sense Phaedrus, as a partner in the teaching of Lysian rhetoric, was "crafty" by association, but not necessarily by design. For example, it never occurred to Phaedrus that Phaedrus was being used by the cunning Lysias; that Lysias's very speech in praise of the non-lover, lent by Lysias, was a speech essentially telling Phaedrus that Lysias did not love him.

Phaedrus needed to become more like Socrates so Phaedrus could become more aware of what is cunning without being cunning himself. Generally, Plato thinks everyone should become as Socratic as possible; so Phaedrus is supposed to be as Socratic as possible. How is Socrates the standard? In what sense is Socrates simple?

Socrates himself raises the issue. Early in the dialogue, Socrates responds to Phaedrus's inquiry as to how seriously Socrates took the myth of Boreas. Socrates, rejecting the rhetoricians' demythologizing, took the myth seriously enough, at least morally:

> All those non-believers employing some boorish sophistication will make everything conform to probability, and they also will need a great deal of free time. But for me there's no such leisure. And, my dear friend, is this: I am still not able to "know myself," as the Delphic inscription enjoins, and it seems laughable for me to think about other things when I am still ignorant about myself. So leaving those matters aside, I believe whatever people say these days about those creatures, and I don't inquire about them but about myself. For me, the question is whether I happen to be some sort of beast even more complex in form and more tumultuous than the hundred-headed Typhon, or whether I am something

---

2. Zuckert, *Plato's Philosophers*, 319.
3. De Vries, *A Commentary on the Phaedrus of Plato*, 52.
4. *Phaedrus*, 242a.

> simpler and gentler, having a share by nature of the divine and the unTyphonic.[5]

Socrates's early reference to the "simpler" (ἁπλούστερον), a predicate Socrates might apply to himself, sets the tone for the later application of ἁπλόος regarding the transformation of Phaedrus.

In *Phaedrus*, the simple is the antidote to everything Typhon, the enemy of Zeus. Given the many meanings of the term, the simple is the "gentle" and that which has a "share by nature of the divine," and more.

With the usual irony associated with Socrates, what accrues after Socrates's appeal to the simple is complexity in the extreme: a triad of speeches identical yet different; a four-fold account of divine madness; an intentionally problematic proof of the inherent immortality of the soul; a complex image of the soul that mirrored the complex relation of the discourses in which the image occurred, etc. Given all of that complexity, where was simplicity?

Also, Socrates's myth about the origin of writing bore ultimately upon the question of the simple. Socrates referred, in a complimentary way, to the simpletons of Dodona who were wise though illiterate: they simply heeded Zeus, even when the god spoke via rocks or trees. Those simple souls were simple in the sense of having "a share in the divine." That divine share was more than implied when Socrates referred to the Essences in the Essence Wheel as "simple" (ἁπλα), calm, and happy apparitions.[6]

Non-simple, *epamphoterious* Phaedrus was pathetic by comparison. Phaedrus, the *Schadenverbesserung eros* Typhon would only listen to clever democrats. This is why in *Phaedrus* Socrates has to be so competitively clever: in the extreme. To keep Phaedrus's attention, Socrates had to dazzle Phaedrus with rhetoric and antilogic in the hopes that Phaedrus would recognize how all of that work was achieved by Socrates's mastery of dialectic; and if Phaedrus could learn to appreciate dialectic, in turn he would recognize Ones, Essences, simples.

What is implied then in Phaedrus's transformation? How can a mortal's soul move to a divine state?

For Socrates, a person can make the transition from human to the opposite, the divine, only if the person is, in some sense, divine already; and the "simple," in one sense, is that which "has a share in the nature of the divine." Socrates assumes that a person, if inherently immortal, is in some

---

5. Ibid., 229a–b.
6. Ibid., 250.

sense a god or like a god. Thus Socrates's compelling pedagogical principle: one could become a god or like a god, only if one were a god, or like a god, in the first place.

For Leibniz in the modern world this pedagogical principle was one of the many reasons for taking Plato seriously. Even if, to Leibniz, *qua* Christian, belief in the inherent immortality of the soul does not square with the Judeo-Christian notion of creation *ex nihilo*, Plato's operating premises and pedagogical implications are intriguing:

> The innate concepts of Plato, which he concealed by the term "reminiscence," are therefore by far to be preferred to the blank tablets of Aristotle, Locke, and other exoteric philosophers. So I believe that, to philosophize correctly, Plato must be combined usefully with Aristotle and Democritus, though a number of the principal doctrines would have to be stricken from each of them.[7]

Leibniz in particular takes Plato's pedagogical principle seriously because Leibniz, *qua* Christian, can both humbly criticize Plato's principle while raising it an exponent. For Plato, if the soul is inherently immortal, if a person cannot not be, then one cannot not know Essences because they likewise cannot not be. For Leibniz, the soul, which is created and therefore not inherently immortal, is nonetheless made in God's likeness, and therefore knows not only Essences but everything at birth, but mostly in a confused state. For Plato, a real education for a human being is, in a sense, to become a god of a sort in the sense in which one is to maintain diligent concentration upon Essences that are also inherently immortal: the simple knowing the simple. For Leibniz, the cure for confusion in the soul is also simplification: recognize all necessary truths, and render all contingent truths intelligible relative to the analytical judgments that operate with a principle of necessity.

β) From Simple to Simple

According to Plato's pedagogical principle, Phaedrus could only be transformed from *epamphoterious* to simple if Phaedrus were *already* simple, or had a share in the divine in the first place. In moral terms, for Socrates, Phaedrus had that better, simpler, more divine soul before he was corrupted.

---

7. Leibniz, "The Spiritual Reality of the Soul," 53.

Who Is Phaedrus?

Here, in part, Socrates seems like just another sophist putting some weird spin on the problem of the One and the Many. His use of simple makes us ask: what is the simple meaning of simple?

In one sense, Plato seems to be playing into the hands of the deconstructionists. Derrida suggests, after all, that when Plato was necessarily involved in writing, Plato was involved in a logic outside his own control. Could this be an instance that verifies Derrida's claim? Or does Plato have the anticipatory better of Derrida?

For Derrida, the very act of writing usurps the logocentrism Derrida argues the West has assumed as its dominant intellectual motif. For Derrida, the Bible, for example, may be a book, but its alleged author, God, is essentially a speaker; and as speaker a commander; and as commander a kind of fascist. Christ speaks, he does not write; and the rest follows. Socrates speaks, he does not write; and the rest follows. God, Christ, Socrates: speakers/fascists all, or so the argument seems to go. And, allegedly, when the speaker speaks, a word can have only one meaning lest the speaker lose his authority. The speaker's authority is bound to the apparent necessity of the univocal.

Derrida argues that Plato, though a writer, opts for the priority of speech over writing because the immediacy of speech recommends only one meaning for a term:

> On the one hand, Plato decides in favor of a logic that does not tolerate [such] passages between opposing senses of the same word, all the more so since such a passage would reveal itself to be something quite different from simple confusion, alternation, or the dialectic of opposites. And yet, on the other hand, the *pharmakon*, if our reading confirms itself, constitutes the original medium of that decision, the element that precedes it, comprehends it, goes beyond it, can never be reduced to it, and is not separated from it by a single word (or signifying apparatus) operating within the Greek and Platonic text.[8]

It seems Derrida gives writing too much credit; or Plato too little. Derrida did not meet Plato's test to discern the opposite senses in the single, play intended, most important term relative to Phaedrus's transformation, απλα: single; simple; that which has a share by nature in the divine.

If we must think in Derrida's terms for the moment, Plato's employment of απλα shows that Plato seemed to know very well where his writing

---

8. Derrida, "Plato's Pharmacy," 127–28.

might meet the margin of a logic that is a non-logic, a logic of endless equivocation. In ἁπλα or ἁπλως, Plato not only tolerates passages between opposing senses of the same word, he urges them.

In sum, the whole of *Phaedrus* offers many hints that ἁπλόος may mean more than one thing in various contexts. Yet, given the many descriptions of Phaedrus by Socrates, the complimentary ones all convene in a determination that seems, well, simple.

When we ask, "Who Is Phaedrus?" we cannot help but think of the particular nature of Phaedrus that makes him, on the one hand, likable. Yet, on the other, he is easy to abuse: he is "naïve" (ἀτέχνος). In a sense, Phaedrus has to remain "naïve," as that very trait is just about the only one that lends him a certain charm. For Socrates, however, Phaedrus should add "that which has a share by nature of the divine" to his character. This is the Socratic equivalent of being wise as a serpent but harmless as a dove, much like the silly simpleton, Socrates.

13

Two Final Triads

α) Homer, Solon, Lysias

SOCRATES SENDS PHAEDRUS BACK to Athens to address three groups: speechwriters, poets/lyricists, and lawmakers. Phaedrus is to inform all three groups as to his conversation with Socrates.

Each of the three groups has a single representative respectively: Lysias, Homer, and Solon. Something should dawn on Phaedrus at once about this peculiar triad: two of the figures are dead. Yet, Socrates says Phaedrus is to return to Athens and "repeat to Lysias . . . and to Homer . . . and to Solon . . ." what was said in the grove.[1] What does Socrates mean? This may just be a quirky way of suggesting Phaedrus say "to the next would-be Homer" or "to the next would-be Solon," etc., what was said. Yet, surely Socrates means something else.

Phaedrus was supposed to learn the lesson of the cicadas: how the cicadas had died and did not realize it. Phaedrus is supposed to be an inverse cicada. He should return to Athens to move from philosophically dead to philosophically alive, and know it. Phaedrus's realization of his coming to life might occur after he returns to Athens and sees how dead the living Lysias seems when compared with the actually dead, but culturally living, Homer and Solon.

Socrates hints, at the very least, that Phaedrus is to entertain this living/dead comparison. Some triad-dyad reduction would be the way Phaedrus could see how alive he had become; and that very activity of discernment would be proof, in itself, of his coming to life, and realizing it.

1. *Phaedrus*, 278b–c.

Phaedrus seems almost there in part, even within the dialogue at times. It is Phaedrus who refers to "the living and breathing word of him who knows, of which the written word may justly be called an image."[2] This is close to a distinction between the living and the dead; and Phaedrus knew Homer was transmitted orally, and that Solon was not strictly a writer. Lysias, though alive, is little more than a dead-letter dealer.

The difference between the living and the dead even carries over to a comparison between Lysias and Isocrates. After Socrates recommends Phaedrus return to Athens to inform Lysias of the conversation in the grove, Phaedrus has a suggestion of his own. Phaedrus suggests that Socrates return to Socrates's favorite. Yet, Socrates has no favorite in mind: "Who is that?" Phaedrus is apparently mistaken about Isocrates being one of Socrates's favorites. Socrates does offer an explicit comparison between Isocrates and Lysias: Isocrates "has a more noble character" than Lysias; and there is a "higher level of speech" in the work of Isocrates compared with Lysias; and there is some "love of wisdom" in Isocrates already, with the implication that there is none in Lysias. Yet, Socrates is not so fond of Isocrates that Socrates is preoccupied with Isocrates.

The recognition of the "love of wisdom," in fact, is that about which Phaedrus is to inform Lysias, Homer, and Solon. The lover of wisdom is capable of three phenomena interconnected. He can: a) arrange his work in such way as to be aware of where the truth is; b) defend his work in cross-examination; and, c) deliver a spoken analysis of that which is trivial in the written.

All three functions carry a critique of Lysias, and, by implication, a critique of Phaedrus as a fan of written sophistry. Lysias will reveal just how dead he is if, upon cross examination by Phaedrus, Lysias will not be able to reveal what is trivial in his own text. Would Lysias even admit that there is anything trivial in his text?

β) The Ridiculous, the Clever, the Enemy

Phaedrus might finally see that, even if he had to return to a superficial, democrat Athens, he did not have to embrace it. He could, should, like Socrates, be an aristocrat, if only of the soul, and try to persuade his fellows of a nobler way.

---

2. Ibid., 276a.

Who Is Phaedrus?

Yet, would Phaedrus really be aware of how dead the living Lysias was? Rhodes writes for many when he expresses doubts about such an outcome: "It may be that, against all odds, Socrates has won Phaedrus to true opinion, or to the beginnings of it. Perhaps Phaedrus can eventually be rewinged. However, I would not count on it. Phaedrus is returning to Lysias, and he leans whichever way the last wind blows."[3]

Phaedrus would certainly have to muster a lot of courage to cross-examine his *Schadenverbesserung eros* lover, Lysias. Were Phaedrus to rile Lysias, the latter might bring more charges of impiety against Phaedrus like those brought against the famous Andokides.

It is hard to see within the confines of the dialogue how Phaedrus might muster the courage to disown or try to change a man as successful as Lysias. Moreover, Plato gives us no clear indication Phaedrus will ever change and challenge Lysias. Yet, to the end, Socrates tries to help Phaedrus change.

It is not odd that *Phaedrus* should end with Socrates's prayer that all but expresses a criticism of Lysias. Socrates prays to Pan: "grant that I become beautiful within and that my worldly belongings be in accord with my inner self. May I consider the wise man rich and have only as much gold as a moderate man can carry and use."[4] This is the prayer of a poor aristocrat of the soul, the antithesis to Phaedrus and Lysias.

By contrast, Phaedrus's last words leave no indication as to whether he has changed or will change. Phaedrus ends with the dubious slogan: "Friends share all in common." Yet, how are these words, "friends share all in common," to be taken?

There are three competing systems in *Phaedrus* that could use this phrase as a motto. In the Eleusinian mysteries, rich and poor initiates alike were called "friends." They were willing to see a certain "all" they had in common: their faith that their special god had descended to dwell among them for a time. Would Phaedrus embrace this, the premise of the mysteries he had once profaned?

More, "friends share all in common" could have been a stock phrase of Athenian democrats. If Phaedrus was giving lip-service at the end to superficial democracy, Phaedrus will not have changed as Socrates's prayer intended. Phaedrus was to be pleased with a little wealth while being an aristocrat of the soul, unlike Lysias, an extremely wealthy democrat.

3. Rhodes, *Eros, Wisdom, and Silence*, 539.
4. *Phaedrus*, 279b.

Two Final Triads

Finally, the claim "friends share all in common" is equivocally true for Socrates. Yet, the proper "all" for Socrates is the sum of universals available for contemplation in the Essence Wheel, and the principles operative in dialectical discernment, not the universe of material goods.

Phaedrus will make a good, if tragic, return to Athens if he sees that the way to improve Athens starts with a troubling recognition: Athens is dominated by merely "clever" money-lovers like Lysias and other "lowly scoundrels," an epithet used by the anonymous writer known as "pseudo-Xenophon," or "the Old Oligarch," to describe the likes of Lysias and Epicrates.[5] The Old Oligarch's reference to lowly scoundrels is sarcastic because scoundrels like Lysias and Epicrates are only ostensibly "low." Alleged champions of "the people" or the "low," Lysias and Epicrates, promote "low" living for others while they live high.

Whatever course Phaedrus chooses, he is supposed to distance himself from, or convert, Lysias. If there is one line from the dialogue Phaedrus might want to revisit, it is this from Socrates: "Is it not better to be ridiculous than to be clever and an enemy?"[6] These are the attributes of the triad of persons who function explicitly or implicitly in every line: Socrates is ridiculous; Lysias is clever; and Phaedrus had been, at one time, an enemy of the state.

Phaedrus, upon his return to Athens, should realize that Socrates loves him, not Lysias; and the love of wisdom is the source.

---

5. Ober, *Political Dissent in Democratic Athens*, 14.
6. *Phaedrus*, 260c.

Bibliography

Allen, R. E. "The Argument from Opposites in *Republic V.*" In *Essays in Ancient Greek Philosophy*, edited by John Anton and George Kustas, 165–75. Albany, NY: State University of New York Press, 1971.
Anton, J. "Dialectic and Health in Plato's *Gorgias*: Presuppositions and Implications." *Ancient Philosophy* Fall (1980) 49–60.
Arieti, J. *Interpreting Plato: The Dialogues as Drama*. Savage, MD: Rowman and Littlefield, 1991.
Barrett, H. *The Sophists: Rhetoric, Democracy, and Plato's Idea of Sophistry*. Novato, CA: Chandler & Sharp, 1987.
Bateman, J. J. "Lysias and the Law." *Transactions and Proceedings of the American Philological Association* 89, edited by Donald Prakken, 276–85, 1958.
Bentley, R. "On Plato's *Phaedrus*: Politics Beyond the City Walls." *Polis* 22 (2005) 230–48.
Buccioni, E. "Keeping It Secret: Reconsidering Lysias' Speech in Plato's *Phaedrus*." *Phoenix* 61 (Spring–Summer, 2007) 15–38.
Calvo, T. "Socrates' First Speech in the *Phaedrus* and Plato's Criticism of Rhetoric." In *Understanding the Phaedrus*, edited by Livio Rossetti, 47–60. Sankt Augustin, Germany: Academia, 1992.
Chardin, J. "Les Contrariétés Merveilleuses de *Coriolan*." In *Lectures de* Coriolan *de William Shakespeare*, edited by Guillaumme Winter and Delphine Lemonnier-Texier, 27–38. Rennes, France: Presses Universitaire de Rennes, 2006.
Cobb, W. S. "Anamnesis: Platonic Doctrine or Sophistic Absurdity?" *Dialogue* 12 (1973) 604–28.
———. *Plato's Erotic Dialogues: The Symposium and the Phaedrus*. Albany, NY: State University of New York Press, 1993.
Crosby, H. L. "An Unappreciated Joke in Aristophanes." *Classical Philology* 10 (1913) 326–30.
De Vries, G. J. *A Commentary on the Phaedrus of Plato*. Amsterdam: Hakkert, 1969.
Demos, M. "Stesichorus' Palinode in the *Phaedrus*." *The Classical World* 90 (1997) 235–49.
Derrida, J. "Plato's Pharmacy." In *A Derrida Reader*, edited by Peggy Kamuf, 112–42. New York: Columbia University Press, 1991.
Dillon, J. "Comments on John Moore's Paper." In *Patterns in Plato's Thought*, edited by J. M. E. Moravcsik, 72–77. Dordrecht: Reidel, 1973.
Dorter, K. "The Method of Division and the Division of the *Phaedrus*." *Ancient Philosophy* 26 (2006) 259–73.
Dušanić, S. "Alkidamas of Elaea in Plato's *Phaedrus*." *Classical Quarterly* 42 (1992) 347–57.
Dyer, L. "Plato as a Playwright." *Harvard Studies in Classical Philology* 12 (1901) 165–80.

Bibliography

Emerson, R. W. "On Plato's Universal Wisdom." In *The Great Thinkers on Plato*, edited by Barry Gross, 121–33. New York: Putnam's Sons, 1968.

Ferrari, G. R. F. *Listening to the Cicadas: A Study of Plato's Phaedrus*. Cambridge: Cambridge University Press, 1987.

Frank, E. "The Fundamental Opposition of Plato and Aristotle." *American Journal of Philology* 61 (1940) 166–85.

Furley, W. D. "A Note on [Lysias] 6, against Andokides." *The Classical Quarterly* 39 (1989) 550–53.

———. *Andokides and the Herms: A Study of Crisis in Fifth-Century Athenian Religion*. London: Institute of Classical Studies, 1996.

Gaudin, C. "*Lectio Difficilior*: Le système dans la théorie platonicienne de l'âme selon l'interprétation de M. Gueroult." *Phronesis* 35 (1990) 47–82.

Gill, C. "Dialectic and the Dialogue Form." In *New Perspectives on Plato, Modern and Ancient*, edited by Julia Annas and C. J. Rowe, 145–72. Washington, DC: Center for Hellenic Studies, 2002.

Gottfried, B. "Pan, the Cicadas and Plato's Use of Myth in the *Phaedrus*." In *Plato's Dialogues: New Studies and Interpretations*, edited by Gerald Press, 179–96, Lanham, MD: Rowman & Littlefield, 1993.

Griswold, C. L. "Comments on Kahn." In *New Perspectives on Plato, Modern and Ancient*, edited by Julia Annas and C. J. Rowe, 129–44. Washington, DC: Center for Hellenic Studies, 2002.

———."Plato's Metaphilosophy: Why Plato Wrote Dialogues." In *Platonic Writing/Platonic Readings*, edited by Charles Griswold, Jr., 143–70. University Park, PA: Pennsylvania State University Press, 1988.

———. *Self-Knowledge in Plato's Phaedrus*. New Haven: Yale University Press, 1986.

Hackforth, R. *Plato's Phaedrus*. Cambridge: Cambridge University Press, 1952.

Hamel, Debra. *The Mutilation of the Herms: Unpacking an Ancient Mystery*. Amazon Media. Kindle edition, 2012.

Hans, J. *Socrates and the Irrational*. Charlottesville, VA: University of Virginia Press, 2006.

Hegel, G. W. F. *Phänomenologie des Geistes*. Hamburg: Meiner, 1952.

———. *Plato and the Platonists*. Lincoln, NE: University of Nebraska Press, 1995.

Heitsch, E. "τιμιότερα." *Hermes* 117 (1989) 278–87.

Hunter, R. *Plato's Symposium*. Oxford: Oxford University Press, 2004.

Hyland, D. *Questioning Platonism*. Albany, NY: State University of New York Press, 2004.

Jaspers, K. *Plato and Augustine*. New York: Harcourt, Brace, and World, 1962.

Jowett, B. *Gorgias and Timaeus*. Mineola, NY: Dover, 2003.

Kahn, C. "On Platonic Chronology." In *New Perspectives on Plato: Modern and Ancient*, edited by Julia Annas and C. J. Rowe, 93–128. Washington, DC: Center for Hellenic Studies, 2002.

———. *Plato and the Socratic Dialogue: The Philosophic Use of a Literary Form*. Cambridge: Cambridge University Press, 1996.

Lateiner, D. "'The Man Who Does Not Meddle in Politics': A Topos in Lysias." *The Classical World* 76 (1982) 1–12.

Leask, I. "Statuary Presence: *Phaedrus* 235d–236b." *Yearbook of the Irish Philosophical Society* (2001) 96–102.

Leff, M. "The Forms of Reality in Plato's *Phaedrus*." *Rhetoric Society Quarterly* 11 (1981) 21–23.

Bibliography

Lefkowitz, M. R. "Aristophanes and Other Historians of the Fifth-Century Theater." *Hermes* 112 (1984) 143–53.
Leibniz, G. "The Spiritual Reality of the Soul." In *The Great Thinkers on Plato*, edited by Barry Gross, 50–58. New York: Putnam's Sons, 1968.
Levin, D. "Some Observations Concerning Plato's *Lysis*." In *Essays in Ancient Greek Philosophy*, edited by John Anton and George Kustas, 236–58. Albany, NY: SUNY, 1971.
Levine, D. L. "The Tyranny of Scholarship." *Ancient Philosophy* 4 (1984) 65–72.
Levinson, R. B. "Language, Plato, and Logic." In *Essays in Ancient Greek Philosophy*, edited by John Anton and George Kustas, 259–84. Albany, NY: SUNY, 1971.
Lind, H. "Sokrates am Ilissos: IG I³ 1 257 und die Eingangsszene des Platonischen *Phaidros*." *Zeitschrift für Papyrologie und Epigraphik* 69 (1987) 15–19.
Lysias. *The Orations of Lysias*. Online: http://www.gutenberg.org/catalog/world.
MacDowell, D. *Andocides, On the Mysteries*. Oxford: Clarendon, 1989.
Martin, T. *Ancient Greece*. New Haven: Yale University Press, 2000.
Mazur, J. *The Motion Paradox*. New York: Dutton, 2007.
McCabe, M. *Plato's Individuals*. Princeton: Princeton University Press, 1994.
McAdon, B. "Plato's Denunciation of Rhetoric in *Phaedrus*." *Rhetoric Review* 23 (2004) 21–39.
McCoy, M. *Plato on the Rhetoric of Philosophers and Sophists*. Cambridge: Cambridge University Press, 2008.
McGlew, J. "Politics on the Margins: The Athenian 'Hetaireiai' in 415 B.C." *Historia: Zeitschrift für Alte Geschichte* 48 (1999) 1–22.
Missiou, A. *The Subversive Oratory of Andokides*. Cambridge: Cambridge University Press, 1992.
Moes, M. *Plato's Dialogue Form and the Care of the Soul*. New York: Lang, 2000.
Moore, J. "The Relation between *Symposium* and *Phaedrus*." In *Patterns in Plato's Thought*, edited by J. M. E. Moravcsik, 52–71. Dordrecht: Reidel, 1973.
Morgan, K. "Comments on Gill." In *New Perspectives on Plato, Modern and Ancient*, edited by Julia Annas and C. J. Rowe, 173–88. Washington, DC: Center for Hellenic Studies, 2002.
Nails, D. *The People of Plato*. Indianapolis: Hackett, 2002.
Natorp, P. *Plato's Theory of Ideas: An Introduction to Idealism*. Sankt Augustin, Germany: Academia, 2004.
Nichols, J. *Plato: Phaedrus*. Ithaca, NY: Cornell University Press, 1998.
Nicholson, G. "The Discourses in *Phaedrus*." In *Retracing the Platonic Text*, edited by John Russon and John Sallis, 19–31. Evanston, IL: Northwestern University Press, 2000.
———. *Plato's Phaedrus*. West Lafayette, IN: Purdue University Press, 1999.
Nietzsche, F. *The Basic Writings of Nietzsche*. New York: Modern Library, 1968.
Nussbaum, M. *The Fragility of Goodness*. Cambridge: Cambridge University Press, 2001.
Ober, J. *Political Dissent in Democratic Athens: Intellectual Critique of Popular Rule*. Princeton: Princeton University Press, 1998.
Owen, G. E. L. "A Proof in the '*peri ideon*.'" In *Studies in Plato's Metaphysics*, edited by R. E. Allen, 293–312. London: Routledge and Kegan Paul, 1965.
Pater, W. "The Artistry in Plato's Work," In *The Great Thinkers on Plato*, edited by Barry Gross, 205–18. New York: Putnam's Sons, 1968.
Pickstock, Catherine. *After Writing: On the Liturgical Consummation of Philosophy*. Challenges in Contemporary Theology. Oxford: Blackwell, 1997.

Bibliography

Planinc, Z. *Plato through Homer: Poetry and Philosophy in the Cosmological Dialogues*. Columbia: University of Missouri Press, 2003.

Plato. *Euthyphro*. Translated by Harold Fowler. Cambridge: Harvard University Press, 1999.

———. *Gorgias*. Translated by James Arieti and Roger Barrus. Newburyport, MA: Focus Philosophical Library, 2007.

———. *Phaedo*. Translated by Harold Fowler. Cambridge: Harvard University Press, 1998.

———. *Phaedrus*. Translated by Harold Fowler. Cambridge: Harvard University Press, 1999.

———. *Protagoras*. Translated by W. R. M. Lamb. Cambridge: Harvard University Press, 1924.

———. *Republic*. Translated by Allan Bloom. New York: Basic, 1968.

———. *Statesman*. Translated by Harold Fowler. Cambridge: Harvard University Press, 1925.

———. *Symposium*. Translated by W. R. M. Lamb. Cambridge: Harvard University Press, 1946.

Polansky, R. "Reading Plato: Paul Woodruff and the *Hippias Major*." In *Platonic Writings/Platonic Readings*, edited by Charles Griswold, Jr., 200–209. University Park, PA: Pennsylvania State University Press, 1988.

———. *Philosophy and Knowledge: A Commentary on Plato's Theaetetus*. Lewisburg, PA: Bucknell University Press, 1992.

Press, G. "Principles of Dramatic and Non-Dramatic Plato Interpretation." In *Plato's Dialogues: New Studies and Interpretations*, edited by Gerald Press, 107–28. Lanham, MD: Rowman & Littlefield, 1993.

Raven, J. E. *Plato's Thought in the Making*. Westport, CT: Greenwood, 1985.

Rhodes, J. *Eros, Wisdom, and Silence: Plato's Erotic Dialogues*. Columbia: University of Missouri Press, 2003.

Rinella, M. "Supplementing the Ecstatic: Plato, the Eleusinian Mysteries, and Phaedrus." *Polis* 17 (2000) 61–78.

Robinson, R. *Plato's Early Dialectic*. Oxford: Oxford University Press, 1953.

Rojcewicz, R. "The Festive and the Workady in Plato's *Phaedrus*," *Collection du Cirp* 1 (2007) 160–79.

Rosen, S. "The Non-Lover in Plato's *Phaedrus*." *Man and World* 2 (1969) 432–77.

Rowe, C. J. "Killing Socrates: Plato's Later Thoughts on Democracy." *The Journal of Hellenic Studies* 121 (2001) 63–76.

Sallis, J. *Being and Logos*. Pittsburgh: Duquesne University Press, 1975.

Sauvage, M. *Socrates and the Human Conscience*. New York: Harper and Brothers, 1960.

Scully, S. *Plato's Phaedrus*. Newburyport, MA: Focus Philosophical Library, 2003.

Stern-Gillet, S. "Le Principe Du Beau Chez Plotin: Réflexions sur *Enneas* VI.7.32 et 33." *Phronesis* 45 (2000) 38–63.

Stoeber, M. "Phaedrus of the *Phaedrus*: The Impassioned Soul." *Philosophy and Rhetoric* 25 (1992) 271–80.

Stumpf, S. *Philosophy: History and Readings*. New York: McGraw-Hill, 2012.

Taylor, C. *Sources of the Self*. Cambridge: Harvard University Press, 1989.

Thompson, W. H. *The Phaedrus of Plato, with English Notes and Dissertations*. London: Whittaker, 1868.

Timmerman, D. "Isocrates' Competing Conceptualization of Philosophy." *Philosophy and Rhetoric* 31 (1998) 145–59.

Bibliography

Van Hook, L. "Alcidamas versus Isocrates: The Spoken Word versus the Written Word." *The Classical Weekly* 12.12, (1919). http://www.classicpersuasion.org/pw/alcidamas/alcsoph1.htm

Vlastos, G. "Plato's Testimony Concerning Zeno of Elea." *The Journal of Hellenic Studies* 95 (1975) 136–62.

———. "Socratic Piety." *Proceedings of the Boston Area Colloquium in Ancient Philosophy*, edited by John Cleary, 213–37. Lanham, MD: Rowman & Littlefield, 1989.

Warnek, P. *Descent of Socrates*. Bloomington, IN: University of Indiana Press, 2005.

White, D. A. *Rhetoric and Reality in Plato's Phaedrus*. Albany, NY: State University of New York Press, 1993.

Wohl, V. "The Eros of Alcibiades." *Classical Antiquity* 18 (1999) 349–85.

Wohl, V. *Love among the Ruins: The Erotics of Democracy in Classical Athens*. Princeton: Princeton University Press, 2002.

Zeruneith, K. *The Wooden Horse: The Liberation of the Western Mind from Odysseus to Socrates*. New York: Overlook Duckworth, 2007.

Zuckert, Catherine H. *Plato's Philosophers: The Coherence of the Dialogues*. Chicago: University of Chicago Press, 2009.

Zwicky, J. "Plato's *Phaedrus*: Philosophy as Dialogue with the Dead." *Apeiron* 30 (1997) 19–48.

Index

Academy, 80
Achelous, 82
Acumenus, 51, 57
Adeimantus, 26
Aesop, 106, 150
aesthetics, 6
Alcestis, 47
Alkibiades, xvii, 21, 48, 58, 59, 63–72, 91, 100–102, 132, 160–61
Alkidamas, 148, 155–58, 160
"All Soul," 122–23
Allen, Richard E., 27, 149
amphoterious, 63
anamnesis, 44, 124
Anaxagoras, 47
Andokides, 19–21, 61–63, 159
Antidosis, 160
antilogic, 11, 145–48, 153, 154, 156, 157, 164
Anton, John, 52
Apology (Plato), 3, 86, 108, 155, 157, 158
Apollonian, 43
Arieti, James, 68
aristocrat, 19, 22, 34, 40–42, 45, 58–61, 67, 71, 77–80, 83, 85–87, 137, 160, 161, 169–70
Aristodemus, 45
Aristophanes, 67, 77, 78, 82, 101
Aristotle, 28, 97, 138, 148, 150, 165
art (*techne*), 8, 17–19, 22, 29, 50–52, 80, 82, 101–3, 132, 138–46, 149, 150, 152, 153, 159
ascending, 7, 28, 29, 32, 33, 50, 79, 88, 90, 91, 110, 115, 124, 128, 135

Bateman, John, 85
beauty, 13, 32, 46, 50, 53, 54, 89, 95, 124, 130–33
Beauty, 28–33, 44, 48, 52, 53, 119, 121, 124, 134, 151
Bentley, Russell, 136
Burkert, Walter, 37
business (-man), 18, 22, 71, 80, 81, 92, 95–97, 133

Callicles, 22
Cephalus, 82
Chaos, 46, 122
Charmides (Plato), 56
Charmides, 113
Christ, 42, 166
Christians, 32, 42, 43, 97, 165
chronology, 1–3
cicada(s), 129–33, 137, 168
collection, 3, 19, 24, 29, 123, 157
"common folk," 105, 131
CO (Compresence of Opposites), xiv, xvi, xviii, 16, 27, 28, 33, 34, 87, 90, 91
contemplation, 29, 31, 33, 44, 52, 55, 90, 99, 119–21, 135, 151, 156, 171
contingency, 13
corruption, 53, 65, 108, 112
cosmology, 46–48, 50
courage, 14, 22, 47, 53, 98, 108, 170
Cratylus (Plato), 1, 2
creative non-fiction, 2, 3, 8, 48, 79, 80, 117
Critias, 56

Index

Crito (Plato), 92

Davies, John, 21
de-corruption, 36, 59, 60, 86, 132
De Vries, G. J., 3, 4, 77, 131
definition, 2, 6, 13, 19, 24, 25, 28, 29, 107, 108, 110, 141, 148
Demeter, 44, 63, 70, 75, 129
democrat, xvi, 18, 19, 22, 34, 42, 43, 45, 51, 53, 57–62, 65, 67–69, 71–74, 77, 79, 80, 83, 83, 85–88, 91, 95, 132, 134, 137, 159–61, 164, 169, 170
Democritus, 165
Demos, M., 20
Demosthenes, 68
demythologizing, 45, 46, 71, 82, 89, 163
Derrida, Jacques, 5, 99, 136
descending, 7, 28, 32, 33, 78, 88, 90, 91, 110
dialectic, xxii, 3, 6, 9, 11, 15–33, 37, 52, 60, 73, 80, 90, 97, 98, 100, 103, 105, 108, 111, 118, 123, 127, 128, 135, 136, 138–41, 143, 145, 146, 148, 150, 151, 153–57, 159, 160 164, 166, 171
dianoia, 4, 9–11, 26–29, 31–33, 53, 83, 90, 105, 110, 121, 124, 159
Diodorus (Siculus), 68
Dion, 42, 66
Dillon, John, 50
Diogenes, 65
discernment, 16, 19, 18–20, 23, 25, 29, 33, 37, 41, 108, 123, 136, 148, 155, 156, 168, 171
Divided Line, xv, xvi, 9–12, 26, 28, 33
Divine (God), 28–33, 44, 78, 121, 122, 124, 165–67
division, 3, 19, 24, 29, 123, 157
Dodona, 102, 164
domination, 82, 112
Dorter, Kenneth, 109
Dover, Kenneth, 21

drama, xiii, xviii, xxiii, 1, 2, 6, 7, 16, 29, 56, 57, 66, 74, 76, 79, 83, 117, 127, 129, 146
Dušanić, Slobodan, 154–55
Dyer, Louis, 1–3

Earth, 46–49, 54, 122
Eleatic, 6, 105, 144, 147, 149–52, 154
Eleusinian Mysteries, xvii, xviii, xxiii, 35–37, 39–45, 60, 61, 70, 71, 75, 129, 170
Emerson, Ralph W., 8, 9, 12
epamphoterious, 38, 57–59, 98, 101, 148, 161–62, 164–65
Empedocles, 46, 47
Epicrates of Ambracia, 80–83, 103
Epicrates of Athens, 7, 12, 43, 53, 55, 76–84, 90, 91, 98, 103, 132, 171
epistemology, 8, 26, 28, 47, 73, 144, 145
erastes, 18, 20, 21, 49–52, 58, 59, 66, 74, 96, 103, 104, 107, 111–13, 132
Erixymachus, 49–52, 54, 57, 59
Essence Wheel, 11, 29, 36, 44, 45, 48, 52, 53, 55, 90, 97–99, 115, 119–21, 123, 124, 135, 151
Essence(s), xvi, xvii, 2, 3, 11, 23, 26, 28, 29, 31–33, 36, 38, 44, 45, 48, 52, 53, 55, 83, 90, 95, 97–99, 104, 115, 119–21, 123–24, 135, 140, 151, 159, 160, 164, 165, 171
Euripides, 82
Euthyphro, 83
exile, 11, 12, 17, 19, 25, 39, 41, 51, 55, 57, 58, 62, 79, 87, 88, 91, 107, 113, 132, 152, 159

Ferrari, G. R. F., 12, 13, 14, 84, 99, 100, 131
Forms (or Essences), xvi, xxii, 2, 12, 30, 32
Frank, Erich, 31
friendship, 42–44, 88, 93, 127, 133
Furley, William D., 60–63, 67, 70

Index

Gill, C. 83
Glaucon, 26
Good, xxii, 10, 25, 26, 28, 29–31, 33, 44, 52
Gorgias (Plato), 22, 38, 52, 81, 82, 101, 138
Gorgias, 22, 142, 148, 154–56, 158
Gottfried, Brian, 124, 131
Griswold, Charles, 1, 8, 9
Gueroult, Martial, 32
guilt, 21, 40, 41, 61–63
Guthrie, W. K. C., 37

Hackforth, Reginald, 20, 119, 131
Hades, 40, 89, 90
HH (Socrates's Half-comical Halting), xiii, xiv, xviii, 5, 99, 114–18, 125–26, 129–30, 137
Hamel, Debra, 56n4
Hans, James, 93
Hegel, G. W. F., xvi, 6, 125, 136
Heidegger, Martin, 5, 138
Heitsch, Ernst, 100
Hermes, 60, 69, 70, 79, 82, 89
Herms (see *MH*)
Hesiod, 46
heteratai, 71–73
homecoming, 11, 29
Homer, 12, 15, 103, 132, 133, 168, 169
honor-love (*philotimia*), xxii, 4, 18, 19, 21, 23, 24, 42, 46, 47–49, 52, 53, 58, 75, 85, 86, 89, 94–96, 98, 99, 121, 122, 125, 130, 134, 137
Hunter, Richard, 45, 46
Hyland, Drew, 5, 6, 138
hypotheses, 32, 83

Ibycus, 99
image(s), 6, 28–31, 33, 44, 45, 48, 50, 52, 67, 74, 93, 94, 96, 98, 99, 102, 104, 113, 115–20, 123, 125–28, 146, 153, 164, 169
immortality, 122–23, 164–65
Isocrates, 10, 11, 32, 33, 42, 103, 156, 160, 169

Jaspers, Karl, 23
Jowett, Benjamin, 7, 9
justice, 5, 13, 14, 33, 108, 123

Kant, Immanuel, 9, 26, 30
Kahn, Charles, xxiv, 1, 7–9
Kinds, 2
Kore, 63, 75, 129
Kristalnacht, 60

Leask, Ian, 136–37
Leff, Michael, 44
Lefkowitz, Mary, 77, 78
Levin, Donald, 110
Levinson, Ronald, 108
Lind, Hermann, 88
Locke, John, 165
L'/P' (Lysias's/Phaedrus's Speech) xiii, xiv, 10, 12, 23, 73, 74, 96, 103–18, 126, 127, 129, 131, 134, 136, 137, 139, 141, 149, 153, 154, 160
Lydus, 57
Lysis (Plato), 2

MacDowell, Douglas, 91
Mazur, Joseph, 150
McCoy, Marina, 135
McGlew, James, 71, 72
Menedemus, 80
metaphysics, 8, 144, 145, 158
Moes, Mark, 5, 64
money-love (*philochrematia*), xxii, 23, 85, 86, 94–99, 119, 121, 122, 171
Morgan, Kathryn, 4, 17
MH (Mutilation of the Herms), xviii, 12, 21, 56, 57, 60–65, 67–73, 79, 91, 133, 158, 159, 161
Morychus, 12, 43, 76–80, 82, 83, 103

Nails, Debra, xvii, 20, 61, 62
Natorp, Paul, xxiii, 3, 24, 29, 30
necessity, 13, 157, 165
Nestor, 142, 154
Nichols, James, 57

181

Index

Nicholson, Graham, xiv, 37, 107
Nietzsche, Friedrich, 43, 78, 82, 147
nihilism, 61, 71, 72, 75
9/11, 60
Nussbaum, Martha, xvii, 56, 65, 66, 105

Odysseus, 155
Odysseus, 93, 142, 154, 158–59
oligarch (-y), 71–73, 85, 159, 160, 171
Olympieum, 7, 76, 78, 79, 88, 91, 127
ontology, 46, 49, 50, 53, 54, 144–45, 149–50, 156–58
Orphic, 35, 37–40
Owen, G. E. L., xv, xvi, 12

pais, 18, 20, 74, 103, 104, 107, 108
Palamedes, 65, 105, 142, 144, 147, 149–52, 154–60
PL (Palinode to Love), xiii, xiv, xvii, 3, 12, 16, 18, 23, 29, 31, 32, 39, 40, 44, 45, 48, 52, 55, 73, 88, 90, 97, 99, 103, 105, 107, 114–18, 121–26, 129, 135, 137, 149, 151, 153
Pan, 82, 89, 93, 170
Panagiotou, Spiro. 3
paradox, 148–52, 156–57
Parmenides (Plato), 1
Parmenides, 147–51, 155, 157
Pater, Walter, 30, 33
Pausanias (Atticistas), 68
pederasty, 18, 20, 23, 52, 66, 74, 94, 95, 103, 104, 106–8, 111–13, 127, 132–35
Peisandros, 160
penance, 137
Phaedo (Plato), 1, 3, 35, 38, 39, 47, 98
P'/S' (Phaedrus's/Socrates's Speech), xiii, xiv, xviii, 12, 20, 45, 73, 74, 85, 99, 103, 105–18, 126–27, 129–30, 136–37, 151
Pickstock, Catherine, 29
Pindar, 22
Planinc, Zdravko, 93
Plutarch, 70
Polansky, Ronald, xvii, xviii, 146

Polemarchus, 26
Polus, 22
pragmatism, 42, 160
Press, Gerald, 5, 6
PEM (Profanation of the Mysteries), xviii, 12, 19, 21, 35, 36, 41, 45, 56, 57, 60–68, 70, 71, 79, 82, 91, 101, 112, 133, 152, 158, 159, 161
Protagoras (Plato), 20, 46, 57
Protagoras, 72, 73
prudence, 23

Quintillian, 147, 155

recollection, 53
reflexivity, 16, 146
Republic (Plato), xv, xvi, xxiii, 1–4, 7–14, 26, 27, 29–32, 52, 53, 76, 83, 90, 94–96, 103, 119, 124
rhetor (-ic) xiv, xxiii, xxiv, 8, 10, 15–19, 22, 23, 33, 34, 44, 45, 51, 52, 56, 57, 60, 67, 73, 76, 80–82, 86, 96–102, 104–8, 110–11, 113–14, 116, 127–28, 136–51, 153–58, 160, 163–64
Rhodes, James, xvii, 7, 8, 20, 21, 31, 46, 47, 56, 64, 66, 91, 93, 95, 111, 112, 170
Rinella, Michael, 35, 36
Robin, Léon, 88
Rojcewicz, Richard, 7, 8
Rosen, Stanley, 4, 5, 105, 109
Rowe, Christopher, J. 2

Sallis, John, 8, 12, 27, 28, 31, 90
satyr, 16
Sauvage, Micheline, 83
Schadenverbesserung (shame-improvement), 48–54, 64, 69, 71, 91, 94–99, 107, 113, 121, 135, 164, 170
Schiller, Friedrich, 30
Schleirmacher, Friedrich, 4
Scully, Stephen, 112, 115–16

simple, 2–4, 17, 23, 38, 59, 94, 135, 162–67
Solon, 12, 103, 132, 133, 136–37, 168–69
Sophist (Plato), 2, 147–48
sophist (-ry) (-ical), xxiii, 33, 45, 49, 57, 58, 82, 89, 95, 101–2, 109, 111, 136–39, 147–48, 154–55, 160, 166, 169
soul, xv, 4, 6, 14, 17, 25, 28, 29, 31, 33, 37, 38, 44, 45, 52, 53, 55, 58, 59, 73, 83, 85, 87, 90, 94, 95, 98, 108, 114, 115, 117–28, 130, 132–35, 138, 141, 164, 165
"soul-leading," 138, 141
speaking, 10, 18, 36, 73, 81, 100–101, 109, 132, 135, 140–46, 153, 155–56, 158
Speusippus, 80
Stern-Gillet, Suzanne, 32
Symposium (Plato), 1–3, 17, 20, 21, 23, 24, 31, 37, 45–47, 50–53, 58, 64, 70, 91, 96, 98, 110, 122–24, 132

Taylor, Charles, 52
Teisamenos, Decree of, 91–93
Teleclides, 77
Theaetetus (Plato), 1, 97
theatre, 41, 81, 82
theology, 44, 78, 89, 92, 96
Thompson, William H., 77,
Thrasymachus, 9, 26, 142, 154
Timmerman, David, 32
transformation, 38, 97, 130, 131, 136, 137, 154, 162, 164, 166

Triptolemus, 43–45
truth, xvi, xviii, 11, 16, 17, 22–24, 26, 29, 31–33, 36, 40, 42, 48, 53, 73, 90, 96, 116, 119, 121, 124, 130, 140, 142, 149, 151, 158, 165, 169
Typhon (-ic), 18, 21, 23, 38, 48–53, 64, 69, 71, 89, 91, 93–96, 98, 99, 107, 113, 121–22, 127, 134, 163–64

utilitarian, 104–5

virtue, 14, 23, 41–43, 53, 56, 72, 73, 105, 108, 109, 137, 143
Vlastos, Gregory, 39, 92, 147, 148, 155

wisdom-love (*philosophia*), xxii, 4, 11, 13, 23, 44, 52, 53, 75, 85, 86, 92, 94–96, 98, 99, 113, 121, 130, 132, 134, 140, 153, 156, 169, 171
Wohl, Victoria, 20, 59, 69, 100–01
writing, 12, 18, 99, 100, 141, 143, 145, 150, 155–57, 164, 166

Xenophon, 171

Zeno, 24, 105, 144–58
Zeus, 7, 11, 16, 31, 44, 53, 69, 70, 75–79, 86–102, 114–15, 120, 125–28, 133–34, 151, 164
Zuckert, Catherine, 162
Zwicky, Jan, 2, 128